Macworld Guide To Microsoft Word 5 By Jim Heid

IDG
BOOKS
QUICK
REFERENCE
CARD

Formatting characters with the ribbon

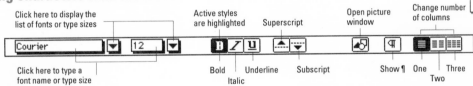

Click here to display the list of fonts or type sizes

Active styles are highlighted

Superscript

Open picture window

Change number of columns

Click here to type a font name or type size

Bold — Italic

Underline

Subscript

Show ¶

One — Two — Three

Formatting paragraphs with the ruler

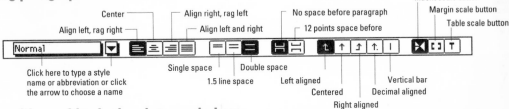

Center

Align right, rag left

No space before paragraph

Indent scale button

Margin scale button

Align left, rag right

Align left and right

12 points space before

Table scale button

Click here to type a style name or abbreviation or click the arrow to choose a name

Single space — Double space

1.5 line space

Left aligned

Centered

Right aligned

Decimal aligned

Vertical bar

Working with graphics in the picture window

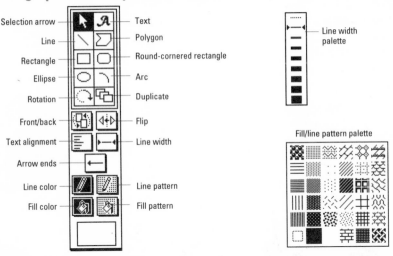

Selection arrow — Text
Line — Polygon
Rectangle — Round-cornered rectangle
Ellipse — Arc
Rotation — Duplicate
Front/back — Flip
Text alignment — Line width
Arrow ends
Line color — Line pattern
Fill color — Fill pattern

Line width palette

Fill/line pattern palette

Word 5.1 Toolbar

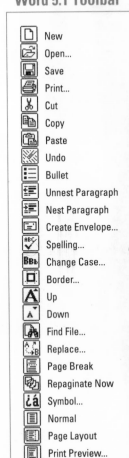

- New
- Open...
- Save
- Print...
- Cut
- Copy
- Paste
- Undo
- Bullet
- Unnest Paragraph
- Nest Paragraph
- Create Envelope...
- Spelling...
- Change Case...
- Border...
- Up
- Down
- Find File...
- Replace...
- Page Break
- Repaginate Now
- Symbol...
- Normal
- Page Layout
- Print Preview...

Making your text look typeset

The special characters and tips below can make your text look professionally typeset.

Character	Key Combination	Example of usage
"	Option-[	He said, "I think so."
"	Shift-Option-[	
'	Option-]	That's the way to do it.
'	Shift-Option-]	She said, "That's 'odd.'"
—	Shift-Option-hyphen	I'll be back — you'll see.
–	Option-hyphen	5 – 10 feet long.

More type tips

- ✦ Type one space after punctuation, not two.
- ✦ Don't type "l" for 1 or "O" for zero.
- ✦ Commas and periods go inside quotes.
- ✦ Colons and semicolons go outside quotes.
- ✦ Use italics, not underlines, for emphasis.
- ✦ Use tabs, not the spacebar, to align text.
- ✦ For better legibility, avoid all CAPITALS.

Macworld Guide To Microsoft Word 5

QUICK REFERENCE CARD

Selection shortcuts

To select this...	Do this...
a word	double-click on the word
a sentence	Command-click within the sentence
a paragraph	triple-click within the paragraph or double-click the selection bar adjacent to the paragraph
a single line	click once in the selection bar adjacent to the line
a carriage return character	double click to the right of the last line of the paragraph
the entire document	Command-click in the selection bar, triple-click in the selection bar, or choose Select All from the Edit menu
a table column	press Option and then click anywhere within the column
an entire table	press Option and then double-click anywhere within the table
a table cell	click within the cell selection bar on the cell's left edge

Table-editing shortcuts

To do this...	Press...
Delete a selected row or series of rows	Command-Control-X
Insert a row or series of rows	Command-Control-V
Insert a paragraph above the row containing the insertion point	Command-Option-spacebar

Character formatting shortcuts

For this style...	Press Command-Shift and...
Bold	B
Italic	I
Underline	U
Word underline	] (closing bracket)
Double underline	[(opening bracket)
Dotted underline	\ (backslash)
Strikethru	/ (slash)
Outline	D
Shadow	W
Small caps	H
All caps	K
Hidden (appears as dotted underline)	X

Outlining shortcuts

To do this...	Do this...
Promote the heading containing the insertion point	Option-left arrow
Demote the heading containing the insertion point	Option-right arrow
Move the paragraph containing the insertion point up	Option-up arrow
Move the paragraph containing the insertion point down	Option-down arrow
Expand or collapse the entire outline to a specific level	Command-Option-T and then press 1, 2, 3, or 4
Expand the heading containing the insertion point	The plus sign key (+) on the numeric keypad
Collapse the heading containing the insertion point	The minus sign key (-) on the numeric keypad
Expand the entire outline	The multiply key (*) on the numeric keypad

About *Macworld Guide To . . .* Books

Macworld Guide To Microsoft Word 5 is part of the *Macworld Guide To . . .* series of books, brought to you by IDG, the leading publisher of computer information worldwide. This is a new kind of book designed to meet your growing need to quickly find what you want to do and learn how to do it.

These books work the way you do: They focus on accomplishing specific tasks — not learning random functions. *Macworld Guide To . . .* books are not long-winded tomes, manuals, or even quick reference guides, but are the result of drawing from the best elements of these three types of publications. These books have the easy-to-follow step-by-step sections of a manual; the comprehensive coverage you'd expect to find in a long tome; and the brevity you need from a quick reference guide — it's all here.

The designers of the *Macworld Guide To . . .* series use the following visual elements to make it easy to find the information you need:

Overview sections provide a summary of the Topic's subject and are meant to be read when you want help accomplishing your goals without having to work through the tutorials. This is a good learning tool for the intermediate user who does not need/want any hand-holding.

Step-by-Step sections demonstrate the concepts given in the Overview sections with easy-to-follow instructions. If you're a beginner, these Step-by-Step sections will go a long way toward getting you up to speed on unfamiliar topics.

Quick Tip sections include tips and insights contained on the material in each Topic which enable you to get the most out of your application or operating system no matter what level user you are.

The authors of the *Macworld Guide To . . .* books are leading *Macworld* columnists, technology champions, and Mac gurus, who are uniquely qualified to provide you with expert advice and insightful tips and techniques not found anywhere else. We're sure you'll agree that the *Macworld Guide To . . .* approach is the best.

— David Solomon
Publisher

MACWORLD

GUIDE TO MICROSOFT
WORD 5

MACWORLD
GUIDE TO MICROSOFT
WORD 5

By Jim Heid

Macworld "Getting Started" Columnist

Foreword by Adrian Mello

Editor-in-Chief, *Macworld*

IDG BOOKS

IDG Books Worldwide, Inc.
An International Data Group Company

CALIFORNIA ✦ INDIANA ✦ MASSACHUSETTS

Macworld Guide to Microsoft Word 5

Published by
IDG Books Worldwide, Inc.
An International Data Group Company
155 Bovet Road, Suite 310
San Mateo, CA 94402
(415) 312-0650

Library of Congress Catalog Card No.: 91-77219

ISBN 1-878058-39-8

Printed in the United States of America

10 9 8 7 6 5 4

Distributed in the United States by IDG Books Worldwide, Inc. Distributed in Canada by Macmillan of Canada, a Division of Canada Publishing Corporation; by Woodslane Pty. Ltd. in Australia and New Zealand; and by Computer Bookshops in the U.K and Ireland.

For information on translations and availability in other countries, contact Marc Jeffrey Mikulich, Foreign Rights Manager, at IDG Books Worldwide. Fax: (415) 358-1260.

For sales inquiries and special prices for bulk quantities, write to the address above or call IDG Books Worldwide at (415) 312-0600.

Acknowledgments

My sincere thanks go to everyone who helped make this book a reality. At Microsoft, the entire Word development team deserves thanks — and a vacation — for putting together the best Word yet. In particular, David Pearce answered questions promptly and guided me through the minefield of pre-release software.

I also want to thank Felicity O'Meara, copy editor extraordinaire, for polishing the manuscript until it glittered. Nobody picks nits better. Thanks also go to technical editor Dennis Cohen, who made sure what I said was right.

My gratitude also goes to everyone at IDG Books, especially to John Kilcullen, for his enthusiasm and support; and to project editor Jeremy Judson, for shepherding the book through the production process and for listening to my whining — and my answering machine.

Finally, my deepest gratitude and eternal love go to my wife and colleague Maryellen Kelly, who read every page and tried every exercise. Her efforts have made this book more accurate and more useful; her love has made my life worth living. This book is dedicated to her, to my mother, and to Trixie, who still knows when it's time for a squeak-squeak break.

(The publisher would also like to thank Patrick J. McGovern, without whom this book would not have been possible.)

About IDG Books Worldwide

Welcome to the world of IDG Books Worldwide.

IDG Books Worldwide, Inc., is a division of International Data Group (IDG), the world's largest publisher of computer-related information and the leading global provider of information services on information technology. IDG publishes over 190 computer publications in 61 countries. Thirty million people read one or more IDG publications each month.

If you use personal computers, IDG Books is committed to publishing quality books that meet your needs. We rely on our extensive network of publications, including such leading periodicals as *Macworld, InfoWorld, PC World, Computerworld, Publish, Network World*, and *SunWorld*, to help us make informed and timely decisions in creating useful computer books that meet your needs.

Every IDG book strives to bring extra value and skill-building instruction to the reader. Our books are written by experts, with the backing of IDG periodicals, and with careful thought devoted to issues such as audience, interior design, use of icons, and illustrations. Our editorial staff is a careful mix of high-tech journalists and experienced book people. Our close contact with the makers of computer products helps ensure accuracy and thorough coverage. Our heavy use of personal computers at every step in production means we can deliver books in the most timely manner.

We are delivering books of high quality at competitive prices on topics customers want. At IDG, we believe in quality, and we have been delivering quality for over 25 years. You'll find no better book on a subject than an IDG book.

John Kilcullen
President and C.E.O.
IDG Books Worldwide, Inc.

IDG Books Worldwide, Inc. is a division of International Data Group. The officers are Patrick J. McGovern, Founder and Board Chairman; Walter Boyd, President; Robert A. Farmer, Vice Chairman. International Data Group's publications include: **ARGENTINA's** Computerworld Argentina, InfoWorld Argentina; **ASIA's** Computerworld Hong Kong, PC World Hong Kong, Computerworld Southeast Asia, PC World Singapore, Computerworld Malaysia, PC World Malaysia; **AUSTRALIA's** Computerworld Australia, Australian PC World, Australian Macworld, Network World, Reseller, IDG Sources; **AUSTRIA's** Computerwelt Oesterreich, PC Test; **BRAZIL's** Computerworld, Mundo IBM, Mundo Unix, PC World, Publish; **BULGARIA's** Computerworld Bulgaria, Ediworld, PC World Bulgaria; **CANADA's** Direct Access, Graduate Computerworld, InfoCanada, Network World Canada; **CHILE's** Computerworld, Informatica; **COLUMBIA's** Computerworld Columbia; **CZECH REPUBLIC's** Computerworld Elektronika, PC World; **DENMARK's** CAD/CAM WORLD, Communications World, Computerworld Danmark, Computerworld Focus, Computerworld Uddannelse, Lotus World, Macintosh Produktkatalog, Macworld Danmark, PC World Danmark, PC World Produktguide, Windows World; **EQUADOR's** PC World Ecuador; **EGYPT's** Computerworld Middle East, PC World Middle East; **FINLAND's** MikroPC, Tietoviikko, Tietoverkko; **FRANCE's** Distributique, GOLDEN MAC, InfoPC, Languages & Systems, Le Guide du Monde Informatique, Le Monde Informatique, Telecoms & Reseaux; **GERMANY's** Computerwoche, Computerwoche Focus, Computerwoche Extra, Computerwoche Karriere, edv aspekte, Information Management, Macwelt, Netzwelt, PC Welt, PC Woche, Publish, Unit; **HUNGARY's** Alaplap, Computerworld SZT, PC World, ; **INDIA's** Computers & Communications; **ISRAEL's** Computerworld Israel, PC World Israel; **ITALY's** Computerworld Italia, Lotus Magazine, Macworld Italia, Networking Italia, PC World Italia; **JAPAN's** Computerworld Japan, Macworld Japan, SunWorld Japan; **KENYA's** East African Computer News; **KOREA's** Computerworld Korea, Macworld Korea, PC World Korea; **MEXICO's** Compu Edicion, Compu Manufactura, Computacion/Punto de Venta, Computerworld Mexico, MacWorld, Mundo Unix, PC World, Windows; **THE NETHERLANDS'** Computer! Totaal, LAN Magazine, MacWorld Magazine; **NEW ZEALAND's** Computer Listings, Computerworld New Zealand, New Zealand PC World; **NIGERIA's** PC World Africa; **NORWAY's** Computerworld Norge, C/World, Lotusworld Norge, Macworld Norge, Networld, PC World Ekspress, PC World Norge, PC World's Product Guide, Publish World, Student Data, Unix World, Windowsworld, IDG Direct Response; **PANAMA's** PC World Panama; **PERU's** Computerworld Peru, PC World; **PEOPLES REPUBLIC OF CHINA's** China Computerworld, PC World China, Electronics International, China Network World; **IDG HIGH TECH BEIJING's** New Product World; **IDG SHENZHEN's** Computer News Digest; **PHILLIPPINES'** Computerworld, PC World; **POLAND's** Computerworld Poland, PC World/Komputer; **PORTUGAL's** MacIn; **RUSSIA's** Computerworld-Moscow, Mir-PC, Sety; **SLOVENIA's** Monitor Magazine; **SOUTH AFRICA's** Computing S.A.; **SPAIN's** Amiga World, Computerworld Espana, Communicaciones World, Macworld Espana, NeXTWORLD, PC World Espana, Publish, Sunworld; **SWEDEN's** Attack, ComputerSweden, Corporate Computing, Lokala Natverk/LAN, Lotus World, MAC&PC, Macworld, Mikrodatorn, PC World, Publishing & Design (CAP), Datalngenjoren, Maxi Data, Windows World; **SWITZERLAND's** Computerworld Schweiz, Macworld Schweiz, PC & Workstation; **TAIWAN's** Computerworld Taiwan, Global Computer Express, PC World Taiwan; **THAILAND's** Thai Computerworld; **TURKEY's** Computerworld Monitor, Macworld Turkiye, PC World Turkiye; **UNITED KINGDOM's** Lotus Magazine, Macworld, Sunworld; **UNITED STATES'** AmigaWorld, Cable in the Classroom, CD Review, CIO, Computerworld, Desktop Video World, DOS Resource Guide, Electronic News, Federal Computer Week, Federal Integrator, GamePro, inCider/A+, IDG Books, InfoWorld, InfoWorld Direct, Laser Event, Macworld, Multimedia World, Network World, NeXTWORLD, PC Games, PC World, PC Letter, Publish, Sumeria, SunWorld, SWATPro, Video Event, Video Toaster World; **VENEZUELA's** Computerworld Venezuela, MicroComputerworld Venezuela; **VIETNAM's** PC World Vietnam.

 The text in this book is printed on recycled paper.

About the Author

Jim Heid has been writing for *Macworld* since 1984, and has appeared in every issue since March 1985. He writes the award-winning monthly "Getting Started" column as well as features and reviews. He specializes in printers, desktop publishing, typography, MIDI, and digital audio — a mix that exploits his background as a typographer, musician, and audio buff. (He grew up in his father's recording studio, which was Pittsburgh's first.) He's also written columns and features on word processing, and has been a user and beta tester of every version of Microsoft Word.

Heid has been working with and writing about personal computers since the late '70s, when he computerized his home-built ham radio station with one of the first Radio Shack TRS-80s. He is the author of seven books on Macintosh and IBM PC personal computing, and is a frequent speaker at user's groups, developer's conferences, and Macworld Expos. He and his wife live north of San Francisco on California's scenic Mendocino coast.

Credits

Publisher
David Solomon

Managing Editor
Mary Bednarek

Acquisitions Editor
Terrie Lynn Solomon

Project Editor
Jeremy Judson

Production Manager
Beth J. Baker

Copy Editor
Felicity O'Meara

Technical Reviewer
Dennis Cohen

Text Preparation
Shirley E. Coe

Indexer
Steve Rath

Editorial Assistant
Dana Bryant Sadoff

Manufacturing Manager
Lana J. Olson

Book Design and Production
Peppy White
Francette M. Ytsma
Tracy Strub
(University Graphics, Palo Alto, California)

university graphics

Contents at a Glance

Table of Contents

Topic 3: Moving Text 16

Topic 4: Formatting Characters 20

Part II: Editing and Proofing 131

Topic 15: Finding and Replacing 133

Topic 25: Adding Borders and Shading 237

Foreword

If you are like most Macintosh users, you spend more time on writing, editing, and formatting documents with a word processor than on any other activity. So why not learn to be really good at it? One of the great joys of using a personal computer is that you can continue to discover seemingly minor techniques, any one of which can save you hours of work. It's remarkable how many users are willing to spend thousands of dollars on hardware to provide their computers with more power and flexibility, when the greatest unmined source of power is learning how to use more effectively the software that they already own. By learning additional, simple keystrokes you can uncover the hidden power of Microsoft Word with a small investment of your time.

After working closely with Jim for seven years I can assure you — there's no better guide to Microsoft Word's powerful word processing abilities. As one of *Macworld's* first contributing editors, Jim has covered word processing on the Mac from its earliest beginnings, when only a couple of programs (one of which was the first version of Microsoft Word!) were available, until the present, when a number of fully featured programs compete for consumers' attention. Having written about the Mac since its inception, Jim is one of the few authors who has actually used and written about every version of Microsoft Word.

Not only is Jim one of the foremost experts on Microsoft Word for the Mac, he has a broader knowledge of the Macintosh market than any other author writing about the Mac today. Every month in his "Getting Started" column in *Macworld,* Jim introduces readers to areas of the Macintosh ranging from color printers to word processors. As such, he is uniquely qualified to explain new concepts to beginning users as well as to more-experienced users who are venturing into new territory or simply looking for a lucid refresher on application areas that continue to change rapidly. Jim also spent five years as a professional typesetter, so he thoroughly understands the most demanding publishing applications that a word processor may be expected to perform.

Jim Heid's ability to successfully address both novices and power users is evident in the format of this book. If you are new to Word or need a refresher, Jim first introduces the key concepts of each new facet of the program in a brief overview section. The Step-by-Step sections show you how to implement what you have just learned — or if you are impatient with concepts, you can just jump in and start using the program, with this section to guide you through the process. The Step-by-Step sections are followed by Quick Tips — which help you discover the buried treasure of Word, whether you have just learned its basic operation or are already familiar with the program and are looking for quick and immediate techniques to make your software really work for you.

However you decide to use this book, you will get more out of Microsoft Word. It's fashionable for people to talk about working smarter, but most won't show you how to do it. Jim Heid shows you not only how to work smarter, but also how to work smarter *more effectively* with his thoughtful and concise presentation.

Adrian Mello
Editor-in-Chief
Macworld magazine

Introduction

About this book

Welcome to a new kind of computer book. The *Macworld Guide to Microsoft Word 5* is different from other computer books — it isn't a quick reference guide, it isn't a manual, and it isn't a 700-page tome.

So what is it?

First, a brief history. When IDG Books approached me about writing the first book in the *Macworld Guide To . . .* series, we looked at manuals, quick reference guides, and those long, forest-leveling books so many publishers are producing these days. The manuals software companies provide vary in quality, but generally, they have one strength: step-by-step sections that you can work through while sitting at the computer. Quick reference guides have the advantage of brevity, and their structure lets you find topics quickly. They're useful if you need a quick refresher on a topic you've forgotten, but they rarely provide insights into the subtleties of a program.

As for the long-winded tomes, they're just too long. Do people really read 700-page computer books from cover to cover? Usually, no. Most people read sections or chapters of immediate interest, and refer to the rest later as needed.

Then it occurred to us that the ideal book on a specific program should combine the best strengths of all three types of publications — the brevity and structured layout of a quick reference guide, the step-by-step tutorials of a manual, and the insights and tips of a tome.

And that describes the *Macworld Guide to Microsoft Word 5*. Think of it as a travel book for Microsoft Word. A travel guide lets you look up a place and then learn about it and find out what to do and where to do it. Similarly, this book lets you look up a topic and learn what to do and how to do it. And just like a travel guide, this book is designed to allow you to quickly look up the information you need when you find yourself in unfamiliar territory.

And as you travel in the Mac world, look for IDG Books's other books in this series: *Macworld Guide to Microsoft Works, Macworld Guide to Aldus PageMaker,* and *Macworld Guide to Microsoft Excel.*

Whom this book is for

The *Macworld Guide to Microsoft Word 5* is for anyone who uses version 5 of Microsoft Word for the Macintosh:

✦ If you're a beginner, the step-by-step tutorials in this book will help you get up to speed on unfamiliar topics.

✦ If you're an intermediate Word user — someone who doesn't know every aspect of Word but doesn't want hand-holding, either — the quick overviews of each subject area will help you accomplish your goals without having to work through the tutorials.

✦ If you're an expert, the tips and insights in each subject area will help you use this powerhouse word processor to its fullest. You'll also appreciate the succinct summaries of Word's workings, the lists of shortcuts, and the quick reference card that you can pull out and keep alongside your Macintosh.

How this book is organized

This book doesn't have chapters, it has smaller sections called *topics*. Each topic covers a specific task you might perform in Word — formatting a paragraph, creating automatic page numbers, or adding footnotes. When you want to perform a certain task, check the table of contents to locate the topic that covers your needs. Or, simply fan the pages of the book — each topic's name appears at the edges of each page to allow you to quickly spot the one you need. Each topic contains three sections:

Overview provides a summary of the topic's subject. This is the section to read when you want the big picture of how to accomplish a certain job.

Step-by-Step elaborates on the information in the overview by providing succinct, step-by-step instructions that walk you through the task at hand. If you want to master a particular Word feature, you might want to work through all the steps in a given topic's Step-by-Step section. If you're looking for a specific set of instructions, just skim the "To do" lines that precede the numbered steps until you find the instructions you need.

Quick Tips provides tips related to the topic's subject. Look here for the little insights that will help you wring the most out of Word.

Within each topic's margins, you'll find occasional illustrations that serve as reminders of important points. You might also use the margin to jot down your own Word discoveries.

This book's topics are organized into four sections:

◆ **Part I, "Word Basics,"** describes how to perform basic formatting and editing tasks.

◆ **Part II, "Editing and Proofing,"** describes how to find and replace text and formatting information, how to cut down repetitive typing with Word's glossary feature, and how to use Word's spelling checker and other proofing features.

◆ **Part III, "Advanced Formatting,"** explains how to create multiple columns of text on a page, how to create tables, outlines, tables of contents, indexes, and long documents, and how to create personalized form letters using Word's print merge feature.

◆ **Part IV, "Streamlining Your Work,"** shows how to use Word's document-management features to organize and quickly locate the Word documents on your hard disk, and how to create stationery documents — templates for the types of documents you create most often. This section also describes how to exchange information between Word and other programs and how to tailor Word to your own tastes by customizing its menus and creating macros that perform repetitive sequences.

The back of the book contains three appendices.

◆ **Appendix A** provides tips on installing Word and adjusting its memory requirements. Look here when you want to fine-tune Word's memory and disk space requirements.

◆ **Appendix B** lists Word's huge array of keyboard shortcuts. If you hate to grope for the mouse in the middle of a writing session, you'll be glad to know you can issue almost any Word command without taking your hands from the keyboard. I describe Word's most common and most useful keyboard shortcuts throughout the book, but Appendix B is the place to turn when you want to see them all in one place.

◆ **Appendix C** is a glossary of common Word and word processing terminology. If you encounter an unfamiliar term while reading this book, chances are you'll find its definition here.

◆ **Appendix D** is a unique *task index* that lists all of the "To do" instructions that appear in each topic's Step-by-Step section.

◆ **Appendix E** discusses the new features provided in Word 5.1 which make using Word easier than ever.

How to use this book

If you're new to Word, you should work through the first few topics to get a feel for the program. Otherwise, plow in wherever you like — one advantage of the way this book is organized is that you don't have to read it sequentially.

This book has several features designed to allow you to locate the information you need quickly. Here are some tips for using these features effectively.

When you want to . . .	Use . . .
learn how to accomplish a certain word processing task, such as adding a header to the top of every page	the table of contents to locate the topic that describes the task
look up a specific set of instructions within a topic — for example, those that describe how to create a different header for odd-and even-numbered pages	the task index
find information pertaining to a particular Word feature, regardless of where the information is located	the general index

Sometimes browsing is the easiest way to look something up. We've made it easy to do that, too. Notice that this book's topic and section headings appear vertically in the page margins — you'll find that if you fan the pages, you can scan the headings at lightning speed. ·

What you should already know

This book assumes you know the basics behind operating a Macintosh. Specifically, you should know how to start programs and choose menu commands, and you should know basic Macintosh terms such as point, click, and double-click. If you're unfamiliar with these concepts, you might want to work through the tutorials in the manual that accompanied your Macintosh.

Get Word help — while you work

At the back of this book, you'll find an offer for Jim Heid's Word Companion (sold separately), a set of disks containing an electronic version of this book that you can refer to as you use the program. Also included is a library of attractively designed document templates, glossaries, custom settings files, and much more. If you want to get the most out of Microsoft Word 5, see the order form for details on Jim Heid's Word Companion.

Part I
Word Basics

Topic 1

Document Basics

Overview

Starting a new document

In Word, as in most Macintosh programs, the information that you enter, modify, look at, save, and print is stored on disk as a *document*. You manage documents — copy them, delete them, move them into folders, and more — by using the Macintosh Finder. A document that you save on disk is also often called a *file*.

When you start Word, it creates a new, untitled document window for you. A new document is automatically set up to use 8½ × 11 inch paper and has top and bottom margins of 1 inch and left and right margins of 1.25 inches. (Topic 7 describes how to change margin sizes.)

To start working on a new document, simply begin typing in the untitled document window. You don't need to press Return at the end of each line as you would with a typewriter. Word's *word wrap* feature brings a word that doesn't fit at the end of a line down to the beginning of the next line. So press Return only at the ends of paragraphs or after text that you want to have appear on its own line (for example, after each line of an address).

You can create another untitled document window by choosing New from the File menu. You can have as many document windows on the screen as you have memory for, up to Word's limit of 23.

Saving a document

As you enter text into a document, the text is temporarily stored in the Mac's memory. If you shut your Macintosh off or a power failure or system error occurs, any untitled documents disappear. To keep a document so that you can use it again later, you must *save* it on disk.

To save a document on disk, choose Save from the File menu. When you choose Save for an untitled document, Word presents a dialog box with a space for you to type a name into, as the following tutorial shows. Word also displays a Summary Info dialog box that lets you enter descriptive information about the file. If you enter summary information about your documents, you can use Word's Find File command to locate documents based on that information, as shown in Topic 33.

Choosing Save once isn't enough if you want to save all changes you've made to the document since the first save. As you work on a document, you need to choose Save from time to time to commit the latest version to disk — and to avoid losing work due to a problem. Each time you choose Save, Word makes a disk copy of the version of the document that exists in your Mac's memory. How often should you save? Any time you do something that you wouldn't want to have to do over again.

Closing a document

After you've finished working with a document, you might want to *close* it by using the File menu's Close command or clicking the document window's close box (in the upper-left corner of the document window). Closing a document is like putting a piece of paper back in a drawer — you aren't throwing it away, but simply setting it aside. You don't have to close a document in order to work on another one (unless Word reports that you don't have enough memory to work with another document). Still, closing documents that you aren't actually using is a good idea — it frees up memory and reduces clutter on the screen. If you try to close a document that you've changed since the last time you saved it, Word asks if you'd like to save the changes before closing.

Opening a document

When you want to work with a document that isn't on the screen, you need to *open* the document. To open a document, choose Open from the File menu, and then double-click the document's name (or select the name and click Open or press Return). If you're working in the Finder, you can open a document by double-clicking it. Doing so starts Word (if it isn't already running) and opens the document.

Step-by-Step

This section shows how to create, save, close, and open a document. First, you'll type a paragraph and then save it on disk. (As you type, notice how Word's word wrap feature eliminates the need to press Return at the end of each line.) Then, you'll close the document and then open it again.

1. **If you haven't already, start Word by selecting the Word icon and then selecting Open from the Finder's File menu, or just by double-clicking the Word icon.**

An untitled document window appears:

If you're running System 7, you
can get help using the Help menu

Click the close box when you want to close the document

New text you type appears here, at the blinking *insertion point*

Use the *ribbon* for quick character formatting (see Topic 4)

Use the *ruler* to adjust margins, line spacing, and tabs (see Topics 5 and 8)

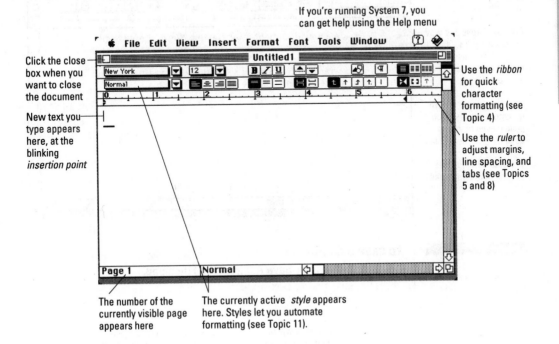

The number of the currently visible page appears here

The currently active *style* appears here. Styles let you automate formatting (see Topic 11).

2. **Type the following paragraph, pressing Return at the end of the last line. To indent the first line of the paragraph, press the Tab key.**

To create a new document after starting Word, simply begin typing in the untitled document window. You don't need to press Return at the end of each line as you would with a typewriter. Word's word wrap feature brings a word that doesn't fit at the end of a line down to the beginning of the next line.

Your screen should look like this:

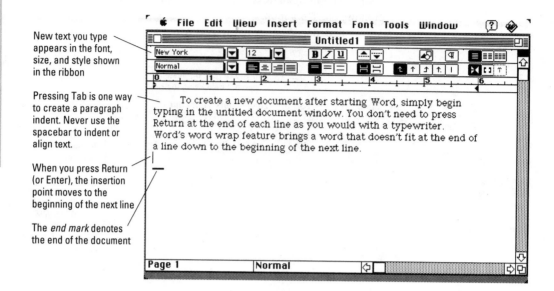

New text you type appears in the font, size, and style shown in the ribbon

Pressing Tab is one way to create a paragraph indent. Never use the spacebar to indent or align text.

When you press Return (or Enter), the insertion point moves to the beginning of the next line

The *end mark* denotes the end of the document

Command-key shortcuts let you choose commands without using the mouse

To save a document:

1. Choose Save (or Save As) from the File menu.

The Save dialog box appears:

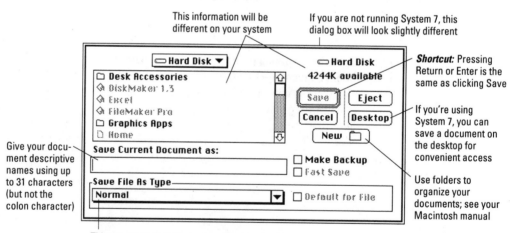

This information will be different on your system

If you are not running System 7, this dialog box will look slightly different

Shortcut: Pressing Return or Enter is the same as clicking Save

If you're using System 7, you can save a document on the desktop for convenient access

Use folders to organize your documents; see your Macintosh manual

Give your document descriptive names using up to 31 characters (but not the colon character)

This pop-up menu lets you save the document in other *formats,* which can be useful if you plan to use it with other programs (see Topic 32)

2. Type a name for the document and then click Save.

Word saves the document on disk.

3. The Summary Info dialog box appears.

Here you can enter descriptive *summary information* about the document. You can use Word's Find File option to locate documents based on their summary information. If you don't want to save any summary information, simply click OK or Cancel. If you click Cancel, Word will ask for summary information the next time you save the document.

```
╔══════════════ Summary Info ══════════════╗
║  ┌─────────┬──────────────────────────┐ ┌────────┐ ║
║  │ Title:  │                          │ │   OK   │ ║
║  ├─────────┼──────────────────────────┤ └────────┘ ║
║  │ Subject:│                          │ ┌────────┐ ║
║  ├─────────┼──────────────────────────┤ │ Cancel │ ║
║  │ Author: │ Your Name Here           │ └────────┘ ║
║  ├─────────┼──────────────────────────┤            ║
║  │ Version:│                          │            ║
║  ├─────────┼──────────────────────────┤            ║
║  │ Keywords:│                         │            ║
║  └─────────┴──────────────────────────┘            ║
╚═══════════════════════════════════════════════════╝
```

To close a document:

1. Click its window's close box or choose Close from the File menu.

Regardless of which technique you use, if you've made any changes to the document since you saved it, Word asks if you want to save changes. If you do, click Yes. If you don't, click No. If you don't want to close the document after all, click Cancel.

To open a document:

1. Choose Open from the File menu.

The Open dialog box appears.

2. Locate the document, and then double-click its name.

Word opens the document. As an alternative to double-clicking the document's name, you can click its name once and then click the Open button or simply press Return. You can also locate a document by quickly typing the first few characters of its name.

Quick Tips

Avoid that spacebar

Don't use the spacebar to align or indent text; if you do, you're likely to have trouble when you reformat or print the text. To align or indent text, use paragraph indents or tab stops as described in Topics 5 and 8.

Don't forget to save

Remember that you must save a document in order to store it on disk. If the document window's name begins with "Untitled," the document isn't saved.

You can use the Preferences command (in the Tools menu) to tell Word to remind you to save at intervals you specify. After choosing Preferences, click the Open and Save option, and then click the Save Reminder check box and type the number of minutes you'd like between reminders. Topic 34 describes more customizing options.

Save versus Save As

You can make a new copy of an already-saved document by choosing Save As from the File menu. Doing so displays the Save dialog box: Type a name for the document and click OK. One reason to use Save As might be to create two different versions of a document.

You can choose a bold-bordered button by pressing Return or Enter

Keyboard shortcuts

As an alternative to clicking the Save button in the Save dialog box, simply press Return. This eliminates having to reach for the mouse after you type the document name. Any time a dialog box has a button with a bold border, you can choose that button by pressing Return or Enter. You'll find additional keyboard shortcuts for the Save dialog box in Appendix B.

Switching between open documents

When you have more than one document open at once, you can switch between them in several ways. You can activate a different window by clicking anywhere within it. Or, choose the desired window's name from the Window menu. You can also page through the open windows by pressing Command-Option-W.

Accessing recently opened documents

On large Macintosh monitors, Word's File menu lists the last four documents you opened. You can open them by choosing their names instead of having to use the Open command. If you have a small-screen compact Mac such as a Classic, the File menu doesn't automatically include this list. You can tell Word to display the list, however, by using the Preferences command in the Tool menu. Choose Preferences, click the View option, and then select the List Recently Opened Documents check box. If you have a large-screen Mac and you don't want to see the list, use the Preferences command to uncheck the option.

Stationery documents

Do you always create a certain kind of document? You can save time and effort by creating a *stationery pad* for it as described in Topic 33.

Making your text look typeset

By following a few simple rules, you can make your text look professionally typeset. See the quick reference card in the front of this book for details.

Topic 2
Basic Editing and Scrolling

Overview

Not making you press Return after each line is just one of the reasons word processors have sent typewriters to the scrap heap. Another is the way they enable you to insert and delete text and jump to different parts of a document.

Word's basic editing features resemble those of other Mac programs, so you may already have a head start in learning them. If not, this topic's Step-by-Step section will get you started.

Inserting text

When you're inserting text, you'll often need to move the insertion point (the blinking vertical bar that indicates where new typing will appear). You can use the mouse to move the insertion point to a specific location by pointing there and then clicking once. You can also tap-tap your way there using the keyboard's arrow keys.

To move the insertion point with the mouse, point with the I-beam pointer and then click

Selecting text

Before deleting or formatting text, you must first *select* it — mark it so that Word knows what you plan to delete or format. The most basic selection technique is to drag across the text. Word also provides selection shortcuts: To select a word, for example, double-click it. To select an entire sentence, press the Command key and click within the sentence. You can also select lines, paragraphs, and the entire document by clicking in the *selection bar,* the area along the left edge of the document window. A list of Word's selection shortcuts appears later in this topic as well as in the pull-out quick reference card in the front of this book.

Report of Operations

Board of Directors
The Board of Directors met

The pointer is a right-pointing arrow when it's in the selection bar

Scrolling

As you work with a document, you'll do a fair amount of *scrolling* to access portions of the document that aren't currently visible within the document window's boundaries. Word's scroll bars work just like the scroll bars in other Mac programs:

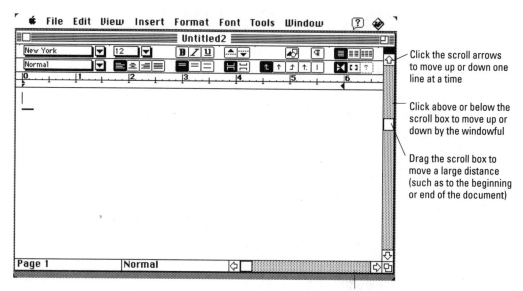

Click the scroll arrows to move up or down one line at a time

Click above or below the scroll box to move up or down by the windowful

Drag the scroll box to move a large distance (such as to the beginning or end of the document)

The horizontal scroll bar lets you scroll left and right when the document won't fit within the window's width

Word also lets you scroll using the keyboard's arrow keys and numeric keypad keys. If you have an extended keyboard (one with a row of function keys across the top), you can also scroll using the Home, End, Page Up, and Page Down keys. Some scrolling keys work differently when you press them along with the Command key — pressing Command along with the left arrow key, for example, moves you to the previous word, not the previous character. Pressing the Shift key as you scroll with the keyboard causes Word to select text.

Some selecting tasks may require you to combine the keyboard and mouse along with scrolling. For example, to select a large passage of text, first move the insertion point to the beginning of the passage. Next, use the mouse to scroll to the end of the passage. Finally, press and hold down the Shift key while clicking at the end of the passage. This *Shift-click* technique works in most Macintosh programs.

The quick reference card in the front of this book summarizes Word's scrolling and selecting shortcuts, including some that let you leap tall passages in a single bound.

Step-by-Step

The instructions in this section show how to insert text, delete it, and replace selected text with new text. For details on selecting text, see the table "Selection strategies" in the Quick Tips section of this topic.

To insert new text:

1. Move the insertion point to the spot where you want the new text to appear.

Remember that you can use the keyboard's scrolling keys or the mouse to move the insertion point.

2. Type the new text.

Keep an eye on the spaces surrounding the new text — it's easy to wind up with extra spaces or no space at all before or after a text passage you insert.

Move the insertion point to the location where the new text will appear...

Dear Mom and Dad,

I'm writing to let you know that I'll be moving back home next week. After paying rent and utility bills for all these years, I've realized that living with parents is actually a pretty good deal. So stock up the 'fridge and clear the clothesline--my old room is going to be back in use!

...and then type the new text

Dear Mom and Dad,

I'm writing to let you know that I'll be moving back home next week. After paying rent and utility bills and going to the coin-operated laundry for all these years, I've realized that living with parents is actually a pretty good deal. So stock up the 'fridge and clear the clothesline--my old room is going to be back in use!

To delete some text:

1. Select the text.

Word highlights the text to show it's selected.

2. Press the Delete key. If you have an extended keyboard (with function keys across the top), you can press the Del key located above the arrow keys. You can choose Clear from the Edit menu.

Word deletes the text and adjusts the paragraph's line endings if necessary.

Select the text you want to delete
(including word spaces, if necessary)...

Dear Mom and Dad,

I'm writing to let you know that I'll be moving back home next week. After paying rent and utility bills and going to the coin-operated laundry for all these years, I've realized that living with parents is actually a pretty good deal. So stock up the 'fridge and clear the clothesline--my old room is going to be back in use!

...and then press Delete (or Del or
Backspace, depending on your keyboard),
or choose Clear from the Edit menu

Dear Mom and Dad,

I'm writing to let you know that I'll be moving back home next week. After paying rent and going to the coin-operated laundry for all these years, I've realized that living with parents is actually a pretty good deal. So stock up the 'fridge and clear the clothesline--my old room is going to be back in use!

To replace text with new text:

1. Select the text.

Word highlights the text to show it's selected.

2. Begin typing the new text.

You don't have to press the Delete key first; your first keystroke clears the selected text.

Select the text you want to replace
(including word spaces, if necessary)...

Dear Mom and Dad,

I'm writing to let you know that I'll be moving back home next week. After paying rent and utility bills and going to the coin-operated laundry for all these years, I've realized that living with parents is actually a pretty good deal. So stock up the 'fridge and clear the clothesline--my old room is going to be back in use!

...and then type the new text (you
don't have to press Delete first)

Dear Mom and Dad,

I'm writing to let you know that I'll be moving back home next week. After paying rent and utility bills and going to the coin-operated laundry for the past twelve years, I've realized that living with parents is actually a pretty good deal. So stock up the 'fridge and clear the clothesline--my old room is going to be back in use!

Quick Tips

Use Undo to restore accidentally deleted text

If you delete some text by mistake, you can restore it by choosing Undo from the Edit menu before doing anything else.

Scrolling: Keyboard vs. mouse

Is it better to use the keyboard or the mouse for scrolling and moving the insertion point? It's often a matter of personal preference, although the keyboard tends to be more efficient when you're busily typing and you need to make a minor edit near the area where you're working. The mouse is usually more efficient when you need to move the insertion point a large distance, and when you're in the editing phase of a project, moving from page to page to make corrections throughout. Become familiar with both keyboard and mouse navigation techniques and use the method that feels most comfortable.

When you use the keyboard to scroll through a document, the insertion point moves as you scroll. By contrast, when you scroll using the mouse and scroll bars, the insertion point does not move. Keep this subtle difference in mind. If you're scrolling to briefly check on something elsewhere in the document, for example, you might not want the insertion point to move. In this case, the mouse might be the better scrolling tool.

Splitting the document window

You can split a document window into two *panes* by dragging or double-clicking the *split bar* located above the vertical scroll bar. When you split a document window, you can scroll each pane independently. It's just the ticket when you want to keep one portion of a document in view at all times or check on something elsewhere in the document without losing your place. To split (or unsplit) a document window from the keyboard, type Command-Option-S.

Double-click the split bar, or click on it and drag down

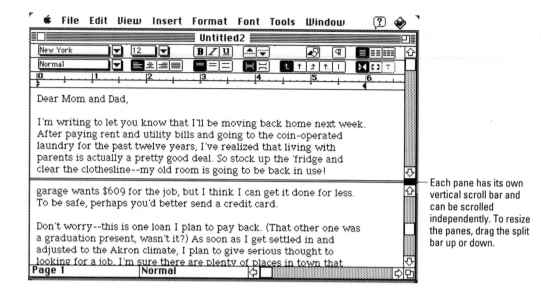

Each pane has its own vertical scroll bar and can be scrolled independently. To resize the panes, drag the split bar up or down.

Opening a second window for a document

Another terrific way to look at different parts of a document at the same time is to create additional windows for the document. Choose New Window from the Window menu, and Word creates another window for the currently active document. Word numbers each window. For example, if you open a second window for a document named Memo, the new window's title bar reads Memo:2, and the original window reads Memo:1. The document's name on disk doesn't change, however. You can create as many additional windows as you like, up to Word's limit of 23. You can close each additional window whenever you like.

You *can* go back

When you're editing, Word's *go back* key is a time saver. The go back key — the 0 on the number keypad — moves the insertion point back to the last three locations where you edited or typed text. Word even stores these locations when you save the document, making it easy to return to where you left off the next time you open it.

Text-selection shortcuts

Dragging across text is only one selection technique. Word provides many selection shortcuts; they're summarized in the following table.

Selection strategies

To select this...	Do this...
a word	double-click the word
a sentence	Command-click within the sentence
a paragraph	triple-click within the paragraph or double-click the selection bar adjacent to the paragraph
a single line	click once in the selection bar adjacent to the line
a carriage return character	double-click to the right of the last line of the paragraph
the entire document	Command-click in the selection bar, triple-click in the selection bar, or choose Select All from the Edit menu

Tell Word where to go

To quickly jump to a specific page in a document, use the Go To command in the Edit menu. You can then type a page number and press Return, or type a code as listed in the following table. You can also double-click the page number area in the lower-left corner of the document window to display the Go To Page dialog box.

Go To command options

To go...	Type this...
to the next page	p (or leave the box empty)
forward three pages from the insertion point	+3
back three pages from the insertion point	-3
to the last page	a number greater than the last page number
to the first page	0

Scrolling to the left of zero

Normally, Word doesn't let you scroll to the left of the zero mark on the ruler. If you want to scroll further left, however, here's how: Press the Shift key while clicking the left arrow in the horizontal scroll bar. One benefit of scrolling "left of zero" is that the selection bar (which you can use to quickly select lines, paragraphs, and the entire document) becomes wider and, therefore, a bit easier to use.

Topic 3
Moving Text

Overview

Moving text around is a common activity — and the ease with which Word and other word processors let you do it is another thing that gives typewriter veterans goosebumps.

The Clipboard

Word provides a variety of ways to move text, but the Edit menu's Cut and Paste commands are the most commonly used. After you select text (highlight it by dragging with the mouse) you can use the Cut command to remove text from the document and place it on the Mac's *Clipboard*, a temporary storage area. You can then insert the text elsewhere by moving the insertion point to a different place in the document (or in a different document or even a different program) and then choosing Paste.

When you
select text and
choose Copy
or Cut...

Weekly Status Report

Week ending September 15

In the production department, a new AX-45 compressor was put on line to assist the AX-35 that was obtained last month.

...the text is
placed on the
Macintosh
Clipboard...

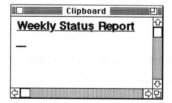

...and you can
insert it
elsewhere by
choosing Paste

Weekly Status Report

Week ending September 21

This week saw the completion of the training program for the new AX-45 compressor. Representatives from the

You can continue choosing Paste to insert multiple copies of the text — anything you put on the Clipboard stays there until you replace it by choosing Cut or Copy again (or until you switch the Mac off or restart it).

If you want to insert text elsewhere without removing it from its original location, use the Copy command instead of Cut. You can use this technique to reuse part of a document, such as a return address, without deleting it from the document.

Moving text with the drag-and-drop feature

Word's drag-and-drop editing feature lets you move text (or graphics, for that matter) by simply dragging it to the desired location — no cutting or pasting required.

To activate drag-and-drop editing, choose Preferences from the Tools menu and then check the Drag-and-Drop Text Editing box.

To drag text elsewhere, simply select it and then point to the selected text. The mouse pointer turns into a left-pointing arrow. Press and hold down the mouse button, and then drag. As you drag, you'll see that a dotted vertical bar follows the mouse pointer. Drag the bar until it's located where you want the text to appear, release the mouse button, and Word moves the text to that location. That's all there is to it.

To make a copy of the text, press Command and then drag to where you want the copy.

You can't drag-and-drop text from one window to another. When you need to move text from one document to another, use the Edit menu commands as described in this topic.

Step-by-Step

This section shows how to cut some text and then paste it elsewhere.

To cut the text:

1. Select it by dragging across it with the mouse or using any of Word's selection techniques.

Word highlights the text to show that it's selected.

2. Choose Cut from the Edit menu.

Word removes the text from the document and places it on the Mac's Clipboard. If you don't want to remove the text from its original location, choose Copy instead of Cut.

To insert the text elsewhere:

1. Move the insertion point to the spot where you want the text to appear.

If you want to move the text to a different document, open that document and then move the insertion point if necessary. If you want to replace existing text or a graphic with the text that's on the Clipboard, select that which you want to replace.

2. Choose Paste from the Edit menu.

Word pastes the text at the insertion point's location. If you selected something prior to pasting, Word replaces the selection with the contents of the Clipboard.

Quick Tips

Undo and the Cut and Copy commands

If you cut or copy the wrong text, choose Undo from the Edit menu before doing anything else. Choosing Undo restores text you cut and also restores any information that may have been on the Clipboard before you cut or copied.

Don't forget to include the paragraph mark

When you're cutting or copying an entire paragraph (and remember, a single line ending with a hard carriage return counts as a paragraph), be sure to include the carriage return when selecting the text — it's easy to miss a carriage return when you select text by dragging across it. The easiest way to be sure you include the carriage return is to select the text by clicking within the selection bar (the area along the window's left edge) or by triple-clicking to select the entire paragraph. See Topic 2 for more selection techniques.

Selection strategies for moving text

When you're moving words or sentences around, you can avoid extra editing by being sure to select the space after a word or sentence. Again, Word's selection shortcuts help: Double-clicking a word selects the space after it, as does Command-clicking a sentence.

Viewing the Clipboard's contents

You can choose Show Clipboard from the Window menu to view the Clipboard's contents. You can't edit the contents of the Clipboard window.

Cut	⌘H
Copy	⌘C
Paste	⌘V

Use Command-key equivalents to avoid having to reach for the mouse

Keyboard shortcuts for Cut, Copy, and Paste

Like most menu commands, the Cut, Copy, and Paste commands have keyboard equivalents that let you choose the commands without groping for the mouse. Word uses the same standard keyboard equivalents for the Edit menu commands that all Mac programs use: Command-X for Cut, Command-C for Copy, Command-V for Paste. If you have an extended keyboard (with 15 function keys along the top), you can also use the F2, F3, and F4 keys to cut, copy, and paste, and F1 to undo.

Saving the Clipboard's contents in the Scrapbook

Remember that the Clipboard's contents vanish when you restart the Mac or switch it off. To save the Clipboard's contents, use the Mac's Scrapbook desk accessory: Choose Scrapbook from the Apple menu, and then choose Paste. Doing so adds a new page to the Scrapbook. To retrieve information from the Scrapbook and put it on the Clipboard, use the Scrapbook's scroll bars to locate the desired page, and then choose Cut or Copy from the Edit menu. Choosing Cut removes the page from the Scrapbook; choosing Copy doesn't.

Other ways to copy and move text

Word provides a couple of clever keyboard shortcuts that enable you to move or copy text without replacing the contents of the Clipboard. First, select the text you want to move, and then press Command-Option-X. In the page number area, Word displays the message *Move To*. Next, move the insertion point — notice it's a dotted bar instead of a solid blinking one — to the location where you want the text to appear (or select a range of text to be replaced). Finally, press the Return key. To copy text instead of move it, use Command-Option-C. To cancel the move or copy operation, press the Esc key or Command-period.

If you find that the preceding Command-Option-letter keystroke sequence twists your fingers into knots, you can use the Commands command (in the Tools menu) to reassign the entire sequence to something a little easier — to one of the function keys on an extended keyboard, perhaps, or to one of the numbers on the numeric keypad. (I've assigned the move sequence to the numeric keypad's 5 key — this enables me, a left-handed mouse user, to select text using the mouse and then invoke the move shortcut with my right hand.) See Topic 34 for details on customizing Word's commands.

Topic 4

Formatting Characters

 ## Overview

In the typewriter world, formatting characters means underlining them or, if you're ambitious, switching type balls from, say, Letter Gothic to Elite. In the Macintosh world, formatting means a great deal more. (Some people might argue it means too much.) Word gives you full access to the Mac's wide variety of type fonts, sizes, and styles. A *font* is a collection of characters in a given design. *Size* refers to the characters' height, and is measured in $1/72$-inch units called *points*; this text, for example, appears in 10-point type. *Style* refers to variations within a font such as *italic* or **bold**.

Formatting alternatives

You can specify a format for characters just before you type them — simply switch into the desired font, size, and style, and then type the text. Or you can format text you've already typed — select the text and then choose the desired font, size, or style. (See Topic 2 if you're unfamiliar with Word's text-selection options.)

As for actually choosing fonts, sizes, and styles, Word gives you four alternatives: You can:

✦ Click Word's on-screen ribbon.

✦ Use the Format menu to choose character styles and the Font menu to choose Fonts.

✦ Use the Character command in the Format menu to choose fonts, sizes, and styles using one dialog box.

✦ Use keyboard shortcuts to change fonts, sizes, and styles.

As this topic's Quick Tips section describes, each of these techniques has its strengths.

(This topic doesn't describe formatting options that control the appearance of paragraphs, such as switching to double spacing, changing indents, or setting tabs. Topic 5 describes these jobs.)

Step-by-Step

This section shows how to format using each of the four techniques just described. You should already be familiar with the text-selection techniques described in Topic 2.

To format using the ribbon:

1. If the ribbon isn't visible, display it by choosing Ribbon from the View menu.

2. If you're formatting existing text, select the text.

3. Choose the desired font, size, and style from the ribbon.

You can also type a font name by first clicking in the Font pop-up menu, or a type size by first clicking in the Size pop-up menu. (See "To change the font from the keyboard," later in this topic, for tips on typing font names.)

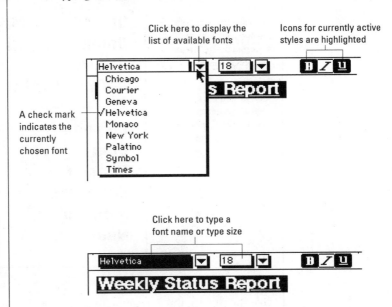

Note that the ribbon gives you access to only three styles: **bold**, *italic*, and underline. If you need other styles such as small caps or strikethru, use the Character command in the Format menu or the style's keyboard shortcut. Also note that you can mix and match style options, choosing, for example, both bold and underlining.

To format using the Format and Font menus:

1. If you're formatting existing text, select the text.

2. To change styles, choose the desired style(s) from the Format menu.

3. Choose the desired font and size from the Font menu. To specify a font size that isn't listed in the Font menu, choose Other from the Font menu, and then type the size and press Return.

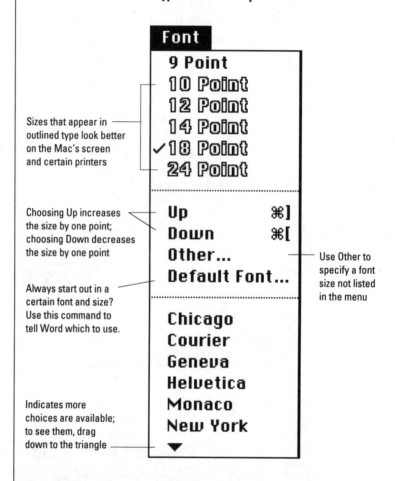

Sizes that appear in outlined type look better on the Mac's screen and certain printers

Choosing Up increases the size by one point; choosing Down decreases the size by one point

Use Other to specify a font size not listed in the menu

Always start out in a certain font and size? Use this command to tell Word which to use.

Indicates more choices are available; to see them, drag down to the triangle

Like the ribbon, the Format menu gives you access to only three styles: **bold**, *italic*, and <u>underline</u>. If you need other styles, use the Character command in the Format menu. If Word's ribbon is displayed, it reflects the choices you made.

To format using the Character command:

1. If you're formatting existing text, select the text.

2. Choose Character from the Format menu.

The Character dialog box appears:

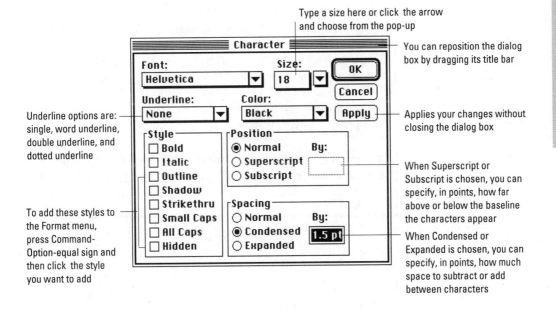

Type a size here or click the arrow and choose from the pop-up

You can reposition the dialog box by dragging its title bar

Underline options are: single, word underline, double underline, and dotted underline

Applies your changes without closing the dialog box

To add these styles to the Format menu, press Command-Option-equal sign and then click the style you want to add

When Superscript or Subscript is chosen, you can specify, in points, how far above or below the baseline the characters appear

When Condensed or Expanded is chosen, you can specify, in points, how much space to subtract or add between characters

You can also display the Character dialog box by double-clicking the ribbon or by choosing Other from the Font menu.

3. Choose the desired font, size, and style attributes.

For the type size, you can either choose a value from the pop-up menu or type a specific value in the Size box.

4. To see your changes applied but leave the Character dialog box open, click the Apply button. To apply your changes *and* close the Character dialog box, click OK.

The Apply button is useful when you're experimenting with formatting options and may need to use the dialog box again. If the dialog box is obscuring the text you're formatting, move the dialog box to a different location by dragging its title bar. (The dialog box will appear in the new location the next time you use it, even if you quit Word in the meantime.)

To change the font from the keyboard:

1. If you're formatting existing text, select the text.

2. Press Command-Shift-E or click *once* on the page number.

The word *Font* appears in the page number area at the lower-left corner of the document window.

3. Type the name of the font you want to use and then press Return.

You don't have to type the font's full name, just enough to allow Word to identify the font. For example, if your system contains only one font that begins with the letter C, you need type only that letter. However, most Macs contain more than one font beginning with C: Chicago and Courier. In this case, you need to type *Ch* or *Co*. You'll hear an error beep if you don't type enough characters for Word to determine which font you want, or if the characters you typed don't correspond to a font. If that happens, backspace the characters you typed and try again. To cancel the font command, press the Esc key or press Command-period.

This week saw the completion of the training program new AX-45 compressor. Representatives from the

Page 1	Normal

Click here or press Command-Shift-E...

This week saw the completion of the training program new AX-45 compressor. Representatives from the

Font	Normal

...and Word awaits your font command...

This week saw the completion of the training program new AX-45 compressor. Representatives from the

helv	Normal

...type all or part of the desired font's name and press Return

To change the type size from the keyboard:

1. If you're formatting existing text, select the text.

2. To increase the type size in single-point increments, press Command-]. To decrease the type size in single-point increments, press Command-[. To increase the type size in standard size increments, press Command-Shift-period. To decrease the type size in standard size increments, press Command-Shift-comma.

Word's standard size increments are 7, 9, 10, 12, 14, 18, 24, 36, 48, 60, 72, and 80. After 80, the size increases (or decreases) by 10, to

90, 100, 110, and so on. Word's smallest type size is 4-point, and the largest is 16,383-point — roughly 227 inches high.

You can also use the Character dialog box to change the type size from the keyboard: Select the text, press Command-D to open the Character dialog box, type the desired size, and then press Return to close the dialog box.

To change the type style from the keyboard:

1. If you're formatting existing text, select the text.

2. Press the key combination for the desired style:

For this style...	Press Command-Shift and...
Bold	B
Italic	I
Underline	U
Word underline	] (closing bracket)
Double underline	[(opening bracket)
Dotted underline	\ (backslash)
Strikethru	/ (slash)
Outline	D
Shadow	W
Small caps	H
All caps	K
Hidden (appears as dotted underline)	X

To remove one formatting attribute (for example, to remove boldfacing):

1. Select the text.

2. Click its style attribute in the ribbon, or choose it from the Format menu, or uncheck its check box in the Character dialog box.
   Word's style settings toggle back and forth: When you choose a style that isn't active, it becomes active, and when you choose a style that is active, it becomes inactive.

To remove multiple formatting attributes and revert to plain text:

1. Select the text.

2. Choose Revert to Style from the Format menu, or use its keyboard shortcut: Command-Shift-spacebar.

The Revert to Style command causes Word to apply the formatting specified in the current style sheet; for details on styles, see Topic 9.

Quick Tips

Which formatting tool is best?

Word's variety of formatting tools — the ribbon, the Font and Format menus, the Character command, and keyboard shortcuts — allows you to choose the formatting technique that's most comfortable and appropriate to what you're doing. For example, the ribbon is handy for formatting text you've already typed, but you might find it cumbersome for formatting text as you type, since you need to reach for the mouse to use it. The Character command is ideal when you want to change a variety of formatting attributes in one fell swoop, while the Font and Format menus are handy when you just need to change one attribute. And the keyboard shortcuts are ideal when you're furiously typing away and don't want to abandon the keyboard.

Set the default font

If you always begin documents in a certain font and size, use the Tool menu's Preferences command and its Default Font option to specify the default font and size (which you can override when necessary). You can also use styles to automate formatting tasks, as described in Topic 11.

Adding other styles to the Format menu

If you frequently use styles such as SMALL CAPS and ~~strikethru~~, you can add them to Word's Format menu. With the Character dialog box open, press Command-Option-equal sign. (The mouse pointer turns into a plus sign.) Next, click the style you want to add to the Format menu. See Topic 34 for more details on customizing Word.

Hidden text revealed

Word's *hidden text* format is an unusual one. Generally, you'll use it to create the special codes Word uses to create tables of contents, equations, and indexes. But you can also use hidden text to type notes or comments in a document. Simply type the comment and then format it as hidden text. When you want to hide the hidden text, use the Preferences command's View option to specify that hidden text not be shown. When you print a document, you can print the hidden text by checking the Print Hidden Text box in the Print dialog box. If the box is unchecked, hidden text will not print.

Topic 5

Formatting Paragraphs

Overview

The tasks you can perform with paragraph formatting include:

+ Changing line spacing — the amount of space between each line of a paragraph and between paragraphs.

+ Changing paragraph indents — the distance between the document's margins and the left and right edges of a paragraph.

+ Changing the alignment of text within paragraphs — centered, aligned against the left or right margins, or *justified* (aligned against the left *and* right margins).

+ Setting tab stops — to create special indents or tables (the Table command is often preferable for creating tables; see Topic 25).

+ Controlling the pagination of paragraphs — whether a paragraph can be divided across two pages, for example, or whether Word automatically keeps all of its lines together on one page.

This topic describes all but the last two of Word's paragraph formatting options. See Topic 7 for details on setting and changing tabs, and Topic 9 for information on controlling pagination.

Word lets you format paragraphs using the ruler or the Paragraph dialog box. Word also provides keyboard shortcuts for many paragraph-formatting options; they're summarized on the quick reference card in the front of this book.

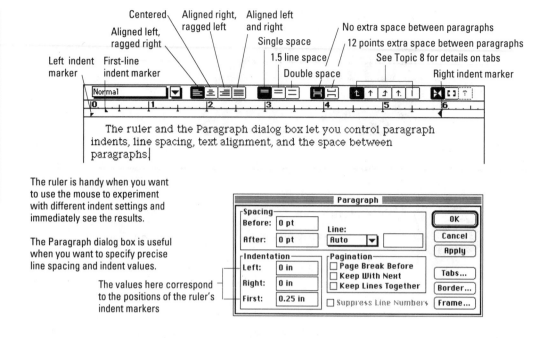

The ruler and the Paragraph dialog box let you control paragraph indents, line spacing, text alignment, and the space between paragraphs.

The ruler is handy when you want to use the mouse to experiment with different indent settings and immediately see the results.

The Paragraph dialog box is useful when you want to specify precise line spacing and indent values.

The values here correspond to the positions of the ruler's indent markers

Paragraph marks

Word's numerous paragraph-formatting options can be confusing when you're just getting started. One key to success is to remember that, in Word, a paragraph is any amount of text (and/or graphics) followed by a carriage return. In Word parlance, the carriage return is called a *paragraph mark*. You can display paragraph marks and formatting codes such as tabs by choosing Show ¶ from the View menu. The following illustration shows a document with paragraph marks visible. Notice there are seven paragraphs in this document.

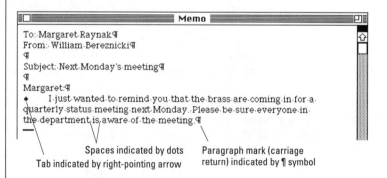

Spaces indicated by dots
Tab indicated by right-pointing arrow

Paragraph mark (carriage return) indicated by ¶ symbol

Word stores a paragraph's formatting in that paragraph's paragraph mark. When you press Return or Enter to start a new paragraph, Word copies the formatting instructions to the new paragraph. This lets you continue using the same paragraph formatting as you type new paragraphs.

Formatting tips

The fact that Word stores each paragraph's formatting in its own paragraph mark has a few important ramifications that can sometimes trip you up. Here are the Golden Rules of paragraph formatting and paragraph marks:

✦ To change the formatting of an existing paragraph, the insertion point must be in that paragraph or its paragraph mark must be selected. (An easy way to select a paragraph mark, whether it is showing or invisible, is to double-click to the right of the paragraph's last line.) If you want to change the paragraph formatting of several paragraphs, select them all *before* changing their formatting.

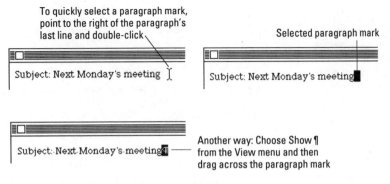

To quickly select a paragraph mark, point to the right of the paragraph's last line and double-click

Selected paragraph mark

Subject: Next Monday's meeting

Subject: Next Monday's meeting

Subject: Next Monday's meeting

Another way: Choose Show ¶ from the View menu and then drag across the paragraph mark

✦ When you delete a paragraph mark, the text before the paragraph mark becomes part of the following paragraph, and takes on its paragraph formatting. This explains why you might suddenly see margins or tab settings change when you delete a paragraph mark. If you inadvertently delete a paragraph mark, you can restore it (and its paragraph's formatting) by immediately choosing Undo from the Edit menu or typing Command-Z.

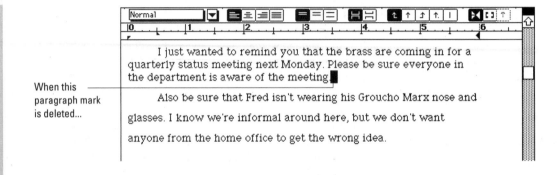

When this paragraph mark is deleted...

...the first paragraph takes on the formatting of the following paragraph, which is double-spaced

✦ When two paragraphs have different paragraph formatting, you can't delete the first paragraph's carriage return by backspacing. If you try, Word beeps. When you find yourself saying "I'm trying to backspace and the #!$@&% program just keeps beeping," it's because the two paragraphs have different formatting. If you're backspacing in order to remove the paragraph mark, select the paragraph mark and press Delete instead (but note that the first paragraph will take on the second paragraph's formatting, as just described). If you're backspacing in order to correct a typo near the end of the previous paragraph, correct the typo by moving the insertion point instead.

✦ If you select more than one paragraph and the paragraphs have different formatting (perhaps one is single-spaced and another is double-spaced), the bottom portion of the ruler turns gray and its formatting icons become deselected as in the following illustration. You can still use the ruler when it appears this way.

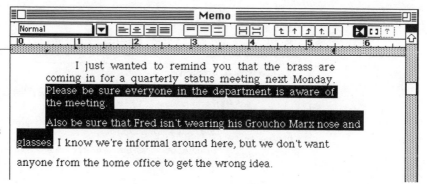

When the bottom half of the ruler is gray and no formatting icons are selected, it means that the selected text spans paragraphs with different formatting

Here, the selected text spans paragraphs with the same formatting, so the ruler appears normal

Indents

As for indents, don't confuse them with margins (which are covered in Topic 7). Margin settings apply to an entire document, while indents work on the paragraph level. Topic 1 showed one way to create a basic paragraph indent: Press the Tab key at the beginning of a paragraph. Word provides other ways to indent that don't require you to remember to press Tab at the start of each paragraph. You can use the Paragraph command (Format menu) to specify a *first-line indent* for the first line of the paragraph. You can also change the first-line indent by dragging the ruler's first-line indent marker (the upper half of the triangle that appears at the ruler's left edge).

If you're typing a series of numbered or bulleted paragraphs and you want runover lines to align, you can create a *hanging indent*— press the Shift key while dragging the lower half of the triangle, called the *left indent marker*. You can also create a *negative indent* to create a paragraph that extends into the left or right margin of the page. The following illustration shows these types of indents.

Drag the upper triangle...

...to create a first-line indent

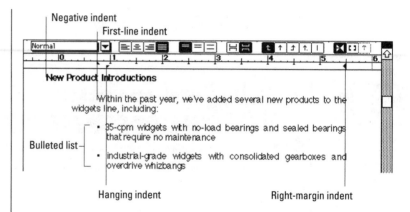

Negative indent
First-line indent
Bulleted list
Hanging indent
Right-margin indent

Finally, a word about line spacing. When you use different type sizes in a line (including ^{super}script or _{sub}script characters), Word adjusts line spacing to accommodate the largest size you used. This often results in inconsistent spacing between lines within a paragraph. You can force Word to apply an exact amount of space between lines: Choose Paragraph from the Format menu, and then choose Exactly from the Line pop-up menu. Finally, type the amount of space desired between lines.

Step-by-Step

This section shows how to change line spacing, paragraph margins, and text alignment, as well as how to create hanging indents and indented paragraphs. Many of these techniques involve using the ruler; if the ruler isn't displayed, you can display it by choosing Ruler from the View menu.

To change line spacing or paragraph alignment using the ruler:

1. **Be sure the insertion point is in the paragraph whose spacing you want to change. If you want to change the spacing of several paragraphs, select them all.**

2. **Click the desired spacing or alignment icon on the ruler.**

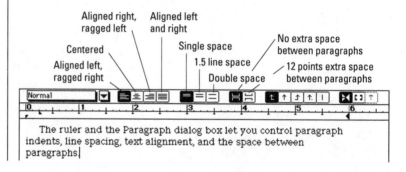

The ruler and the Paragraph dialog box let you control paragraph indents, line spacing, text alignment, and the space between paragraphs.

To adjust the paragraph's left and right indents using the ruler:

1. **Be sure the insertion point is in the paragraph whose spacing you want to change. If you want to change the margins of several paragraphs, select them all.**

2. **Drag the left indent marker to change the left indent, and the right indent marker to change the right indent.**

   When adjusting the left indent, be sure to click on the bottom half of the indent marker; if you click and drag only the top half, you'll change the first line indent, not the overall indent. When you release the mouse button, Word reformats the text to fit the new indents.

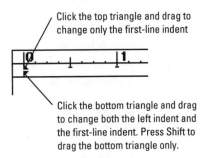

Click the top triangle and drag to change only the first-line indent

Click the bottom triangle and drag to change both the left indent and the first-line indent. Press Shift to drag the bottom triangle only.

To adjust line spacing, indents, or alignment using the Paragraph command:

1. **Be sure the insertion point is in the paragraph you want to change. If you want to change several paragraphs, select them all.**

2. **Choose Paragraph from the Format menu.**

   The Paragraph dialog box appears.

You can use the ruler while the Paragraph dialog box is open

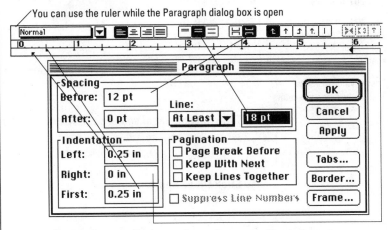

Shortcut: Press the Tab key to advance from one text box to the next

3. **Type the desired values in the appropriate boxes (to create a negative indent, type a minus sign before the indent value). Or use the ruler's icons and indent markers.**

If you use the ruler, Word shows the indent or spacing values in the appropriate areas of the dialog box. The changes aren't applied until you click Apply or OK in the dialog box, however.

4. **Click Apply or OK.**

The Apply button is useful when you're experimenting with formatting options and may need to use the dialog box again. If the dialog box is obscuring the paragraph you're formatting, move the dialog box to a different location by dragging its title bar.

To specify fixed line spacing that doesn't change to accommodate the tallest item in a line:

1. **Be sure the insertion point is in the paragraph you want to change. If you want to change several paragraphs, select them all.**

2. **Choose Paragraph from the Format menu.**

The Paragraph dialog box appears.

3. **From the Line pop-up menu, choose Exactly.**

Word adjusts the line spacing to accommodate the tallest character or graphic in the line

Word adjusts the line spacing so that it's no less than the value you specify; Word may increase the spacing if necessary

Line spacing is the value you specify; Word won't increase or decrease the spacing

Specify value in points, lines, inches, or centimeters

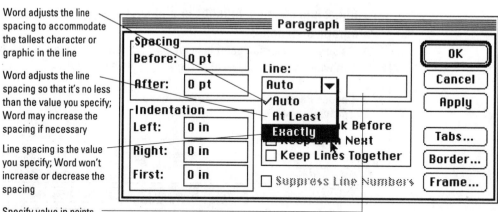

4. **Type the amount of space desired between lines.**

Word assumes the value is in points unless you follow the value with the li (lines), in (inches), or cm (centimeters) abbreviation.

5. **Click OK or Apply.**

To create a hanging indent to align the left margins in numbered or bulleted lists:

1. **Type at least one of the items in the numbered or bulleted list. The item you type should be long enough that it spills over to the next line.**

   You can separate the bullet or number from its text by typing a space or by pressing Tab. Generally, a space is sufficient unless the text is justified against the left and right margins, in which case the varying width of the spaces may cause misalignment.

2. **Be sure the insertion point is within the item you just typed.**

3. **Press the Shift key and drag the lower indent marker to the right roughly ¼ inch.**

   When you release the mouse button, the runover line indents to the right.

4. **If necessary, adjust the lower indent marker until the runover line aligns with the line above it.**

First, type one of the bulleted or numbered items
(to get the bullet character, press Option-8)...

• $609 to get the car repaired (actual amount may be less if I can get used parts)

...and then press Shift while dragging the lower
indent marker until the runover line aligns

Drag this
marker

• $609 to get the car repaired (actual amount may be less if I can get used parts)

Correct runover alignment

5. **Move to the end of the item, press Return, and type the remaining items in the numbered or bulleted list.**

6. **To restore the indent to its previous setting, drag the lower indent marker to its previous position.**

To create a first-line indent:

1. **Be sure the insertion point is in the paragraph for which you want to create an indent. If you want to create an indent for several paragraphs, select them all.**

2. **Drag the first-line indent marker (the upper triangle of the left indent marker). Or choose Paragraph from the Format menu and type the desired indent value in the First box.**

Select the paragraph(s) for which you want to create a first-line indent...

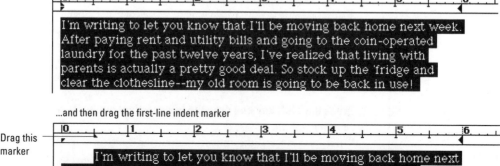

...and then drag the first-line indent marker

Drag this marker

One problem with creating a first-line indent is that you'll have to reformat subheadings and other single-line paragraphs that you don't want to indent. If you find yourself doing too much reformatting, you might just prefer to keep the first-line indent and left indent the same and rely on pressing the Tab key to create first-line indents.

To nest a paragraph (indent it from the paragraph that precedes it):

1. **Be sure the insertion point is in the paragraph you want to nest. If you want to nest several paragraphs, select them all.**

2. **Press Command-Shift-N.**

   Word nests the paragraph — that is, it indents the entire paragraph by ½ inch. To nest the paragraph by a larger amount, continue pressing Command-Shift-N, see illustration at top of next page.

To unnest a paragraph (move its left indent ½ inch to the left):

1. **Be sure the insertion point is in the paragraph you want to unnest. If you want to unnest several paragraphs, select them all.**

2. **Press Command-Shift-M.**

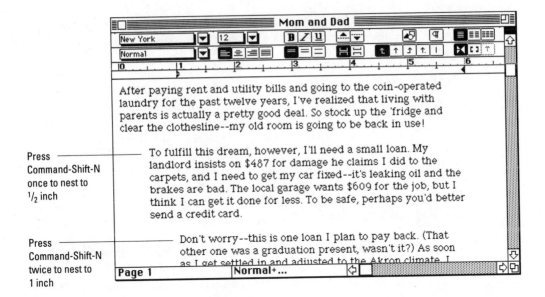

Mom and Dad

New York   12   B / U

Normal

After paying rent and utility bills and going to the coin-operated laundry for the past twelve years, I've realized that living with parents is actually a pretty good deal. So stock up the 'fridge and clear the clothesline--my old room is going to be back in use!

Press Command-Shift-N once to nest to ½ inch

To fulfill this dream, however, I'll need a small loan. My landlord insists on $487 for damage he claims I did to the carpets, and I need to get my car fixed--it's leaking oil and the brakes are bad. The local garage wants $609 for the job, but I think I can get it done for less. To be safe, perhaps you'd better send a credit card.

Press Command-Shift-N twice to nest to 1 inch

Don't worry--this is one loan I plan to pay back. (That other one was a graduation present, wasn't it?) As soon as I get settled in and adjusted to the Akron climate, I

Page 1   Normal+...

Quick Tips

Applying one paragraph's formatting to another paragraph

Because Word stores paragraph formatting in the paragraph mark, it's easy to apply the formatting of one paragraph to a different paragraph. First, format the first paragraph as desired. Next, select its paragraph mark (double-click to the right of the last character in the paragraph to select the paragraph mark, or choose Show ¶ from the View menu and then drag across the ¶ symbol) and choose Copy from the Edit menu. Finally, select the paragraph mark of the paragraph you want to change, and then choose Paste. Because Word stores paragraph attributes in the paragraph mark, the second paragraph takes on the format of the first. You can continue applying the first paragraph's format to other paragraphs (even ones in other Word documents) by moving the insertion point as appropriate and then choosing Paste.

Other ways to save time with paragraph marks

The ability to copy and paste paragraph marks opens up all kinds of opportunities for automating complex paragraph formatting chores. You can save paragraph marks in the Scrapbook desk accessory and copy them into documents later. (You need to copy and save some descriptive text along with the paragraph mark, since the Scrapbook window won't show the paragraph symbol or the formatting it represents.) Better still, save paragraph marks as glossary entries (see Topic 16 for details on using glossaries). You can even use Word's Replace command to search for paragraph marks and then replace them with the Clipboard's contents. If you have a paragraph mark on the Clipboard, you can use this technique to replace every paragraph mark with one that stores different formatting. Topic 15 describes the Find and Replace commands.

Starting a new line without starting a new paragraph

You can start a new line in Word without starting a new paragraph: Simply press Shift-Return instead of Return. Text before and after the new line is considered a single paragraph, and its formatting is governed by one paragraph mark. The Shift-Return is called a *soft return*. If you choose Show ¶, the soft return is indicated by an arrow pointing down and to the left. One reason to use a soft return might be to override a first-line indent when typing a subheading or other single line that you don't want to indent.

Inserting a paragraph mark without moving the insertion point

You can insert a paragraph mark without moving the insertion point to the beginning of the next line by pressing Command-Option-Return.

The bigger the left indent, the bigger the selection bar

When you create a large left indent for a paragraph, the width of the selection bar — that invisible area between the left margin of your text and the left edge of the document window — grows accordingly. This makes it easier to select text using the selection bar — and that means it also makes it easy to accidentally select an entire line of text when all you want to do is move the insertion point to the beginning of a paragraph. The moral? Keep an eye on the screen as you click and be sure you aren't clicking in the selection bar if you don't want to be. Remember the feedback the mouse pointer gives you: When you're in the selection bar, the pointer is a right-pointing arrow. When you're in the text area, the pointer is an I-beam.

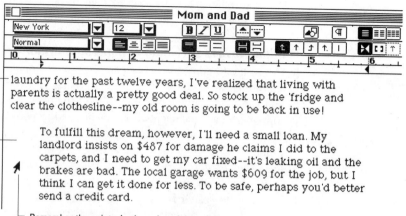

When a paragraph has no left indent, the selection bar is narrow...

...but when a paragraph has a left indent, the selection bar's width grows accordingly

laundry for the past twelve years, I've realized that living with parents is actually a pretty good deal. So stock up the 'fridge and clear the clothesline--my old room is going to be back in use!

To fulfill this dream, however, I'll need a small loan. My landlord insists on $487 for damage he claims I did to the carpets, and I need to get my car fixed--it's leaking oil and the brakes are bad. The local garage wants $609 for the job, but I think I can get it done for less. To be safe, perhaps you'd better send a credit card.

Remember the pointer's shape is a right-pointing arrow when the pointer is in the selection bar

Topic 6

Ways to View Documents

Overview

Word lets you look at a document in a variety of ways, and each method has advantages and drawbacks. Using the View menu, you can switch between *normal, outline,* and *page layout* views.

All text and graphics displayed in a single column

Page break indicated by dotted line

Outline bar lets you promote and demote headings and specify the level of detail you want to see

Multiple columns appear in position along with headers, footers, and footnotes

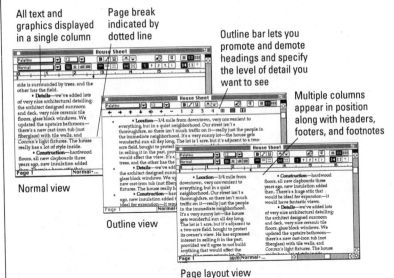

Normal view

Outline view

Page layout view

The normal view is, as its name implies, the one you'll probably use most often. In normal view, Word indicates the breaks between pages with a dotted line and displays text in one continuous column, even if you've formatted a page to have multiple columns. Also, Word doesn't show the running header or footer text, automatic page numbers, or footnotes that you may have created for a document. In short, Word makes a few display compromises that allow you to scroll and manipulate text more quickly.

The outline view lets you use Word's built-in outlining features to sketch out and change the structure of a document. You can create headings and subheadings and change their order and priority. Using the *outline bar* that appears at the top of the screen, you can choose to display all headings or subheadings, or step back from the big picture and hide the details, displaying only main headings or certain levels of subheading. Some people use outline view for basic outlining; others use it to create to-do lists or even to manage small lists of names and addresses. Some additional tips for applying the outlining mode to your work appear in Topic 30.

In page layout view, Word works hardest, showing not only the character and paragraph formatting that appears in other views, but also page formatting. In page layout view, running headers and footers appear in position, multiple columns appear alongside one another, and page breaks really look like page breaks instead of just dotted lines. The page layout view shows your document as it will appear when printed, making it the ideal view for checking your overall formatting. But there's a price to pay: Scrolling is considerably slower in page layout view since Word must work harder to create the accurate screen display.

The File menu's Print Preview command lets you view your pages reduced to fit the size of the screen. In print Preview mode, you can't edit or type new text, but you can adjust document margins (not paragraph indents), change the breaks between pages, add page numbers, print the document, and perform other tasks. Word's Print Preview command shows a reduced view of what your document will look like when printed out. Unlike in page layout view, you cannot edit or type new text while in print preview mode.

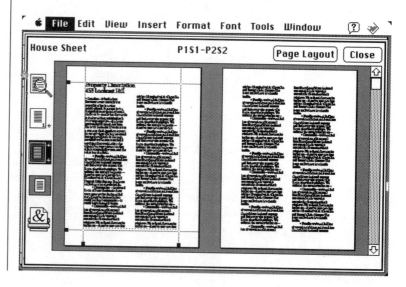

When you save a document, Word records which view you're using. The next time you open the document, it opens in that view.

You can even mix and match views in a single document window by splitting the window using the split bar (see Topic 2) and then choosing the desired view for each of the window's panes.

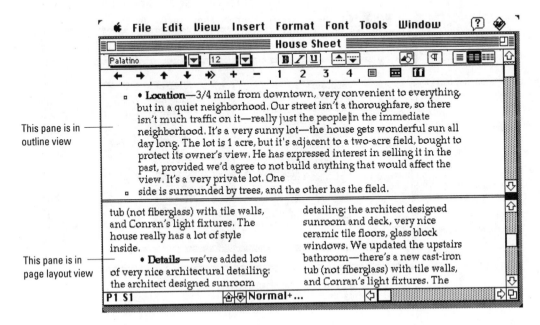

This pane is in outline view

This pane is in page layout view

Step-by-Step

In this section are instructions for switching between Word's views, mixing views in a single document window, and switching in and out of Print Preview mode.

To switch views:

1. **Choose the desired view from the View menu.**

   The current view appears with a check mark next to it.

To mix views in a document window:

1. **Split the document window by dragging or double-clicking the split bar located above the vertical scroll bar. Or, split the window by pressing Command-Option-S.**

   Word splits the document window into two panes.

2. **Click the I-beam pointer within the pane whose view you want to change.**

3. **Choose the desired view from the View menu.**

To activate Print Preview:

1. Choose Print Preview from the File menu.

Word switches into print preview mode.

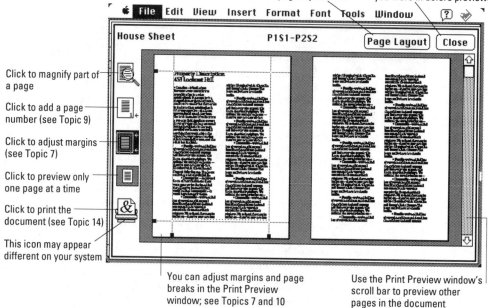

Click to close the Print Preview window and switch the document to page layout view

Click to close the Print Preview window and return to the view you were in before previewing

Click to magnify part of a page

Click to add a page number (see Topic 9)

Click to adjust margins (see Topic 7)

Click to preview only one page at a time

Click to print the document (see Topic 14)

This icon may appear different on your system

You can adjust margins and page breaks in the Print Preview window; see Topics 7 and 10

Use the Print Preview window's scroll bar to preview other pages in the document

To magnify part of a page in Print Preview:

1. Click the Magnifying Glass icon in the upper-left corner of the Print Preview window.

The mouse pointer turns into a Magnifying Glass icon.

2. Click the portion of the page you want to magnify.

Word magnifies that part of the page. You can scroll to view other portions of the page, but you can't make any changes to the magnified page.

3. To return to the Print Preview window, click the Magnifying Glass icon again.

As a faster alternative to using the Magnifying Glass icon, you can magnify part of a page by simply double-clicking the portion of the page you want to magnify. Double-click the page again to return to the print preview display.

To close the Print Preview window and return to the view that was last in use:

1. Click the Close button in the Print Preview window, press the Esc key, or press Command-period.

Quick Tips

Controlling document views

If you want the document to appear in a certain view the next time you open it, save the document after switching to the new view.

Headers, footers, and footnotes in page layout view

In page layout view, you can edit headers, footnotes, and footers directly in position, without having to open a separate window — simply scroll until you can see the text you want to edit, and then make your changes. (A *header* appears at the top of every page; a *footer* appears at the bottom of every page.) But what if you want to create a header or footer for a document that doesn't have one? Simply choose Header or Footer from the View menu. Instead of a new Header or Footer window opening, Word moves the insertion point to the top (or bottom) of the currently displayed page.

Mixing and matching views: A reminder

Remember that you can mix and match views between the documents you have open. If you're working in page layout view, for example, and you open another document, the second document will open in the view that was active when you saved it — which might not necessarily be page layout view.

Background on background pagination

As you work in any view, Word works behind the scenes to keep the page number in the lower-left corner of the document window accurate (this is called *background pagination*). If you're making extensive edits, it may take a few seconds for Word to repaginate the document. If the page number is gray, the page numbers are not accurate. Either wait until Word has repaginated the document, or force it to do so by choosing Repaginate Now from the Tools menu.

It's also worth noting that you can turn off Word's Background Pagination feature using the Preference command's (Tools menu) General option. Turning off background pagination speeds up Word slightly, especially when you're making extensive edits on a slower Macintosh such as a Classic, SE, or Plus. The drawback, of course, is that Word's on-screen page number will be inaccurate; you'll need to use the

Repaginate Now command when you want accurate on-screen page numbers. (The page numbers Word *prints* are always accurate, since Word repaginates when printing.)

Print Preview and frames

Using the Print Preview window along with Word's frames, you can position text and graphics on the page by dragging them around — much as you would in a desktop publishing program. Topic 23 describes how to work with frames.

Topic 7

Setting Paper Size, Orientation, and Margins

Overview

Word's preset paper size, orientation, and margin settings may be all you need for most documents, but you can change these settings when you need to create documents with special formatting requirements. If you always use special paper or margin settings, you can easily customize Word to apply those settings to new, untitled documents.

The margin settings, page size, and page orientation options you choose apply to the entire document. You can't mix and match page sizes, orientations, or margins within a single document. If you need different margin settings within a document, however, you can get the desired results by adjusting paragraph indents as described in Topic 5.

Changing the paper size or orientation

Word is preset for a page size of 8.5 × 11 inches — a standard letter-sized page. To change a document's paper size, choose Page Setup from the File menu and select the name of the desired size. (If you're not sure how big a "B5 letter" is, see the table "Page sizes" at the end of this topic.) You can also use the Preferences command to specify a custom page size, although many printers don't support custom paper sizes. Dot-matrix printers such as the Apple ImageWriter II do, but most laser printers do not.

Tall — reader holds page vertically

You can also use the Page Setup dialog box to change the print orientation of your document. Word is preset to print in *tall*, or *portrait*, orientation — for example, 8.5 × 11 instead of 11 × 8.5. To change the orientation to *wide*, or *landscape*, choose Page Setup and click the wide icon.

Wide — reader holds page horizontally

If you always use a certain page size or orientation, you can customize Word so that new documents have those specifications. Simply use Page Setup to specify your preferences and, before clicking OK, select the Use As Default check box.

If you have more than one type of printer attached to your Mac, it's a good idea to use the Chooser to select the printer on which the final version of the document will be printed before you configure Page Setup. This ensures that the page sizes and other features provided by that printer will appear in the Page Setup dialog box. (It also prevents the reformatting headaches that can arise when you switch printers after beginning a document.)

To select a printer using the Chooser, choose the Chooser from the Apple menu, and then click the icon for the desired printer. (If your Mac is attached to a network containing several PostScript printers, you'll also need to select the name of the specific printer you want. If your network contains more than one zone, you'll also need to select the appropriate zone.) Click the Chooser window's close box to get rid of the Chooser.

Changing margins

Word gives a new document margin settings of 1 inch from the top and bottom of the page and $1\frac{1}{4}$ inches from the left and right edges. You can change margins in any of three ways:

♦ When you want to type precise measurement values (and access special margin-related options, described shortly), choose Document from the Format menu and type the values in the Document dialog box. If you always use certain margin settings, you can specify them as preset values by clicking the Use As Default button in the Document dialog box.

♦ When you want to experiment with various margin settings and quickly see how they affect the document's overall appearance, use the Print Preview command and then drag the margin boundary lines in the Print Preview window. Another benefit of using the Print Preview window to change margins is that you can see how headers, footers, and page numbers will appear in the margins.

Margin Scale button

♦ When you want to change the left or right margin, you can use the ruler's margin scale. To display the margin scale, click the Margin Scale button at the right edge of the ruler. One benefit of using the ruler is that you can continue editing the document as you make adjustments. (Keep in mind that the ruler isn't available when you're in outline view. You need to be in page layout or normal view to access it.)

Margins and binding considerations

Lengthy documents are often bound in three-ring binders, with office binding equipment, or by a commercial printer's bindery. If you will be creating bound documents, you may want to take advantage of some of the specialized margin options provided by Word's Document dialog box, accessed by choosing Document from the Format menu.

If you will be binding pages that are printed on one side, increase the left margin by ¼ to ½-inch to compensate for the binding. The best value to use will depend on the binding method you use.

If you will be binding pages that are printed on both sides, you may want to do one or both of the following:

◆ Create a gutter. When you will be binding pages printed on both sides, you need to increase the width of the *inside margin* (the margin that will face the binding). The extra space is called a *gutter margin,* and you can create it by typing a measurement value in the Gutter box (in the Document dialog box).

◆ Specify mirrored margins. In a double-sided bound document, you want the width of the inside and outside margins to be the same for odd- and even-numbered pages. To specify this, select the Mirror Even/Odd option in the Document dialog box. When you do, the Left and Right labels in the Margins area of the dialog box change to Inside and Outside.

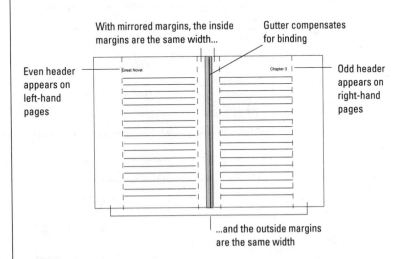

With mirrored margins, the inside margins are the same width...

Gutter compensates for binding

Even header appears on left-hand pages

Odd header appears on right-hand pages

...and the outside margins are the same width

While you're setting up a document for double-sided printing, you might also want to create different headers or footers for the odd- and even-numbered pages. The Document dialog box's Even/Odd Headers option lets you do just that; for more details, see Topic 9.

Step-by-Step

This section shows how to change paper size and print orientation using the Page Setup dialog box, and how to change margins using the Document dialog box, the Print Preview window, and the ruler.

To change the paper size and/or orientation:

1. If you have more than one type of printer, use the Mac's Chooser to select the type of printer on which you plan to print the document.

This enables the Page Setup dialog box to show the page sizes and special features (such as enlargement or reduction) supported by that printer.

2. Choose Page Setup from the File menu.

The Page Setup dialog box appears. The options available depend on your printer:

LaserWriter Page Setup   7.0   OK

Paper: ● US Letter ○ A4 Letter
○ US Legal ○ B5 Letter ○ [Tabloid ▼]   Cancel

Reduce or [100] %   Printer Effects: Options
Enlarge: ☒ Font Substitution?
Orientation   ☒ Text Smoothing?
                      ☒ Graphics Smoothing?
                      ☒ Faster Bitmap Printing?

Personal LaserWriter LS   1.0 f1   OK

Paper: ● US Letter   ○ A4 Letter   Cancel
       ○ US Legal   ○ B5 Letter   Help
       ○ No. 10 Envelope

Orientation: Size: Printer Effect:
                ● 100%
                ○ 75%   ☐ Precision Bitmap Alignment
                ○ 50%   (4% reduction)

StyleWriter   1.0f2   OK

Paper: ● US Letter   ○ A4 Letter   Cancel
        ○ US Legal   ○ Envelope (#10)

Orientation: Scale: 100%

3. **Select the desired page size and/or click the desired orientation icon.**

   If you always use those settings, select the Use As Default check box, and Word will provide them for new, untitled documents.

4. **Click OK or press Return.**

   Word applies your settings to the active document. Other open documents aren't affected; Page Setup changes apply to the active document only.

To change margins using the Document dialog box:

1. Choose Document from the Format menu.

The document dialog box appears:

Type a value here for documents that will be bound

Check this box if document will be printed on both sides

Document

Margins
Left: `1.25 in`   Top: `1 in`   `At Least ▼`
Right: `1.25 in`   Bottom: `1 in`   `At Least ▼`
Gutter: `0 in`   ☐ Mirror Even/Odd

OK
Cancel
Use As Default
File Series...

Footnotes
Position: `Bottom of Page` ▼
○ Restart Each Page
● Number From: `1`

☒ Widow Control
☐ Print Hidden Text
☐ Even/Odd Headers
Default Tab Stops: `0.5 in`

2. Type the desired values in the appropriate text boxes, and then click OK or press Return.

If you want new, untitled documents to have the new settings, click the Use As Default button before closing the dialog box.

To change margins using the Print Preview window:

1. Choose Print Preview from the File menu.

The Print Preview window appears, with *margin handles* indicating the top, bottom, left, and right margins, as shown in the following illustration.

Top and bottom margin handles

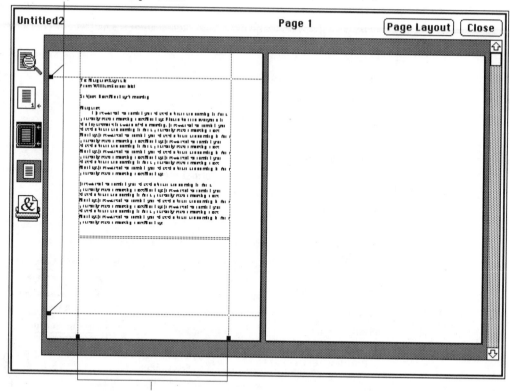

Left and right margin handles

2. Point to the margin handle that you want to adjust.

The mouse pointer turns into a cross-hair (+).

3. Drag a margin handle to the desired location.

Notice that Word displays the margin position at the top of the Print Preview window.

4. Repeat Step 3 to adjust other margins.

Word won't apply your changes until you perform the next step.

5. To apply your changes, click anywhere off the page or click the Print Preview window's Margin icon.

Word repaginates the document to reflect the new margins.

To change the left or right margins using the ruler:

1. Click the Margin Scale button in the ruler.

The ruler's alignment and spacing icons become gray, and its paragraph indent markers are replaced by margin brackets as shown in the following illustration.

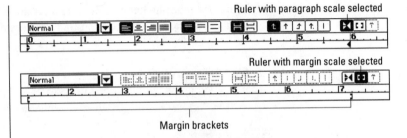

Ruler with paragraph scale selected

Ruler with margin scale selected

Margin brackets

2. Drag the margin brackets to set the margins.

As you drag a margin bracket, the margin width appears in the lower-left corner of the document window.

3. To return the ruler to its paragraph scale, click the Paragraph Scale button.

To set up margins for a double-sided document that will be bound:

1. Choose Document from the Format menu.

2. Click the Mirror Even/Odd check box.

In the Margin section of the dialog box, the Left and Right box labels change to read Inside and Outside:

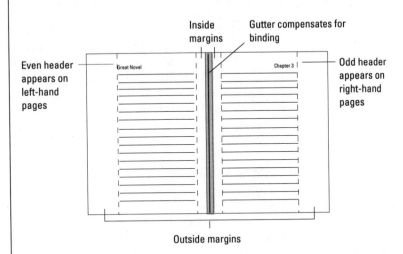

Inside margins

Gutter compensates for binding

Even header appears on left-hand pages

Odd header appears on right-hand pages

Outside margins

3. Type a value in the Gutter box.

The exact value will depend on the binding method you use. Try a value of ¼- to ½-inch for starters, or check the manual that accompanied your binding equipment.

4. To create separate headers or footers for the odd- and even-numbered pages, click the Even/Odd Headers check box.

See Topic 9 for details on creating even and odd headers or footers.

5. Click OK or press Return.

If you want new, untitled documents to have the new settings, click the Use As Default button before closing the dialog box.

Quick Tips

Changing paper size and margins

Oftentimes, you need to adjust Page Setup options and margins at the same time. Word provides a shortcut that lets you do just that: the Document button in the Page Setup dialog box. Click it, and the Document dialog box appears — just as if you had chosen Document from the Format menu. You can make all the margin adjustments you like, and then click OK and return to the Page Setup dialog to continue adjusting its settings.

Specifying exact margins

When using the Document dialog box, you might have noticed that the Top and Bottom margin boxes appear next to a pop-up menu whose choices are At Least and Exactly. Here's the scoop: If you have a header or footer that's more than a few lines long, Word automatically adjusts the top and bottom margins to accommodate the extra header or footer text so that it doesn't overlap the main body text. If you don't want Word to adjust one or both of the margins, choose the Exactly option for either or both. You can use this technique to create a *watermark* — such as the word *CONFIDENTIAL* appearing superimposed over the text on each page. For step-by-step instructions on creating a watermark, see Topic 9. A template for creating a watermark is included with Jim Heid's Word Companion, the disk accompaniment to this guide (sold separately).

Set those defaults

I've mentioned it a few times in this topic, but it bears repeating: If you always use certain margin, orientation, or paper size settings, select the Use As Default options in the Page Setup or Document dialog boxes. Why fuss with margin and paper adjustments for each new document you create when Word will do the work for you? Also remember you can create customized untitled documents by creating stationery pads, as described in Topic 33.

Printing in the margins

As mentioned earlier in this topic, Word prints certain components *in* a document's margins — headers and footers, page numbers, and footnotes. You can also format paragraphs and graphics to print in the margins, however. You might take advantage of this capability to attractively format headings, captions, illustrations, or *pull quotes,* which are excerpts of a document's body text set off in a larger type size to attract a reader's attention.

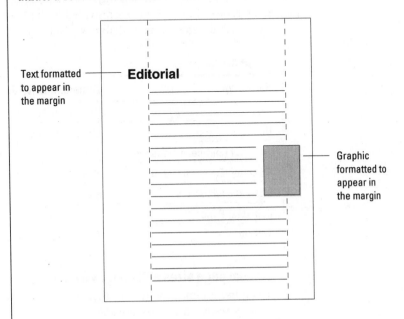

Text formatted to appear in the margin

Editorial

Graphic formatted to appear in the margin

To format a single-line paragraph to appear in the margin, create a negative indent as described in Topic 5. (To recap briefly, you can create a negative indent by dragging the ruler's left-indent marker to the left of the zero mark or by typing a negative value — one preceded by a minus sign — in the Left box of the Paragraph dialog box.)

To format a multiline paragraph or a graphic to appear in the margin, use frames, as described in Topic 23. Frames provide quite a bit of formatting flexibility — you can specify, for example, that a frame move up and down as a paragraph adjacent to it moves. This enables a graphic or a caption to move along with the body text as the document's pagination changes. Another benefit of frames is that you can reposition them by dragging them in the Print Preview window. And remember that you can create a style for frames that allows you to create in-margin text or graphics with a click of the mouse. (Styles are discussed in Topic 11.)

A template containing a variety of predefined styles for in-margin text and graphics (sold separately) is included with Jim Heid's Word Companion disk set.

Staying within the printable area

Many printers — particularly laser printers — can't print to the very edge of a sheet of paper. If you're shrinking margins, keep in mind your printer's *printable area*. For laser printers, avoid margins smaller than ¼ inch.

Page sizes demystified

Just what is an A4 letter, anyway? The table "Page sizes" lists the dimensions of the page sizes provided in the Page Setup dialog box. Note that all sizes aren't available with all printers.

Page sizes

Paper type	Dimensions (width by height)
US Letter	8 ½ × 11 inches
US Legal	8 ½ × 14 inches
A4 Letter (European standard)	21 × 29.7 centimeters
B5 Letter (European standard)	17.6 × 25 centimeters
International Fanfold	8 ¼ × 12 inches
Computer Paper	14 ⅞ × 11 inches
Tabloid	11 × 17 inches

Custom page sizes and ImageWriters

If you use an ImageWriter or other printer that can print on custom paper sizes, you can take advantage of some of the special paper stocks that are available, such as Rolodex cards and index cards. To specify a custom page size, choose Preferences from the Tools menu and be sure the General option is selected. Type the page size's dimensions in the Custom Paper Size boxes.

Topic 8
Setting and Adjusting Tab Stops

Overview

Tab stops — or tabs, for short — enable you to indent text or graphics and perform all manner of alignment feats. You can use tabs for simple tasks such as indenting the first line of paragraphs, or to create tables of contents or complex financial tables. You might also use tab stops to position text so that it prints in the correct location on preprinted forms such as invoices. In short, any task that involves controlling the left-to-right position of text or graphics within a line is a candidate for tabs.

Tab stops live between the left and right margins of a line. When you press the Tab key, the blinking insertion point jumps to the next tab stop to the right.

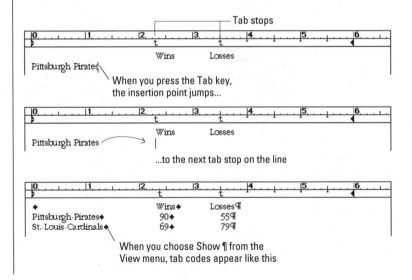

The text within a tab can be aligned left against the tab stop, centered within it, or aligned right. To align columns of numbers, you can create *decimal tabs*. You can also create *leader characters,* which guide the reader's eyes across a line of text (for example, the rows of dots leading to page numbers in a table of contents). You can even create a tab stop that produces a vertical bar (⏐). These tab varieties are illustrated below.

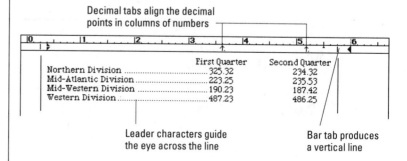

Decimal tabs align the decimal points in columns of numbers

	First Quarter	Second Quarter
Northern Division	325.32	234.32
Mid-Atlantic Division	223.25	235.53
Mid-Western Division	190.23	187.42
Western Division	487.23	486.25

Leader characters guide
the eye across the line

Bar tab produces
a vertical line

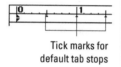

Tick marks for
default tab stops

Word provides default tab stops that are spaced ½-inch apart. These default tabs appear on the ruler as small tick marks. Word's default tab stops may be all you need for simple tasks such as indenting the first line of a paragraph or positioning your address on the right-hand side of the page in a letter. Word's default tabs are always left-aligned and have no leader character.

Word's default tab stops are fine for simple tasks such as
the paragraph indent shown below, but for formatting
jobs like this one, you need to press Tab quite a bit

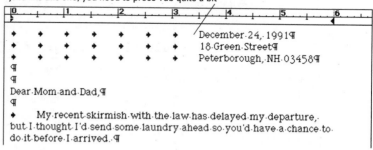

Several templates that allow you to quickly tap into Word's tab features are included with Jim Heid's Word Companion, the disk complement to this book (sold separately).

Creating new tabs

For those times when Word's default tab stops don't cut it, create your own. You can create tabs using either the ruler or the Tabs dialog box. (Remember, if the ruler isn't visible, you can display it by choosing Ruler from the View menu.)

To create a tab with the ruler, first click the tab button corresponding to the type of tab you want, and then click the bottom portion of the ruler in the position where you want to insert the tab. (You can also drag a tab from a tab button to the desired location on the ruler. If you've used programs such as T/Maker's WriteNow or Claris's Mac-Write or Claris-Works, you might find this technique more familiar.)

When you create a tab, Word clears all the default tabs to its left. To create additional tabs with the same alignment (left, center, and so on), continue clicking the bottom portion of the ruler in the desired locations.

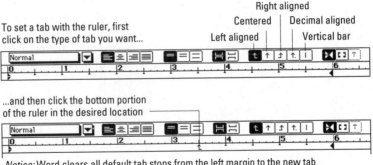

Notice: Word clears all default tab stops from the left margin to the new tab

You can also create tabs using the Tabs dialog box. Use this dialog box when you want to create a tab with a leader character, when you want to specify a tab's position by typing a precise value, or when you want to clear all the tabs in a paragraph. You can open the Tabs dialog box by choosing Paragraph from the Format menu and then clicking the Tabs button, or by simply double-clicking a tab icon in the ruler. When the Tabs dialog box is open, you can use the ruler as described above to create a tab stop, and then assign a leader character to it or fine-tune its position by typing a value in the Position box. Or, you can simply type the value in the Position box to begin with.

You can adjust a tab's position (or create
new tabs) when the Tabs dialog box is open

You can also open the Tabs dialog box
by double-clicking any tab button

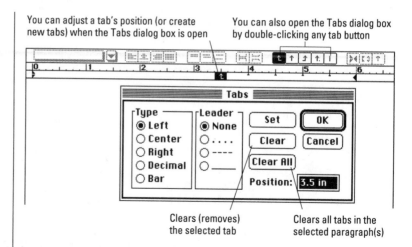

Clears (removes)
the selected tab

Clears all tabs in the
selected paragraph(s)

Tabs belong to paragraphs

Here's an important point to remember when working with tabs: The
tab settings you create apply to the paragraph containing the blinking
insertion point, or to the paragraphs that are selected when you
created the tabs. (And remember, in Word, a paragraph is any text —
even a single line or character — that ends with a carriage return.) If
you want to adjust the tabs of a single paragraph, the insertion point
must be in that paragraph. If you want to adjust the tabs of several
paragraphs, select those paragraphs first. It's Word's attach-the-
formatting-to-the-paragraph approach again — the same scheme we
encountered in Topic 5's discussion of paragraph formatting. Setting
tabs is just another aspect of paragraph formatting.

If you select more than one paragraph and the paragraphs have
different tab settings, the bottom portion of the ruler turns gray and
only the first paragraph's tabs appear in the ruler.

The selected paragraphs have different formatting, so the ruler is
gray and reflects the formatting of the first paragraph only

	Quarterly Earnings	
	First Quarter	Second Quarter
Northern Division	325.32	234.32
Mid-Atlantic Division	223.25	235.53
Mid-Western Division	190.23	187.42
Western Division	487.23	486.25

This side effect of Word's approach to formatting can be an annoyance, and if you're creating a table, you might consider using Word's table-editing features (covered in Topic 24) instead of tabs. The Quick Tips section of this topic provides some guidelines to help you decide when to use tabs and when to use the table feature — and when you might combine both.

Adjusting tabs

Oftentimes you need to fine-tune the positions of your tab stops after typing some text. Perhaps you need to accommodate some text that didn't fit within the original tabs, or you've changed fonts or type sizes and things don't quite align properly. Or perhaps you'd like to change a tab's alignment or add a leader character.

To change the position of tabs, select the paragraph or paragraphs whose tabs you want to adjust, and then drag each tab to the new location. Each time you release the mouse button, Word reformats the selected paragraph(s) to reflect the tab adjustment.

To change the alignment of an existing tab stop, double-click the tab stop and then choose the desired alignment in the Tabs dialog box. Or click and drag the type of tab you want from the ruler's tab buttons, positioning the new tab directly over the old one, as shown below:

Point to the type of tab you want, and then click and drag down until the pointer is directly over the tab you're changing

To remove a tab, simply drag it away from the ruler. When you release the mouse button, Word sends the tab into oblivion. You can also double-click the doomed tab to open the Tabs dialog box, and then click the Clear button. You can clear all the tabs (and restore Word's default tab stops) for a paragraph by clicking the Clear All button in the Tabs dialog box.

Step-by-Step

This section describes how to create, adjust, and remove tabs using the ruler and the Tabs dialog box.

To set tabs using the ruler:

1. **Be sure the insertion point is within the paragraph you want to set a tab for. If you want to set a tab for several paragraphs, select them.**

2. **Click the ruler tab button that corresponds to the type of tab alignment you want.**

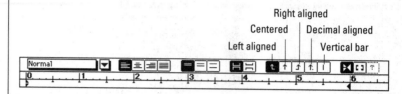

3. **Click the bottom portion of the ruler at the position where you want to insert the tab.**

   To create additional tab stops with the same alignment, continue clicking at the desired ruler positions.

To change a tab position using the ruler:

1. **Be sure the insertion point is within the paragraph whose tabs you want to adjust. If you want to adjust the tabs of several paragraphs that have identical tab settings, select those paragraphs.**

2. **Click the tab whose position you want to adjust, and then drag left or right along the ruler until the tab is in the desired position. You can also double-click the tab to display the Tabs dialog box, and then type a precise position value in the Position box.**

   As you drag, Word displays the tab's position from the left margin in the bottom-left corner of the document window.

To change an existing tab stop to a different type (for example, to change a left-aligned tab to a decimal tab):

1. **Be sure the insertion point is within the paragraph whose tab you want to change. If you want to change the tabs of several paragraphs that have identical tab settings, select those paragraphs.**

2. **Double-click the tab whose type you want to change.**

   The Tabs dialog box appears:

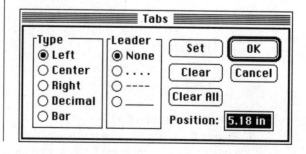

3. In the Type section of the Tabs dialog box, click the type of tab you want.

If you also need to tweak the tab's position, this is a good time to do it. Remember that you can drag the tab left and right along the ruler while the Tabs dialog box is open. You can also type a value in the Position box.

4. Click OK.

To remove a tab stop:

1. Be sure the insertion point is within the paragraph whose tab you want to remove. If you want to remove a tab from several paragraphs that have identical tab settings, select those paragraphs.

2. Point to the tab you want to remove, and then, while pressing the mouse button, drag the tab down into the document window.

When you release the mouse button, the tab disappears. If the tab you deleted was the rightmost tab in that paragraph, Word restores the default tab stops between the end of the line and any tabs to its left:

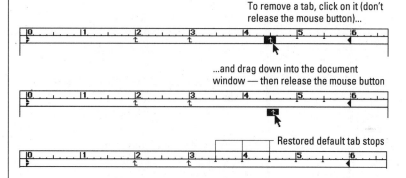

To remove a tab, click on it (don't release the mouse button)...

...and drag down into the document window — then release the mouse button

Restored default tab stops

You can also remove a tab by double-clicking it, and then clicking the Clear button in the Tabs dialog box.

To set tabs using the Tabs dialog box:

1. Be sure the insertion point is within the paragraph whose tab settings you want to change. If you want to change the tabs of several paragraphs, select those paragraphs.

2. Open the Tabs dialog box by double-clicking any tab button in the ruler.

You can also open the Tabs dialog box by choosing Paragraph from the Format menu, and then clicking the Tabs button in the Paragraph dialog box.

3. **In the Position box, type the position of the tab you want to set. Or click the bottom portion of the ruler and drag left and right until the new tab is in the desired position.**

4. **Be sure the type of tab you want is selected in the Type area of the Tabs dialog box.**

5. **If you want to set additional tabs, save the new one first by clicking the Set button. If you're creating just one tab, simply click OK or press Return; you don't have to click Set.**

To set a tab with a leader character:

1. **Be sure the insertion point is within the paragraph whose tabs you want to change. If you want to change the tabs of several paragraphs that have identical tab settings, select those paragraphs.**

2. **Open the Tabs dialog box by double-clicking any tab button in the ruler.**
   You can also open the Tabs dialog box by choosing Paragraph from the Format menu, and then clicking the Tabs button in the Paragraph dialog box.

3. **In the Position box, type the position of the tab you want to set. Or click the bottom portion of the ruler and drag left and right until the new tab is in the desired position.**

4. **Be sure the type of tab you want is selected in the Type area of the Tabs dialog box.**
   Most tabs that have leader characters are left-aligned.

5. **Click the desired leader character.**
   Typesetters generally use dot leaders (the one directly below None in the Leader area of the Tabs dialog box).

6. **If you want to set additional tabs, save the new one first by clicking the Set button. If you're creating just one tab, simply click OK or press Return; you don't have to click on Set.**
   If you're setting additional tabs and you don't want leaders for them, be sure to click None in the Leader area of the Tabs dialog box before setting the additional tabs.

Quick Tips

Changing the default tab spacing

Word's ½-inch default tab stops are good starting points, but you might prefer a different default tab spacing. Your wish is Word's Document command. Choose Document from the Format menu, and then type the desired spacing in the Default Tab Stops box. If you want those defaults to apply to the currently active document only, click OK. If you want the defaults to apply to future documents, click Use As Default, and then click OK.

Tabs or tables? Or both?

If you're creating a table, you might wonder whether it's better to use tabs or to use Word's table-editing features (discussed in Topic 24). It depends. The table feature is often easier, since it provides word wrap within each column, eliminating the hassle of retyping or cutting and pasting if you need to reorganize the table. Using the table editor is also easier for fancy formatting gymnastics such as positioning a caption alongside a graphic or adding shading or borders to a table. And the table feature is unbeatable if you're moving information between Word and the Microsoft Excel spreadsheet program. You can even combine tabs and tables — for example, to add leader characters to one column of the table. (Topic 24 describes how.)

However, many programs can't interpret Word tables, but they can interpret tabs. If you're creating documents that you plan to import into a publishing program, you'll probably want to use tabs.

Tips for creating attractive tables

There's an art to formatting large, multicolumn tables so that they're attractive and legible. Here are some tips for creating effective tables.

◆ *Adjusting space between columns.* Generally, there should be an equal amount of white space between each pair of columns in the table. If the column headings are particularly lengthy — especially in relation to the contents of each topic — consider dividing them into multiple lines.

◆ *Aligning column headings.* Column headings are often centered over their respective columns, but other alignment schemes also have their place. For tables containing lengthy text, consider aligning headings so that they're aligned left with each column. For columns containing numbers, you might align the headings against the column's right edge.

✦ *Typeface considerations.* You're creating a table with numerous columns and you're finding it difficult to fit all the columns on a page. Your first temptation may be to reduce the table's type size until it fits. Resist the urge. A smaller type size may enable a table to fit, but the resulting table is likely to be so illegible that readers will skip over it. Before shrinking the type size, consider using a narrower font. Fonts such as Helvetica Narrow or Helvetica Condensed are space-efficient yet legible.

✦ *Use leaders when appropriate.* For tables containing many lines but not a lot of columns, leader characters can help the reader's eyes across each line, lessening the chance of skipping to the wrong line when moving from column to column.

✦ *Use leaders of the same size.* If you're varying type sizes within a table that contains leaders (as is common in a table of contents, for example), you'll get inconsistently sized leader dots, since Word uses the periods present in whatever type size you're using. To avoid this inconsistency, select the leader characters in the table and choose the same type size, font, and style for each one.

✦ *Use borders, shading, or extra line spacing to separate individual lines or groups of related lines.* A horizontal border (in graphic arts terms, a *rule)* can be an attractive way to separate lines or groups of related lines. To create a horizontal rule below each line in a table, use the Borders command as described in Topic 25. You might also consider shading every other line or group of related lines. Shading is also covered in Topic 25.

If you're interested in learning more about the graphic design considerations of tables, read *Graphic Design for the Electronic Age* by Jan V. White (Watson-Guptill Publications, 1988).

Creating angled table headings

In some tables, column headings are positioned diagonally so that they take up less space. (The tables in *Consumer Reports* magazine are often formatted this way.) By typing headings into Word's Picture window and then rotating them, you can create the same effect, as shown in the following illustration.

	Price	Capacity	Color	Weight	Stock Number
Argon 1200	$105	12	Blue	14	53987
Nova Mark III	85	14	Orange	17	38761
Carousel Model 6	398	17	Pink	38	88712
Eraser Blaster 1400	300	10	Green	39	98777

In this scheme, each heading is a separate picture with its text rotated at a 45-degree angle. I used tabs to align each "heading picture" over its respective column. To create a single heading using Word's picture window, first open the picture window by clicking the picture window icon in the ribbon. Next, use the picture window's text tool to type the heading text, and then rotate the text using the rotation tool. To get a 45-degree angle, rotate the text until the picture window's status bar reads: Rotation 315°. Now position the angled heading so that it's in the upper-left corner of the picture window. Close the picture window and then adjust the size and position of the heading's frame. Be forewarned: Creating angled headings isn't a breeze — if you need to edit a heading, you must undo its rotation, edit its text, and then rotate it again.

A template for creating tables with angled headings (sold separately) is included with the Jim Heid's Word Companion disk set.

Sleuthing for extra tab characters
You can view tab codes (the formatting code that Word inserts when you press the Tab key) by choosing Show ¶ from the View menu. Tab codes appear as right-pointing arrows. You can also use Word's Find command to locate tab codes; see Topic 15 for details.

Applying one paragraph's tabs to other paragraphs
When you're struggling to reformat a table whose tab settings vary, remember that you can copy one paragraph's formatting to other paragraphs. To apply one line's tabs to other lines, select that line's paragraph mark and then copy it to the Clipboard. Next, select the paragraph mark of the line you want to change and then choose Paste.

Topic 9

Creating Headers, Footers, and Page Numbers

Overview

Any document longer than a single page is a candidate for headers, footers, and page numbers. A header appears at the top of every page, a footer appears at the bottom, and page numbers can appear anywhere you like.

Most people create simple headers and footers that contain text describing the document — its name and perhaps a revision number, date, and page number. But headers and footers can contain anything — graphics, borders, even multiple paragraphs and tables. And while headers and footers usually print above and below the top and bottom margins, you can specify that they print within the margins to create special effects.

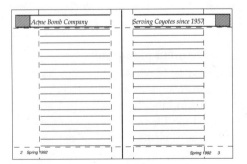

Header containing graphics • Separate odd and even headers and footers • Headers and footers formatted to print outside the document margins

Basic header and footer

Footer formatted to print within margins as a watermark

Word lets you create separate headers and footers for even- and odd-numbered pages — ideal for documents that will be printed on both sides of the paper and then bound. You can also create a special header or footer for the first page of a document, or specify that the header or footer not appear on the first page. You might use this option for reports, memos, and other correspondence for which you want every page except the first to have a header, footer, or page number.

In the Quick Tips section of this topic, you'll find some tips and ideas for applying headers, footers, and page numbers to your documents. Many of these tips have corresponding templates on Jim Heid's Word Companion, the disk set that complements this book (sold separately).

Page numbers

You can create page numbers in either of two ways: You can create them as part of a header or footer, or you can make them independent of the header or footer by creating them with the Section command (in the Document menu) or the Print Preview window. It's generally more convenient to use the Header or Footer window to create page numbers. You *must* use the Header or Footer window if you want to precede the page number with text, as in "Page 15." It's also easier to change the font, size, and style of page numbers if you create them in the Header and Footer window.

If you want to create page numbers that you can position independently of the document's headers and footers, use the Section dialog box's Margin Page Numbers option. Or use the Print Preview window's page number symbol. It's more work to change the font, size, and style of page numbers created with the Section command or page number symbol. Instead of being able to select the page number and modify it, you must modify the Word style sheet named *page number*. (Styles are discussed in Topic 11.)

Regardless of how you create page numbers, you'll find that Word provides plenty of flexibility for their formatting. You can specify several numbering schemes, for example, including uppercase or lowercase Roman numerals (I, II, III, IV or i, ii, iii, iv). You can also specify a starting page number other than 1 — useful when you've broken a large project up into several smaller files. And if you use the first page of a document as a title page, you can eliminate the page number from the first page and begin numbering on the second page.

Creating a header or footer

A new, untitled document has no headers or footers. To create one, choose Header or Footer from the View menu. When you do, the Header or Footer window appears, as shown in the following illustration.

Inserts page number
Inserts date
Inserts time

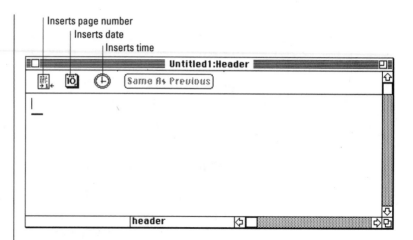

The Header or Footer window works identically to the main document window — you can even display its ribbon or ruler by choosing Ribbon or Ruler from the View menu. You can use the character- and paragraph-formatting techniques discussed in previous topics. And although the Header and Footer windows initially appear smaller than the document window, you can resize them to any size.

Header and Footer
windows have default
tab stops:

A centered tab
at 3 inches

A right-aligned
tab at 6 inches

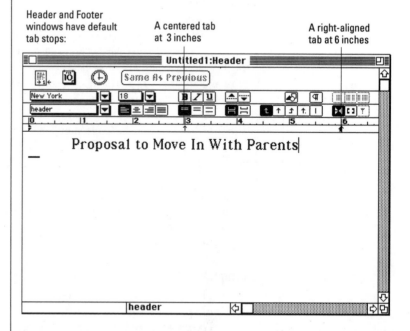

As the above illustration shows, the Header and Footer windows have preset tab stops that simplify centering page numbers and aligning text against the right margin of the header or footer. You can also create your own custom tab settings using the techniques described in the previous topic.

The Header and Footer windows contain icons that you can click to insert the page number, date, and time in the header or footer. The date and time come from your Macintosh's built-in clock; Word updates them for you as time marches on. If you don't want them to be updated — perhaps you want the header or footer to contain the time or date a document was originally created or last edited — don't use the icons. Type the date or time manually instead.

You can delete a header or footer by opening its window and deleting everything in it.

Headers and footers for double-sided documents

If you're creating a double-sided document, you can create separate headers and footers for its odd- and even-numbered pages by using the Document command's Even/Odd Headers option as described in this topic's Step-by-Step section.

Changing the position of headers and footers

Word gives headers and footers the following default positions:

✦ The top of the header appears ½-inch from the top edge of the page.

✦ The bottom of the footer appears ½-inch from the bottom edge of the page.

You can change the vertical position of a header or footer by dragging the header or footer up or down in the Print Preview window. You can also change its position using the Section dialog box.

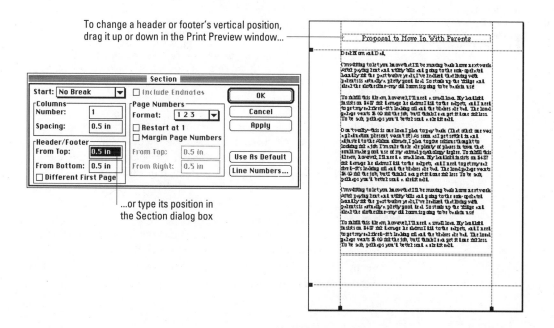

To change a header or footer's vertical position, drag it up or down in the Print Preview window...

...or type its position in the Section dialog box

To change the horizontal position of a header or footer so that it prints in the left margin, use negative paragraph indents as described in Topic 5.

Headers and footers in page layout view

In Word's page layout view, headers and footers appear in the document window, not in separate windows of their own:

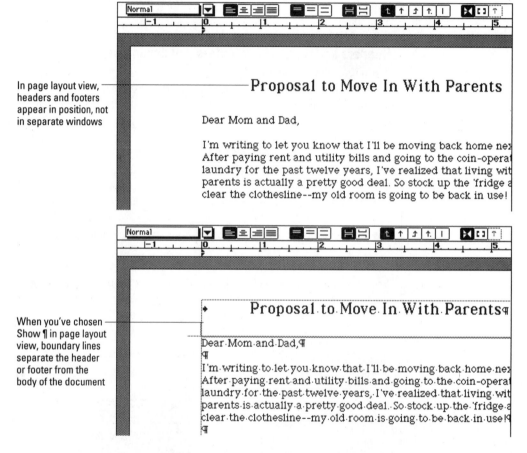

In page layout view, headers and footers appear in position, not in separate windows

When you've chosen Show ¶ in page layout view, boundary lines separate the header or footer from the body of the document

To modify an existing header or footer when in page layout view, scroll the document window up or down as needed to reach the header or footer. Or simply choose Header or Footer from the View menu, and Word moves the insertion point there for you.

Step-by-Step

In this section, you'll find instructions for creating headers and footers, for creating separate headers and footers for the first page of a document, for positioning headers and footers using the Print Preview and Section commands, and for creating page numbers.

To create a header or footer:

1. Choose Header or Footer from the View menu.

A Header or Footer window appears.

2. Type the header or footer's text.

Headers and footers can also contain graphics, tables, and entire paragraphs.

Inserts page number

Inserts date

Inserts time

3. If you want the header or footer to contain the page number, date, and/or time, click the appropriate icon in the Header or Footer window.

To control the position of the page number, use tabs. (The preset tabs in Word's header and footer windows are ideal.) To alter the appearance of a header or footer, use Word's standard character- and paragraph-formatting techniques. You can also display the ribbon and ruler in the Header or Footer window by choosing Ribbon or Ruler from the View menu.

4. When you have finished creating the header or footer, close its window by clicking its close box or by choosing Close from the File menu.

You can also leave the Header or Footer window open, and switch back to the document window by clicking within it.

To create a different header or footer for the first page of a document:

1. Choose Section from the Format menu.

The Section dialog box appears:

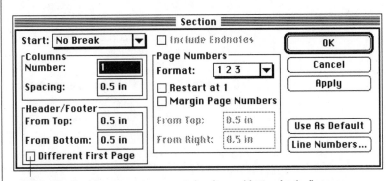

Select this check box to create separate headers and footers for the first page

2. In the Header/Footer section of the dialog box, click the Different First Page check box.

3. Click OK or press Return.

The View menu now contains two new commands: First Header and First Footer.

4. Choose First Header or First Footer to display the Header or Footer window for the first page.

5. Create the first header or first footer using the same techniques used for creating a standard header or footer.

To create a separate header for odd- and even-numbered pages:

1. Choose Document from the Format menu.

The Document dialog box appears:

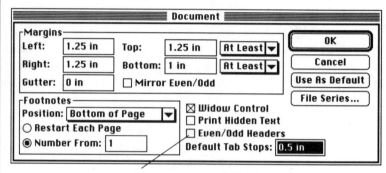

Select this check box to create separate headers or footers for the odd- and even-numbered pages in a document

2. In the Margins area, click the Mirror Even/Odd check box.

This tells Word to mirror the margins on facing pages, as described in Topic 7.

3. Click the Even/Odd Headers check box.

4. Click OK or press Return.

The View menu now contains commands for the even and odd headers and footers.

5. Create the headers and footers using the techniques described earlier.

Even and odd headers and footers are typically formatted as follows:

The header in odd-numbered pages typically contains a document's title

Headers and footers on even pages are typically aligned against the left margin

The header for even-numbered pages usually contains the chapter number and title

Headers and footers on odd pages are typically aligned against the right margin

To delete a header or footer:

1. **Open the window for the header or footer you want to delete by choosing its name from the View menu.**

2. **Select everything in the Header or Footer window.**
   Remember, you can select everything in a window by choosing Select All from the Edit menu or by pressing the Command key while clicking the window's selection bar.

3. **Press Delete or choose Clear from the Edit menu.**

4. **Close the Header or Footer window.**

To change the vertical position of a header or footer using the Print Preview window:

1. **Choose Print Preview from the File menu.**
   In the Print Preview window, headers and footers appear within dotted rectangles.

2. **Drag the header or footer up or down as desired. To position the header or footer so that it prints within the document's margins, press the Shift key as you drag.**
   As you position the header or footer, Word displays the distance between the header or footer from the top or bottom of the page at the top of the Print Preview window. Remember that you can increase the size of the top margin by dragging the top margin boundary. Note that if you position the header or footer so that it prints within the document's margins, its contents will overlap anything that appears within the document's margins. As this topic's Quick Tips section shows, this can be useful for producing a watermark on each page, such as the word *CONFIDENTIAL* printed at an angle behind the body text.

To change the vertical position of a header or footer using the Section command:

1. **Choose Section from the Format menu.**
   The Section dialog box appears.

2. **In the Header/Footer area, type the desired distance between the top or bottom of the page and the header or footer.**
   For the header, the distance is measured from the top of the page to the top of the header. For the footer, the distance is measured from the bottom of the page to the bottom of the footer.

To insert page numbers using the Print Preview window:

1. Choose Print Preview from the File menu.

→1←

Page number
pointer

2. Click the page number symbol.
The mouse pointer turns into a number *1*.

3. Click the page at the position where you want the page number to appear.
Word inserts the page number at that position.

4. Click the Close button to close the Print Preview window.

To adjust the position of a page number using the Print Preview window:

1. Choose Print Preview from the File menu.

2. Click the page number symbol.
The mouse pointer turns into a number *1*.

3. Point to the existing page number, and then press and hold down the mouse button.
At the top of the window, you'll see the page number's position, measured from the top-right edge of the page.

4. While continuing to hold down the mouse button, adjust the page number's position as desired, and then release the button.

5. Click the Close button to close the Print Preview window.

To insert page numbers using the Section command:

1. Choose Section from the Format menu.
The Section dialog box appears.

2. Click the Margin Page Numbers check box.
The From Top and From Right text boxes become active.

3. Specify the page numbers' position by typing measurements in the From Top and From Right boxes.
If you don't specify otherwise, Word positions page numbers ½-inch from the top of the page and ½-inch from the right edge.

4. Click OK or press Return.
To customize Word to always insert margin page numbers at the position you specified, click the Use As Default button before clicking OK.

To adjust the position of page numbers using the Section command:

1. **Choose Section from the Format menu.**

2. **In the From Top and From Right boxes, specify the page numbers' position.**

3. **Click OK or press Return.**
   To customize Word to always use the position you specified, click the Use As Default button before clicking OK.

To specify a starting page number other than 1:

1. **Choose Document from the Format menu.**

2. **Click the File Series button.**

3. **In the Page Numbers area, click the Number From button.**

4. **Type the desired starting page number in the Number From box.**

5. **Click OK or press Return.**
   The File Series dialog box closes.

6. **Click OK or press Return.**

To change the format of page numbers:

1. **Choose Document from the Format menu.**

2. **In the Page Numbers area, choose the desired page number format from the Format pop-up menu.**

3. **Click OK or press Return.**
   If you want to use more than one numbering format in a document, you must break the document into sections as described in Topic 22.

Quick Tips

Inserting a page number at the default position

For page numbers inserted with the Section or Print Preview commands, Word's default page-number position is ½-inch from the top of the page and ½-inch from the right edge. When the Print Preview window is open, you can insert a page number at this default position by simply double-clicking the page number symbol. It's easier than clicking once on the page number symbol and then dragging the pointer around on the page.

How to use odd and even headers and footers

In many manuals or books, the header in odd-numbered pages typically contains the book's chapter number and title, while the header for even-numbered pages contains the title or section name.

Similarly, the footer text for even-numbered pages typically appears aligned against the left margin, while the footer text for odd-numbered pages is generally aligned against the right margin.

Many books don't have footers, but periodicals such as magazines and newsletters often do. In these publications, the footers typically contain the page number, periodical name, and issue date. Headers typically contain the title of the article. (To create a different header for each article, you need to break the document into sections as described in Topic 22. As an alternative, you can also make each article a separate document, and change the starting page number as described in this topic's Step-by-Step section.)

Headers contain the article title and
don't appear on first page of the article

Meet the Boomerangs

Meet the Boomerangs
*They're Broke and Broken—
And They're Moving Back Home*

Baby boomers are realizing life with parents can be inexpensive

2   *HomeBound   December 1991*

HomeBound   December 1991   3

Footers contain the page number,
publication name, and issue date

To number pages in double-sided publications, create the page numbers in the Header or Footer windows so that you can change the position of the page number on odd and even pages. Don't use the Section command or the Print Preview window's page number symbol. Page numbers created with the latter techniques always appear in the same position on every page.

How to omit a header or footer from the first page

You may not want a header or footer to appear on a document's first page — perhaps you've used the first page for a title page, or you don't want a header or footer to foul your attractive letterhead. To omit a header or footer from the first page, choose Section from the Format menu and then click the Different First Page check box in the Section dialog box. If you examine the View menu, you'll see two new commands — First Header and First Footer — which correspond to the header and footer for the first page. Create your document's headers and footers using the *other* commands — Header and Footer — leaving First Header and First Footer empty. Technically speaking, you haven't omitted the header or footer from the first page, you simply haven't created them.

Inserting a page number within a document's text

The page numbers that you can insert in Header and Footer windows are actually glossary entries. (See Topic 16 for information on glossaries.) This means you can insert them anywhere in the body of the text, as often as you like. First, press Command-Backspace to tell Word you want to insert a glossary entry. Next, type *page* and then press Return. The page number appears at the insertion point's position, and is updated as the document's pagination changes. You might use this technique to quickly add a page number to one page of a document without having to open the Header or Footer window or grapple with the Section command.

Inserting other glossary entries in headers or footers

Word provides numerous standard glossary entries that may have a home in your headers or footers. You can include the date and time in several formats other than the ones provided by the date and time icons in the Header and Footer windows. You can also include some or all of the document's summary information (the tidbits you enter in the Summary Info dialog box), including the author name, title, version, keywords, and subject. To see the full list of standard glossary entries, open the Glossary dialog box (choose Glossary from the Edit menu). And remember that you can add often-used glossary entries to the Work menu, as described in Topic 16.

Creating a watermark

As mentioned earlier, you can take advantage of Word's ability to print a header or footer within a document's margins to create a watermark — to mark each page of a document with a large banner, such as *CONFIDENTIAL* or *DRAFT COPY*. Here's how:

1. Open the Header or Footer window that will contain the watermark.

If you're already using a normal header (that is, one that prints outside the top margin), use the Footer window — or vice versa.

2. Open Word's picture window, and type the watermark's text. (See Topic 13 for details on the picture window.)

If you like, rotate the text to a 45-degree angle to give it that official, rubber-stamped look. (Using the Courier font and outline style helps, too.)

3. Close the picture window.

The "picture of text" appears in the Header or Footer window.

4. Choose Print Preview from the File menu.

5. While pressing the Shift key, drag the header or footer containing the watermark into the middle of the page area.

The watermark will appear within the document's margins:

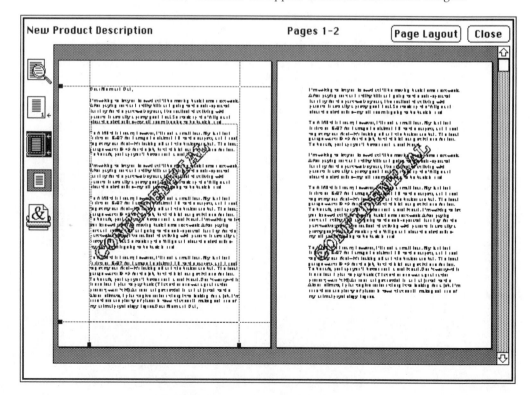

Topic 10

Controlling
Page Breaks

Overview

Like most word processors, Word automatically *paginates* — divides a document into pages based on the margin, line spacing, page setup, and other formatting options you chose. You don't have to worry about when you should start a new page or insert a fresh sheet of paper. Word's automatic page breaks are called *soft* page breaks and appear as dotted horizontal lines when you're in the normal document view.

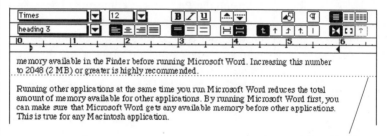

In normal view, Word indicates page breaks with a dotted horizontal line

But there are times when you might want to control where one page ends and the next one begins — in order to keep a heading with its related text, for example, or to avoid breaking a table. You can control page breaks in several ways:

✦ *By inserting a* hard *page break.* A hard page break overrides Word's automatic pagination — it's a way for you to force a page to end where you want it to. You can create a hard page break by choosing Page Break from the Insert menu or by pressing Shift-Enter. (That's Enter — the big key in the numeric keypad — not Return. On older Mac keyboards that lack numeric keypads, the Enter key is to the right of the spacebar.)

✦ *By adjusting soft or hard page breaks in the Print Preview window.* You can drag a soft page break up or down to control where Word breaks the pages. You can also delete a hard page break by dragging it off the page.

✦ *By using Word's Keep paragraph options.* These options, accessed through the Paragraph command in the Format menu, enable you to specify that Word keep certain lines of a paragraph together, or to keep a given paragraph on the same page as the one that follows it.

Notice that the technique of hitting Return until a page breaks is *not* listed here. In the world of word processing, inserting a flock of carriage returns is as heinous a crime as using the spacebar to align or indent text. If you control pagination by using hard carriage returns, you're likely to end up doing a great deal of manual editing should revisions or reformatting change the document's page breaks. In contrast, you can search for and remove hard page breaks in a flash.

When Word paginates

Word's automatic pagination feature is always active unless you turn it off using the Preferences command (Tools menu). As mentioned in Topic 6, the automatic pagination feature works in the background to ensure your page breaks and page numbers are accurate. If the page number in the lower-left corner of the document window is gray, the pagination is *not* accurate; wait a moment while Word catches up, or force it to do so by choosing Repaginate Now from the Tools menu.

Word also repaginates when you print a document, when you switch into page layout view or use the Print Preview window, and when you compile an index or a table of contents.

As mentioned in Topic 6, you can make Word run a bit faster by turning off automatic pagination. To do so, choose Preferences from the Tools menu and then uncheck the Background Pagination check box.

Hyphenating can change page breaks

Using Word's Hyphenate command to automatically hyphenate a document is likely to change a document's page breaks, since hyphenation enables more text to fit on each line. If you plan to hyphenate a document (as described in Topic 19), do so before adjusting page breaks.

Step-by-Step

Here you'll find instructions for inserting, removing, and adjusting hard page breaks, and for using Word's Keep paragraph options.

To insert a hard page break while editing a document:

1. **Position the insertion point at the point where you want to break the page.**

2. **Choose Page Break from the Insert menu, or press Shift-Enter.**
   Word inserts the hard page break just before the insertion point. In normal view, hard page breaks are indicated by a heavier dotted line than is used to denote a soft page break:

Problem: Page break separates a heading from its related text

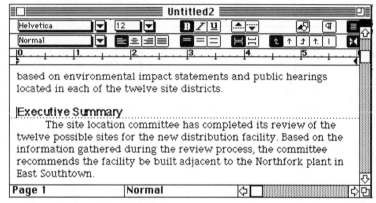

Solution: Insert a hard page break before the heading

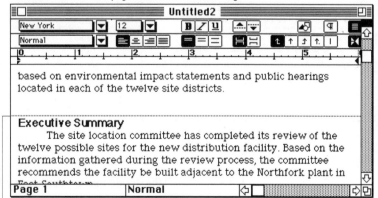

Hard page breaks are indicated with a heavier dotted line than is used for soft page breaks

The margin symbol

To insert a hard page break while using the Print Preview window.

1. **If the Print Preview window isn't open, choose Print Preview from the File menu.**

2. **Be sure the margin symbol is selected.**

3. **If necessary, use the scroll bar or keyboard to scroll to the page whose break you want to adjust or remove.**

4. **Point to a soft page break, and then press and hold down the mouse button.**

   If you're working with the last page in the document, point to the double-dotted line and then press and hold down the mouse button.

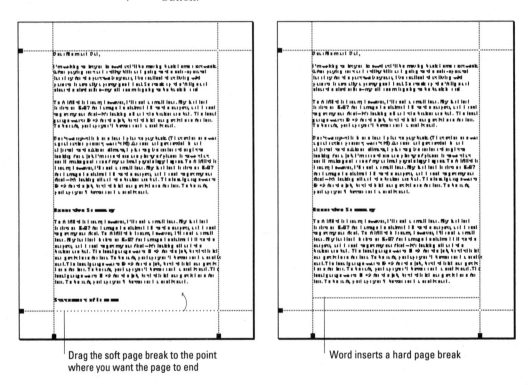

Drag the soft page break to the point where you want the page to end

Word inserts a hard page break

5. **Drag up until the dotted line is positioned where you want the page break.**

6. **Release the mouse button.**

   Word creates a hard page break and repaginates the document.

To remove a hard page break when in normal or outline view:

1. Select the hard page break by clicking the selection bar or by double-clicking the hard page break.

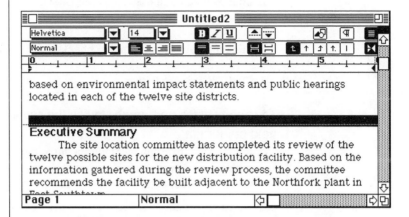

2. Press Delete or Backspace, or choose Clear from the Edit menu.

Word deletes the hard page break. If the background pagination option is active, Word repaginates the document.

To remove a hard page break when in page layout view:

1. Position the insertion point immediately after the hard page break.

You might find it easier to choose Show ¶ and then select the hard page break by double-clicking it.

2. Press Delete (on some keyboards, Backspace).

Word deletes the hard page break. If the background pagination option is active, Word repaginates the document.

To adjust or remove a hard page break using the Print Preview window:

1. If the Print Preview window isn't open, choose Print Preview from the File menu.

2. Be sure the margin symbol is selected.

3. If necessary, use the scroll bar or keyboard to scroll to the page whose break you want to adjust or remove.

4. Drag the hard page break up or down as desired. To remove the hard page break, drag it down and off the page.

Word repaginates the document as necessary.

5. Close the Print Preview window when you've finished.

To keep lines within a paragraph together on one page:

1. Select the lines.

2. Choose Paragraph from the Format menu.
   The Paragraph dialog box appears.

3. Click the Keep Lines Together check box.

4. Click OK or press Return.

To specify that a paragraph stay on the same page with the next paragraph:

1. Position the insertion point within the paragraph you want to keep with the next paragraph. If you want several paragraphs to be kept together, select all of them except the last one:

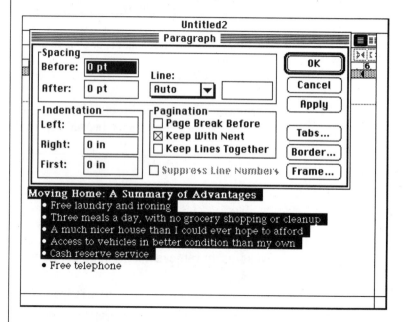

2. Choose Paragraph from the Format menu.
   The Paragraph dialog box appears.

3. Click the Keep With Next check box.

4. Click OK or press Return.

To specify that a paragraph appear at the top of a page:

1. Position the insertion point within the paragraph.

2. Choose Paragraph from the Format menu.
The Paragraph dialog box appears.

3. Click the Page Break Before check box.

4. Click OK or press Return.

Quick Tips

Searching for and deleting hard page breaks

As you work on a document, you may wind up with unwanted hard page breaks littered throughout. Using Word's Replace command, you can conduct a search-and-destroy mission to rid your document of them.

Here's how: Choose Replace from the Edit menu, and in the Find What section of the Replace dialog box, choose Page Break from the Special pop-up menu. Leave the Replace With box empty. If you want to remove every hard page break, click Replace All. If you want to be more selective, use the Find Next and Replace buttons to remove them on a case-by-case basis.

You will want to be more selective if your document also contains section breaks created using the Section command (discussed in Topic 22). Word uses the same find code to represent hard page breaks and section breaks, so clicking Replace All will remove not only all hard page breaks, but all section breaks, too.

Topic 15 contains more details on Word's Find and Replace commands.

Use those Keep paragraph options

Controlling page breaks with Word's Keep and Page Break Before paragraph formatting options is often preferable to using hard page breaks — if you edit or reformat the document extensively, you don't have a large number of hard page breaks to adjust or remove. What's more, the paragraph options can be part of a Word style sheet, making it easy to apply them consistently across a document.

When you've chosen the Show ¶ command from the View menu, Word indicates paragraphs formatted with Keep or Page Break Before options by placing a small black square to their left:

Squares indicate these paragraphs
have a Keep option set

■**Moving·Home:·A·Summary·of·Advantages**¶
  ■ •·Free·laundry·and·ironing¶
  ■ •·Three·meals·a·day,·with·no·grocery·shopping·or·cleanup¶
  ■ •·A·much·nicer·house·than·I·could·ever·hope·to·afford¶
  ■ •·Access·to·vehicles·in·better·condition·than·my·own¶
  ■ •·Cash·reserve·service¶
     •·Free·telephone¶

Pagination and page layout programs

Here are two pagination pointers you may want to keep in mind if you're creating documents that you will import into a desktop publishing program such as Aldus PageMaker.

✦ *Don't use hard page breaks.* Publishing programs generally ignore them. Use the publishing program's own pagination features to control page breaks after you import the document.

✦ *Do use Keep options if your publishing program supports them.* PageMaker 4.0 and later versions support Keep Lines Together and Keep With Next. PageMaker also supports Page Break Before — if PageMaker's Autoflow option is active and the program encounters Page Break Before, PageMaker starts a new page and continues flowing text. QuarkXPress 3.0 and later versions support Keep Lines Together and Keep With Next, but not Page Break Before.

Topic 11

Formatting with Style Sheets

Overview

Style sheets — or styles, for short — allow you to store and recall formatting information with a mouse click or a few keystrokes. A style sheet holds character formatting information (font, size, and style) as well as paragraph formatting information (line spacing, indents, tabs, borders, and so on). Instead of having to thread your way through the Character and Paragraph dialog boxes, to switch from say, 8-point, single-spaced Times Italic to 12-point, double-spaced Helvetica, you can simply switch from one style sheet to another.

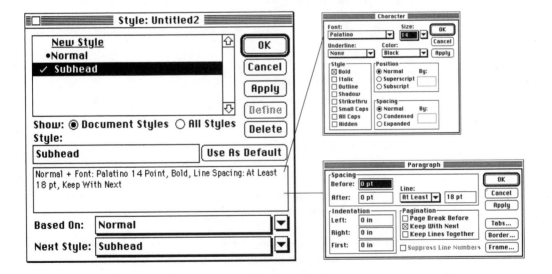

Another significant advantage of styles is that they enable you to quickly change the appearance of one or more components in a document. When you change a style, every paragraph of a document that uses that style is changed accordingly. For example, instead of having to manually scroll through a document to change every 12-point Helvetica heading to 14-point Times Bold, you can simply change the style definition for the heading.

Once you create a set of styles for one document, you can use them in other documents. Obtaining consistent formatting is easier, especially with projects involving many separate documents and writers.

As this topic's Quick Tips section shows, style sheets are also useful when you're creating documents that will be imported into a desktop publishing program.

Standard styles

Word provides numerous predefined standard styles that govern the formatting of headers, footers, tables of contents, indexes, footnotes, and page numbers inserted with the Print Preview window or the Section command. A standard style called Normal determines the default character and paragraph formatting applied to new, untitled documents. If you always begin a document with a certain format, you can change the Normal style to reflect your preferred character and paragraph formatting. The Step-by-Step section of this topic describes how.

All of Word's standard styles are based on the Normal style. You can change the appearance of any of these components by altering the Normal style or the appropriate standard style.

You can add a style of your own to the standard styles by using the Use As Default button in the Style dialog box. When you add a style to the default list, the style will be available in new, untitled documents you create.

Ways to create styles

Word provides two basic ways to create styles. You can also use either of the following techniques to alter an existing style.

+ *By example.* This is the easiest technique to use, and it lets you create styles for documents you've already formatted. First, format the text the way you like. Next, click once within the ruler's Style pop-up menu, type a style name, and then press Return twice. (Guidelines for naming styles appear later in this topic.)

+ *By using the Style dialog box along with the ruler and ribbon and the Format and Font menus.* You might find this approach more convenient when you're defining several styles in one fell swoop. The Style dialog box is also the gateway to Word's most powerful style options: Next Style, which tells Word to automatically switch from one style to another when you press Return; and Based On, which enables you to create a style that's based on an existing style.

The Next Style option

Chances are you'll frequently switch from one style to another after typing a paragraph or section of text. For example, after typing a heading formatted using a style named *heading,* you might begin typing body text using a style named *body.* Word's Next Style option, accessed through the Style command, lets you automatically switch from one style to another. Using the preceding example, when you press Return, Word automatically switches from the heading style to the body style. (When writing the Step-by-Step sections of this book, I used Next Style to automatically switch from the bold type of each numbered step to the plain type of the description that follows it.)

If you don't define a next style, Word automatically uses the current style as the next style. In other words, each time you press Return, Word continues applying the same style to the new paragraphs.

Ways to apply styles

You can apply a style in three ways:

+ *By choosing the desired style from the ruler's Style pop-up menu.* This is often the easiest way to apply a style when you're using the mouse to scroll through and edit a document. To access standard (built-in) styles as well as your own styles, press Shift while opening the pop-up menu.

+ *By using the keyboard.* You can apply a style by pressing Command-Shift-S, typing all or part of the style name, and then pressing Return. This technique is the most convenient of the three when you're in the writing phase and don't want to abandon the keyboard.

+ *By choosing the Style command from the Format menu and then double-clicking the desired style name in the Style dialog box.* You might use this technique if you need to alter a style before applying it.

You can also add style names to the menu bar, enabling you to choose them as you would any other command. Topic 34 describes how.

Because Word's styles work at the paragraph level, Word applies a style you choose to the paragraph containing the blinking insertion point. If you want to apply a style to numerous paragraphs, select them before choosing the style.

Because Word styles also store *character* formatting information, when you apply a style to a paragraph, all of that paragraph's text is changed to the reflect the character formatting stored in the style — even if you didn't have all of the text selected:

Before applying style

Why Renting Just Doesn't Cut it Anymore

After applying style

Why Renting Just Doesn't Cut it Anymore

Guidelines for naming styles

Word isn't too picky where style names are concerned, but there are a few limitations and points you should keep in mind.

✦ Style names cannot contain more than 254 characters. I suspect most of us can live with this limitation.

✦ You can create an abbreviation for a style name by typing a comma and then typing the abbreviation — for example, Main Heading,mh. Abbreviations are extremely useful if you like to use the keyboard to apply styles, since you need type only the abbreviation.

✦ Because Word uses the comma character to separate a style name and its abbreviation, you can't use a comma as part of a style name itself.

✦ Style names are case-sensitive; for example, Word treats *caption* and *Caption* as two different style names. If you like to summon styles using the keyboard, you may want to use all-lowercase style names so that you can type the style names more quickly. Or use all-lowercase style name abbreviations.

Step-by-Step

This section shows how to define and alter styles using the style-by-example technique as well as the Style dialog box, and how to apply styles using the ruler, keyboard, and Style dialog box. You'll also find instructions for using the Next Style and Based On options, for deleting and renaming styles, and for accessing the styles in a different document.

Some of the steps in this section rely on the ruler; if the ruler isn't visible, you can display it by choosing Ruler from the View menu.

To define a style using the ruler's Style pop-up menu:

1. Use the Character and Paragraph commands or the ruler and ribbon to format some text.

If you have a paragraph that's already formatted as desired, be sure the blinking insertion point is within it or that at least part of the paragraph is selected.

2. Click once in the ruler's style box.

The currently visible style name becomes selected.

3. Type a name (and an abbreviation, if desired) for the style and then press Return.

Word asks if you want to define that style based on the selected text. If you decide not to define the style — perhaps you want to give it a different name or tweak the formatting a bit more — click Cancel.

4. Click Define or press Return.

Word defines the new style. Notice that the new style's name appears in the ruler's style box and in the style area at the bottom of the window, indicating that the new style is the currently active style.

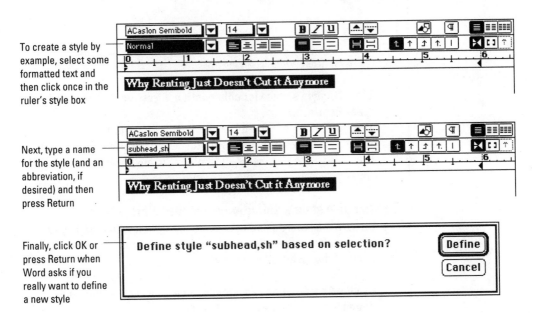

To create a style by example, select some formatted text and then click once in the ruler's style box

Next, type a name for the style (and an abbreviation, if desired) and then press Return

Finally, click OK or press Return when Word asks if you really want to define a new style

To apply a style using the ruler:

1. **Be sure the insertion point is in the paragraph to which you want to apply the style. If you want to apply the style to several paragraphs, select them all.**

2. **Choose the desired style name from the Style pop-up menu.**
   You can also click once in the style box and then type the desired style's name or abbreviation.

To apply a style using the keyboard:

1. **Be sure the insertion point is in the paragraph to which you want to apply the style. If you want to apply the style to several paragraphs, select them all.**

2. **Press Command-Shift-S.**
   The word *Style* appears at the bottom of the document window:

| Style | Normal | | |

Press Command-Shift-S to apply a style from the keyboard

| sh | Normal | | |

Type all or part of the style's name

| Page 2 | subhead | | |

When you press Return, Word applies the style

3. **Type the style's name (or abbreviation, if you created one) and then press Return.**
   You don't have to type all of the style's name, just enough for Word to determine which style you want. For example, if you have a style named *main* and another named *masthead*, you could get away with typing just *mai* or *mas*.

To change a style's definition using the ruler:

1. **Be sure the insertion point is in the paragraph whose style you want to alter. Or use the ruler's Style pop-up menu to select the name of the style you want to alter.**

2. **Use the Character and Paragraph commands or the ruler and ribbon to reformat the text as desired.**

3. **Click once in the ruler's style box.**
   The currently visible style name becomes selected.

4. Press the Return key.

Word asks if you want to redefine the style based on the selected text, or if you want to reapply the style to the selected text.

You might choose this option to restore the formatting of a paragraph whose style you've overridden with manual formatting

Style: subhead,sh

○ **Reapply the style to the selection?**

⦿ **Redefine the style based on selection?**

OK

Cancel

5. Click the Redefine option and then click OK or press Return.

Word changes the style definition to reflect your latest formatting. Word also reformats all paragraphs in the document that are formatted according to that style.

To define a style using the Style dialog box:

1. Choose Style from the Format menu.

The Style dialog box appears:

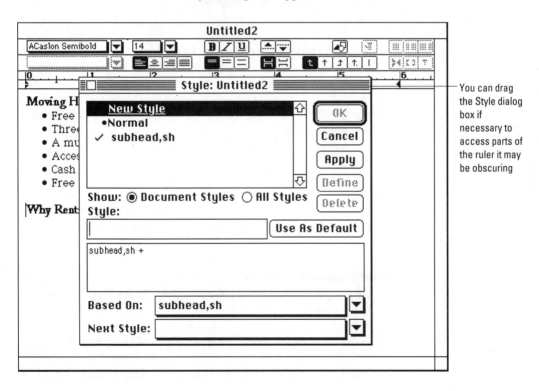

You can drag the Style dialog box if necessary to access parts of the ruler it may be obscuring

2. **Use the ruler and ribbon and the Format and Font menus to specify the format for the style.**

   If you prefer, you can also format the text in advance, before choosing the Style command. In either case, Word displays the formatting options you choose in the lower portion of the dialog box.

3. **Type a name (and abbreviation, if desired) in the Style text box.**

4. **Click the OK, Apply, or Define button.**

   Click OK (or press Return) to define the style and close the dialog box. Click Apply to define the style and leave the dialog box open — perhaps to define another style or tweak the one you just defined. Click Define to define the style but not apply it to the selected paragraph(s).

5. **To define another style, select the New Style entry in the styles list and repeat the preceding steps.**

To change a style's definition using the Style dialog box:

1. **Choose Style from the Format menu.**

   The Style dialog box appears.

2. **Select the style you want to alter by clicking it once.**

   Don't double-click — doing so applies the style and closes the dialog box.

3. **Use the ruler and ribbon and the Format and Font menus to specify the format for the style.**

   Word displays the formatting options you choose in the lower portion of the dialog box.

4. **Click OK, Apply, or Define.**

   If you change your mind and decide not to alter the style, click Cancel, and then click No when Word asks if you want to accept the changes to the style.

To define a next style:

1. **If the Style dialog box isn't already open, choose Style from the Format menu.**

2. **In the list of styles, select the first style by clicking it once.**

3. **Choose the desired next style from the Next Style pop-up menu.**

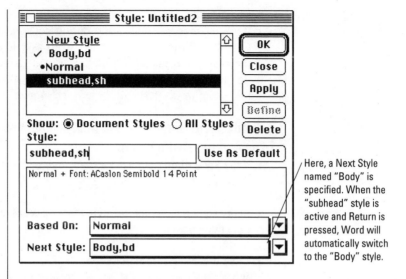

Here, a Next Style named "Body" is specified. When the "subhead" style is active and Return is pressed, Word will automatically switch to the "Body" style.

To change one of Word's standard styles (such as Normal):

1. **If the Style dialog box isn't already open, choose Style from the Format menu.**

2. **Select the All Styles button.**

   The style list now lists Word's standard styles as well as any styles you created.

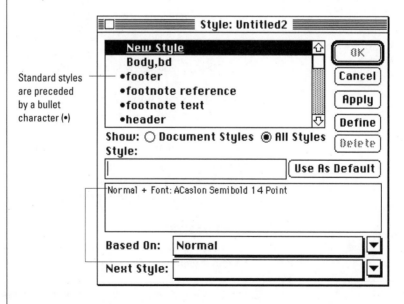

Standard styles are preceded by a bullet character (•)

3. **Use the ruler and ribbon and the Format and Font menus to specify the format for the style.**

   Word displays the formatting options you choose in the lower portion of the dialog box.

4. Click Define.

If you change your mind and decide not to alter the style, click Cancel, and then click No when Word asks if you want to accept the changes to the style. Note that if you change the Normal style, text formatted according to other standard styles will be changed too, since those styles are based on Normal.

To add a style to Word's default style sheet so that it's available in new, untitled documents:

1. If the Style dialog box isn't already open, choose Style from the Format menu.

2. In the style list, select the style that you want to have available in new documents.

3. Click the Use As Default button.

Word asks you to verify that you want to record the style in the default style sheet.

4. Click Yes or press Return.

To delete a style:

1. If the Style dialog box isn't already open, choose Style from the Format menu.

2. In the style list, select the style you want to delete.

3. Click the Delete button.

Word asks if you really want to delete the selected style.

4. Click OK or press Return.

Word deletes the style. If any paragraphs in the document were formatted under that style, Word reformats them according to the Normal style. If the style was recorded in the default style sheet, Word also asks if you'd like to delete it from the default style sheet. Click OK if you do; if you still want the style to be available in other new, untitled documents, click Cancel.

To rename a style:

1. If the Style dialog box isn't already open, choose Style from the Format menu.

2. In the style list, select the style you want to rename.

3. In the Style text box, delete the existing name and then type a new one (including an abbreviation, if you like).

4. Click the Define button.
Word asks if you want to rename the style.

5. Click OK or press Return.

To access the styles in a different document:

1. If the Style dialog box isn't already open, choose Style from the Format menu.

2. Choose Open from the File menu.
Word's Open dialog box appears, instructing you to select a style sheet.

3. Locate the document whose styles you want to use, and double-click its name.
Word loads that document's style sheets. If any styles in that document have the same name as styles in the active document, the imported styles replace the existing ones.

Quick Tips

Use styles for consistency

Consistency is the cornerstone of good graphic design. A document's components — its headings, captions, body text, tables, and so forth — should each have the same formatting throughout the document. Consistency provides a unified appearance that gives the readers familiar reference points and enables them to identify each component. Consider the signs that identify freeways and their on-ramps and exits — if every sign were a different color and shape and used a different typeface, chances are you would get lost more often than you would find your way.

Consistency should also transcend a single document to encompass all related documents you create. Think about your favorite newspaper — its design is consistent within each issue *and* from one issue to the next. Word's style sheet features make this consistency easier to achieve.

Printing a list of styles

You can print a list of the styles defined for a document by choosing the Print command from the File menu while the Style dialog box is open. A style sheet printout can be a useful way to document the formatting specifications for a project.

Using the Repeat command with styles

Word's Repeat command (in the Edit menu) can be handy when you're working your way through a document and applying styles. If you've just applied a style in one paragraph and you want to apply the same style to a different one, click within the second paragraph and choose Repeat Formatting from the Edit menu. You can repeat this routine as many times as needed.

Styles and manual formatting

You can use the ruler and ribbon and Format and Font menus to change the formatting of a paragraph that's already formatted by a style. When you do, Word displays a plus sign after the style's name at the bottom of the document window.

As a general rule, try to avoid frequently overriding a style, since doing so defeats the purpose of styles — to automate formatting and allow for consistency. If you find yourself overriding a style frequently and in the same way, consider creating an additional style that stores the required formatting. For example, if you find yourself frequently overriding a subhead style to add an additional 6 points of line spacing, create an additional style that adds those 6 points for you.

If you've manually formatted a paragraph that is also formatted by a style, you can remove the manual formatting by choosing Revert to Style from the Format menu. Note that Revert to Style reverts character formatting — font, size, and style — not paragraph formatting such as changes in tabs or line spacing. To remove changes in paragraph formatting, reapply the style to the paragraph.

Another way to import styles from a different document

The Step-by-Step section of this topic shows that you can access the styles in a different document by choosing Open from the File menu while the Style dialog box is open. This technique imports every style from a document, however, and there may be times when you want to just import one or two. For times like those, there's another way:

1. Open the document containing the style you want to copy.

2. Copy a paragraph that's formatted in that style.
Be sure to include the paragraph mark. In fact, the paragraph mark is all you really need to copy, since it's what contains the style.

3. Switch to the second document and then choose Paste.
If you copied and pasted some text along with the paragraph mark, delete the text you pasted.

Tips for altering standard styles

If you always begin a document with specific character and paragraph formatting, change the Normal style to reflect that formatting and then click the Use As Default button to record the style in the default style sheet. Each time you start a new, untitled document, you won't have to manually specify the desired formatting. Keep in mind that all of Word's standard styles are based on the Normal style, so if you change the definition of Normal, text formatted in the other standard styles will change accordingly.

You can also modify Word's other standard styles, and here are just a few reasons you might want to.

♦ To change the tab stops in headers or footers (modify the styles named *header* or *footer*).

♦ To change the point size, font, or style of footnotes (modify the style named *footnote*).

♦ To change the annoying formatting that Word applies to outlines (modify the styles whose names begin with *heading* — heading 1, heading 2, and so on).

♦ To change the indents or otherwise reformat the indexes and tables of contents Word generates (modify the styles whose names begin with *index* or *toc,* respectively).

♦ To change the font, style, or style of page numbers inserted with the Print Preview window or the Section dialog box (modify the style named *page number*).

What's a circular style reference?!

You'll see this obtuse alert message if you try to specify the name of the style you're currently defining in the Based On text box. In other words, Word is telling you that you can't base a style on itself. Now why doesn't Word say that in the first place?

Overriding Next Style

You can override the Next Style option by pressing Command-Return to end a paragraph. When you press Command-Return, Word applies the current style to the next paragraph instead of switching to the next style.

Topic 12

Inserting Special Characters

Overview

The Macintosh provides a large cast of characters. Besides the standard alphabet, numerals, and punctuation characters that appear on the Mac's keyboard, most Macintosh fonts also provide a great many special characters, including:

✦ Typesetting characters such as an em dash (—), "curly" quotes, and ligatures (combinations of two characters, such as fi and fl). Proper use of these characters will go a long way toward making your documents look professionally typeset.

✦ Accents and punctuation characters for languages other than English. Examples include the tilde (as in *¡Piñata!*) and the umlaut (as in *üblichen*). Accents are also called *diacritics* or *diacritical marks*.

✦ Math symbols such as not-equal-to (≠) and less-than-or-equal-to signs (≤).

✦ Special grammatical symbols such as the paragraph mark (¶) and section mark (§).

✦ Alternate currency symbols such as the pound (£) and yen (¥) signs.

✦ Copyright (©), trademark (™), and registered trademark (®) symbols.

✦ Macintosh-specific characters such as the Command key symbol (⌘) and the Apple logo (🍎).

Not every font provides every type of special character, however. In some fonts, certain special characters are available only in certain sizes. What's more, the special characters a font does provide are tucked away within key sequences that involve pressing the Option key or Shift and

Option keys along with other keys. Finding little-used sequences summon them can be harder still.

The Symbol command

Word's Symbol command (in the Insert menu) makes it easier to locate and use the special characters a font provides. When you choose Symbol from the Insert menu, a window appears containing the entire character set of the current font and size.

You can insert a special character at the insertion point's location by simply clicking the character's box. You can also display the character set of a different font or size by choosing the desired font or size from the Font menu.

The Mac provides a desk accessory called Key Caps that also makes it easier to locate special characters. In the Quick Tips section of this topic, I'll provide some hints for using Key Caps and explain when you might prefer using Key Caps to Word's Symbol command.

Step-by-Step

In this section you'll find instructions for inserting a special character using the Symbol command and for changing the font and size displayed by the Symbol window.

To insert a special character:

1. **Be sure the blinking insertion point is at the location you want the special character to appear.**

2. **Choose Symbol from the Insert menu.**

   The Symbol window appears. (You can also press Command-Option-Q to open the Symbol window.)

3. **Locate the character you want, and click it once.**

   Word inserts the character at the insertion point's location.

When you select a character, Word displays its decimal character code and key sequence here

4. **Close the Symbol window by clicking its close box.**

To change the font or size displayed in the Symbol window:

1. **With the Symbol window open, choose the desired font or size from the Font menu.**

   Word updates the Symbol window to reflect the font or size you chose.

Quick Tips

Quick access to the Symbol font

PostScript printers such as the Apple Personal LaserWriter NT and the LaserWriter IIf and IIg contain a font named Symbol, which includes the Greek alphabet and many mathematical symbols. Word provides a slick keyboard shortcut that lets you quickly insert a single character from the Symbol font. When you press Command-Shift-Q, Word switches to the Symbol font for the next character you type. After you type that character, Word returns to the font you were using.

Be smart — use smart quotes

It's preferable to use "curly" typographer's quote marks and apostrophes instead of the straight "typewriter" quotes that appear on the key to the left of the Return key. But the curly-quote key sequences — which use the Shift and Option keys along with the [and] keys in various combinations — can tie your fingers in knots. The answer: Word's Smart Quotes option, which automatically gives you typographically correct quotes as you type. To activate the Smart Quotes option, choose Preferences from the Tools menu and check the Smart Quotes check box.

You should not use smart quotes (or em and en dashes) when creating documents that you'll transfer to computers other than Macs, however. The curly quotes are unlikely to be available on the other machines, and will usually appear as the capital letters R, S, T, or U, depending on the quote.

Why no smart dash?

Wouldn't it be nice if Word could automatically translate double hyphens (--) into an em dash (—) as you type? Alas, it can't, but you can have the next best thing by using the Replace command just before printing a document. Choose Replace and tell Word to change all double hyphens into an em dash. While you're being typographically correct, you might want to replace all double word spaces with a single word space. See Topic 15 for more details on the Replace command. The quick reference card in the front of this book contains more tips for making your documents look professionally typeset.

Speaking of dashes, an en dash (–) is often used to represent the word *to* (the San Francisco–Pittsburgh flight) and in compound adjectives containing hyphens (her German–Scotch–Irish heritage). But don't use an en dash as a substitute for the word *and* ("between 10–15 years old" is wrong), or in a phrase containing the word *from* ("I worked from 3–11" is wrong).

Real inch and foot marks

Many people mistakenly refer to the Mac's straight-up-and-down type-writer quotes as foot and inch symbols. They aren't — true inch and foot symbols (technically, they're *prime marks*) are slanted. The only true prime marks are in the Mac's Symbol font. If you don't feel like switching to Symbol for prime marks, you can simulate them by italicizing type-writer quotes.

Shrink those symbols

The register mark (®) and trademark symbol (™) in most Macintosh fonts are so huge you might think they were created by Apple attorneys. You might want to shrink them down by several sizes and then shift them vertically using the superscript style so that their tops align with the top of the text. For 12-point text, try 8- or 9-point symbols.

Quick character entry with glossaries

If you use a certain special character often, consider creating a glossary entry containing it. Putting a special character in a glossary is an especially good idea if you use a smaller, superscripted version of the character as described in the previous tip. For details on using Word's glossary feature, see Topic 16.

Know your Key Caps

The Mac's Key Caps desk accessory displays an on-screen keyboard with a text-entry box above it. When you press keys on the Mac's keyboard, Key Caps updates its graphical keyboard to reflect the characters they summon. To locate a certain character in a given font:

1. **Choose the font's name from the Key Caps menu.**
   This is an important step, since, as mentioned earlier, not all fonts provide the same characters in the same keyboard locations.

2. **Press Option, Shift, and Option-Shift until you locate the character on Key Caps' keyboard.**

3. **When you find the character, continue holding down the Option and/or Shift key, and then click the character's key.**
   The character appears in the text entry window above the keyboard. Repeat this step for any additional characters you need (such as those that would complete a fraction).

4. **Select the character(s) in the text-entry window and choose Copy or Cut from the Edit menu.**

5. **Return to your document, be sure you have a blinking insertion point where you want the character to appear, and then choose Paste.**
If necessary, change the font to the desired typeface.

As an alternative to copying the character to the Clipboard, you can type the character directly by pressing its appropriate key, as displayed by Key Caps. Close Key Caps' window when you're done with it; leaving it open while you type slows the Mac as Key Caps' keys flash merrily in the background.

You'll probably use Word's Symbol window instead of Key Caps to ferret out those elusive special characters. The Symbol window has two advantages over Key Caps: It shows all the special characters at once (you don't have to press Shift and Option to find them) and it lets you change the font size in which characters are displayed. Key Caps shows everything in one size, and that can make finding certain characters difficult when you're working with pictorial fonts (ones whose characters are pictures, not letters or numbers).

Voilà! Accents!

Creating an accented character such as é or ñ requires a two-step key sequence. First, press Option along with the accent's character. Next, type the character that will appear under the accent. For example, to create an *n* with a tilde over it (ñ), press Option-N and then type an *n*.

Topic 13

Working with Graphics

Overview

Word gives you several ways to include graphics in a document. You can:

Picture button

♦ *Use the Insert menu's Picture command to import graphics created in other programs.* Word supports several popular graphics file formats, including PICT, MacPaint, Tagged Image File Format (TIFF), and Encapsulated PostScript (EPS).

♦ *Draw a picture using Word's built-in picture window.* This window is accessed by clicking the ribbon's picture button or through the Insert menu's Picture command.

♦ *Use the Edit menu's Paste or Paste Special commands to paste a picture that you've cut or copied from a different program.* The Paste Special command lets you create a link to the original graphic so that if it's revised, the revised version appears in your Word document. In order to establish a link, the source program (the one you used to create the graphic) must support Microsoft's paste-link feature. Version 3.0 of the Microsoft Excel spreadsheet program supports this feature.

♦ *Use the Edit menu's Subscribe To command to subscribe to an edition file created in Word or another program.* (An edition file, as explained in Topic 32, is created when you use a program's Create Publisher command.) The Subscribe To command is available only if you're using Apple's System 7 software.

This topic doesn't describe the Paste Special or Subscribe To commands, since they can also apply to text and other types of information, such as Excel spreadsheets. For details on these commands, see Topic 32.

Importing graphics files

When you choose Picture from the Insert menu, Word presents a dialog box that enables you to locate and open a graphics file. You can use the dialog box's Find File button to locate all graphics files on your hard disk, and even preview the files to decide which one to import.

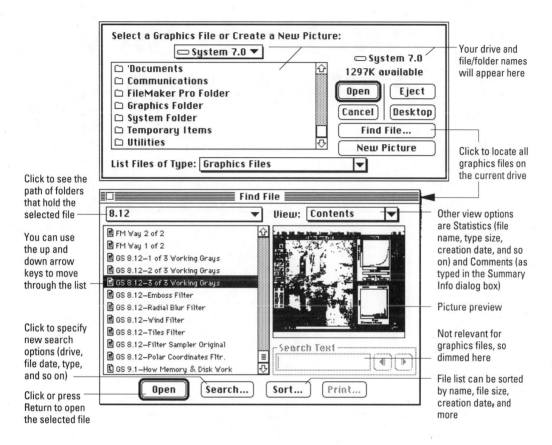

Click to see the path of folders that hold the selected file

You can use the up and down arrow keys to move through the list

Click to specify new search options (drive, file date, type, and so on)

Click or press Return to open the selected file

Your drive and file/folder names will appear here

Click to locate all graphics files on the current drive

Other view options are Statistics (file name, type size, creation date, and so on) and Comments (as typed in the Summary Info dialog box)

Picture preview

Not relevant for graphics files, so dimmed here

File list can be sorted by name, file size, creation date, and more

The preview feature is especially useful if you work with libraries of clip art. (Note that you must have the Find File command installed in the Word Commands folder in order for the Find File button and command to be available.)

For more details on searching for files, see Topic 33.

Word's picture window

Word's picture window is a mini drawing program that you can use within Word. With its tools, you can draw a variety of shapes, including lines, squares, arcs, circles, and polygons. You can also annotate drawings with text in any font, size, or style. You can rotate text or objects you draw (or graphics that you import) in one degree increments. You can change the line thickness of shapes and specify a variety of patterns for the shapes and for the interior of closed shapes such as boxes and circles. You can also flip text or objects to turn things upside down or to invert them, as shown in the following illustration.

Flip tool

Flipped vertical

Flipped horizontal

If you're familiar with drawing programs such as Claris's MacDraw series, you'll feel comfortable with the picture window, although its features don't compare to those of a stand-alone graphics program. In particular, the picture window lacks a Group command for treating multiple objects as one object, and it lacks automatic alignment features such as a grid or an Align command. Still, the picture window is more than adequate for drawing simple diagrams or creating special text effects, and its ability to rotate imported graphics can be handy.

When you close the picture window, the graphic you were working with appears in the document window. You must close the picture window in order to resume editing the document.

Note that the picture window feature is available only if the picture file is installed in the Word Commands folder, located within Word's folder; see Appendix A for details on Word's plug-in modules.

Cropping or scaling graphics

Once you've imported a graphic or created one using Word's picture window, the graphic appears in the document window within a frame that you can manipulate in two ways. You can:

✦ *Crop* it — adjust the frame that surrounds it to remove white space or unwanted portions of the graphic.

✦ *Scale* it — change its size so that it takes up more or less space on a page.

To crop or scale a graphic, you must select it in the document window by clicking it once (don't click twice, or you'll open the picture window). Once you've selected a graphic, you can crop or scale it by dragging the handles on its frame as shown below.

When you drag the corner handle, the percentage of enlargement or reduction appears here

Drag to crop horizontally (to scale horizontally, press Shift and drag)

Drag to crop horizontally and vertically (to scale horizontally and vertically, press Shift and drag)

Drag to crop vertically (to scale horizontally and vertically, press Shift and drag)

If you need to crop *and* scale a graphic, you must go through a somewhat awkward two-step routine. First, use the picture window to scale the graphic to the desired size. Then, crop the scaled graphic by resizing its frame in the document window. This two-step routine is necessary because Word always restores a graphic to its original proportions when you crop its frame. When you resize the graphic using the picture window, however, the graphic's original proportions are discarded and replaced with the proportions of the graphic as it appears in the picture window. See this topic's Step-by-Step section for more detailed directions on cropping and scaling graphics.

Alas, Word's picture window doesn't provide a linear scaling feature — that is, it doesn't let you easily scale a picture while maintaining its proportions. Because of this shortcoming, it's easy to end up with a picture that has a squished or stretched appearance. So if you anticipate having to both scale and crop a graphic, you might want to do the cropping in a graphics program. Then you can import the graphic into Word and scale it by resizing its frame.

Word and true color graphics

These days, more and more people are working with *24-bit color,* also called *true color,* images — graphics that can contain millions of colors and provide photorealistic detail. You can get true color images by using a sophisticated painting or drawing program such as SuperMac Technology's SuperPaint Professional, Deneba's Canvas, or Claris's MacDraw Pro; by using three-dimensional rendering programs such as Ray Dream Designer or Specular's Infini-D; by using a color scanner such as La Cie's SilverScanner or Microtek's ScanMaker 1850S; or by using video-frame grabber hardware offered by firms such as Mass Microsystems, SuperMac, and Radius (to name just a few).

You can import true color graphics into Word, but don't use the picture window to alter them. When you open a true-color graphic with the picture window, Word discards most of the graphic's color information. If you need to add text labels or otherwise tweak a true-color graphic, do so in a program that will retain its color information. For example, you might use a drawing program such as Claris's MacDraw Pro or Aldus FreeHand to add text labels to a true-color graphic, and save the annotated graphic as a PICT or EPS file that you can import into Word. Fortunately, Word warns you before opening the picture window, so you can cancel the operation if you want to retain the true-color information.

If you accidentally open a true-color graphic using the picture window, close the picture window and immediately choose Undo. This restores the graphic's color information.

Step-by-Step

In this section, you'll find instructions for opening and using Word's picture window and for importing, scaling, and cropping graphics.

To open Word's picture window:

1. Click the Picture button in the ribbon.

— or —

1. Choose Picture from the Insert menu.

An Insert Picture dialog box appears.

2. Click the New Picture button.

— or —

2. Double-click an existing graphic in your document.

If you use this technique, the graphic appears in the picture window.

To draw a line, arc, circle, rectangle, or round-cornered rectangle:

1. Select the appropriate tool in the picture window's tool palette.

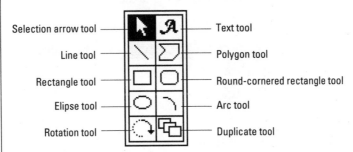

Selection arrow tool — Text tool
Line tool — Polygon tool
Rectangle tool — Round-cornered rectangle tool
Elipse tool — Arc tool
Rotation tool — Duplicate tool

2. Move the pointer within the drawing area.

3. Press and hold down the mouse button, and drag.

As you drag, Word displays the item's dimensions in the picture window's status bar. To draw a perfect square or circle or a perfectly horizontal or vertical line, press and hold down the Shift key as you drag. To draw from the center of the shape out, press Option while dragging. Press Shift and Option to draw a perfect shape from the center out.

4. Release the mouse button when the shape is the desired size.

To draw a polygon (an enclosed, irregular shape):

1. Select the polygon tool in the picture window's palette.

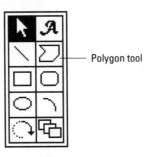

Polygon tool

2. Click within the drawing area to define the starting point of the polygon.

When you move the mouse after clicking, a line appears from the point where you clicked to the mouse pointer's current position.

3. Click where you want to position each corner of the polygon.

4. To close the polygon, click the first point again or simply double-click within the drawing area.

If you double-click, Word draws a line between where you double-clicked and the starting point, completing the polygon for you.

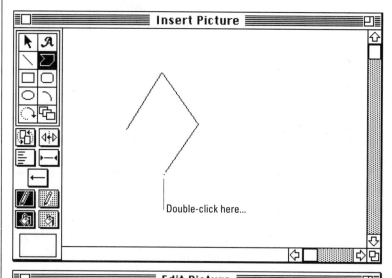

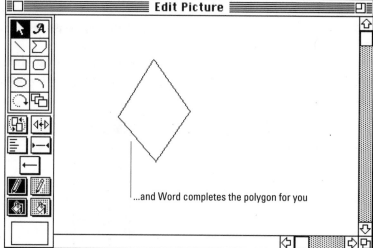

To add text to a picture:

1. **Click the picture window's text tool (the letter A in the tool palette).**

2. **Click within the drawing area to create a blinking insertion point. Or if you want a text box of a specific size, drag within the drawing area, as shown in the following illustration.**

Select the text tool and then drag to create a text box of a specific size (the size appears in the picture window's status bar)

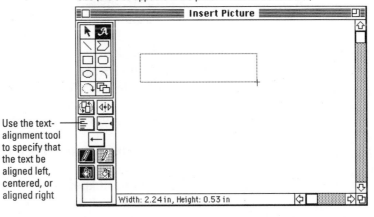

Use the text-alignment tool to specify that the text be aligned left, centered, or aligned right

As you drag, Word displays the item's dimensions in the picture window's status bar. If you simply click within the drawing area, you'll create a wide text box that extends to the picture window's right edge.

3. Type the text. You can also paste text from the Clipboard.
Word wraps text within the box. You can use the Font and Format menus to change the font, size, and style of the text, but all of the text in a text block will change accordingly. You can't mix fonts, sizes, or styles within a single text block. (This is another good argument for using a stand-alone drawing program.)

To resize a shape or text block:
1. Be sure the picture window's selection arrow tool is selected.

2. Select the item you want to resize by clicking it once.
Selection handles appear at the item's boundaries.

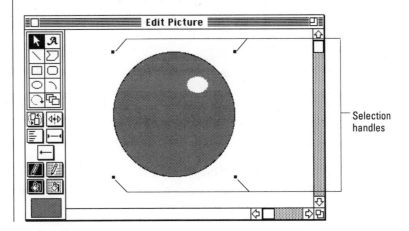

Selection handles

3. Drag a selection handle to resize the item.

As you drag, Word displays the item's dimensions in the picture window's status bar.

To select multiple items:

1. Drag a selection marquee around the items, being sure to completely enclose each one you want to select.

— or —

1. Click the first item you want to select.

2. While pressing the Shift key, click each subsequent item.

To change the line thickness or fill pattern of a shape:

1. Select the shape by clicking it with the selection arrow tool.

Selection handles appear at the shape's boundaries.

2. Choose the desired options from the appropriate palettes.

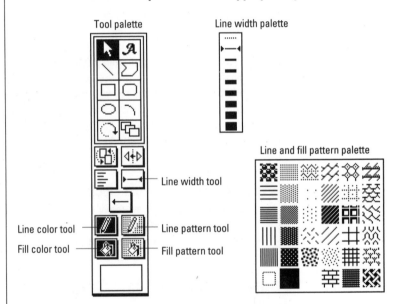

Tool palette   Line width palette

Line and fill pattern palette

Line width tool

Line color tool ──── ── Line pattern tool

Fill color tool ──── ── Fill pattern tool

If you want Word to draw shapes using a specific line width, pattern, or color, select the desired options *before* drawing a shape and while no shapes are selected. (To be sure nothing is selected, activate the selection arrow tool and then click any blank part of the drawing area.)

To rotate a shape or text block:

1. Select the shape by clicking it with the selection arrow tool.

Selection handles appear at the shape's boundaries.

Rotation tool
crosshair

2. Click the rotation tool in the picture window's tool palette.

When you move the pointer back to the drawing area, it appears as a circle with a crosshair.

3. Click and drag one of the shape's selection handles.

As you drag, an outline of the shape follows the pointer and the rotation angle appears in the picture window's status bar.

Flip tool

4. Release the mouse button when the object is rotated as desired.

Note that you can't edit or reformat rotated text. You must first restore its normal position by selecting the rotated text block and choosing Undo All Flips and Rotations from the flip tool's pop-up menu.

To bring an item in front of others, or send an item behind others:

1. Select the shape by clicking it with the selection arrow tool.

Selection handles appear at the shape's boundaries.

Front/Back tool

2. Choose Bring to Front or Send to Back from the front/back tool's pop-up menu.

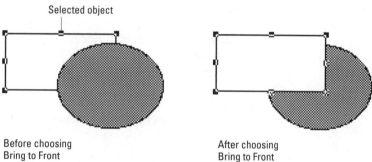

Selected object

Before choosing
Bring to Front

After choosing
Bring to Front

To duplicate one or more items:

Duplicate tool

1. Select the item by clicking it with the selection arrow tool, or select all the items by drawing a marquee or by Shift-clicking.

2. Click the duplicate tool in the picture window's palette.

To import a graphic that's saved on disk:

1. Choose Picture from the Insert menu.

The insert picture dialog box appears.

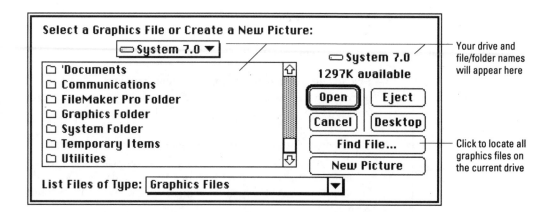

Select a Graphics File or Create a New Picture:

⌐⊃ System 7.0 ▼

☐ 'Documents
☐ Communications
☐ FileMaker Pro Folder
☐ Graphics Folder
☐ System Folder
☐ Temporary Items
☐ Utilities

⌐⊃ System 7.0
1297K available

[**Open**] [Eject]
[Cancel] [Desktop]
[Find File...]
[New Picture]

List Files of Type: [Graphics Files   ▼]

Your drive and
file/folder names
will appear here

Click to locate all
graphics files on
the current drive

2. Locate the desired graphic and then double-click it.
Word imports the graphic. You can work with an imported
graphic in the picture window, but keep in mind the picture
window's color limitations mentioned in this topic's Overview
section.

To paste a graphic from a different program:

1. In the original program, select the graphic and choose Copy from the Edit menu.

2. If you're running MultiFinder or System 7, switch to Word. If you aren't running MultiFinder or System 7, quit the application and then start Word.

3. Position the insertion point where you want the graphic to appear, and then choose Paste from the Edit menu.
Alternatively, you can open the picture window and choose
Paste.

To crop a graphic:

1. Select the graphic in the document window by clicking it once.
Don't click twice — doing so opens the picture window.

2. Drag the selection handles until the graphic is cropped as desired.

Before cropping

After cropping

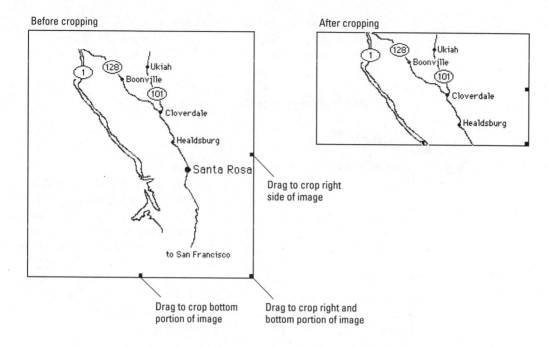

Drag to crop right
side of image

Drag to crop bottom
portion of image

Drag to crop right and
bottom portion of image

Hidden portions of the graphic aren't deleted; you can restore them by dragging the handles to enlarge the picture's frame.

To scale a graphic:

1. Select the graphic in the document window by clicking it once.

2. Press and hold down the Shift key and then drag the selection handles.

Drag the lower-right selection handle to resize the graphic and maintain its original proportions. As you drag the lower-right selection handle, Word displays the percentage of enlargement or reduction at the bottom of the document window.

3. Release the mouse button when the graphic's frame is the desired size.

Word redraws the graphic at the desired size. If you had previously cropped the graphic, the cropping is lost and the entire graphic appears. To crop *and* size a graphic, use the picture window to resize the graphic, and then crop its frame in the document window. See this topic's Overview section for more details.

To place a border around a graphic:

1. Select the graphic in the document window by clicking it once.

2. Choose Character from the Format menu.

3. In the Style area, click the Outline check box.

For a fatter border, also click the Bold check box. To place a shadow along the bottom and right edges of the border, also click the Shadow check box.

4. Click OK or press Return.

Quick Tips

Importing EPS graphics via the Clipboard

You can use the Clipboard to import PostScript illustrations created in Adobe Illustrator and Aldus FreeHand, but there's a special trick to it: Press the Option key while choosing Copy in Illustrator or FreeHand. This tells the program to place the illustration on the Clipboard in two formats: a PICT format that Word will use to display the graphic, and the underlying PostScript instructions that your printer will use to print the graphic. (This format is called *PICT with embedded PostScript*. You can use this technique to include PostScript illustrations in any program that supports graphics.) You can resize the illustration after pasting it into Word, and it will still print sharply.

Graphics and Word's performance

It takes more time to scroll through a document containing graphics than it does to scroll through a document containing mostly text. That's because Word must work harder to redraw the graphic each time you scroll. You can speed up Word's scrolling by using the Picture Placeholders preferences option. (Choose Preferences from the Tools menu, select the View option, and click the Picture Placeholders check box.)

When Picture Placeholders is selected, Word displays a gray box where each picture appears. The picture appears normally if you open it using the picture window, and it prints normally when you print the document.

Converting text to a picture

You can convert any piece of text in a Word document to a picture. Simply select the text, and then press Command-Option-D. This sequence puts a picture of the text on the Clipboard, ready for you to paste into the document. If you don't need the original text you selected, delete it.

You can use this trick along with the picture window to create special text effects such as stretched or condensed headlines. Altered text may appear ragged on the screen, but if you're using Adobe Type Manager, Apple TrueType fonts, or a PostScript printer, it will print sharply.

Another way to import MacPaint documents

Word automatically displays the names of MacPaint-format files in its Open dialog box (the dialog box that appears when you choose Open from the File menu). If you select a MacPaint document, Word creates a new, untitled document and imports the graphic into it. If necessary, you can use the Clipboard to cut the graphic and paste it into a different document.

Importing a chart from Excel? Use Paste Special

If you're importing a chart created in Excel and you suspect the original chart may change over time, consider using the Paste Special command to establish a link with the original file. This will make it easier to update the Word document when the original chart changes.

As Topics 32 describes, you can use Paste Special or the Edit menu's Publish and Subscribe commands to establish this kind of two-way link with other types of documents, too.

Resizing the picture window doesn't resize the picture

You can't change a picture's size by resizing the picture window. You need to select the picture and resize it by dragging one of its selection handles in either the document window or the picture window.

If you've used the picture window's tools to create or embellish a graphic, resize the picture by dragging one of its selection handles in the document window only. Resizing this kind of picture in the picture window involves resizing every object individually — a painstaking process for large pictures (and another good argument for using a stand-alone drawing program to create complex drawings).

Frame your pictures

If you enclose a picture in a frame, you can position it freely on the page and create attractive *runaround* effects, as shown in the following illustration.

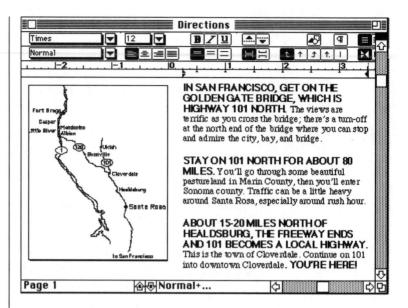

To enclose a picture in a frame, put the picture in its own paragraph (be sure there is a paragraph marker to the immediate right of the picture), and then choose Frame from the Format menu. Click OK or press Return when the Frame dialog box appears, or click the Position button to open the Print Preview window, where you can drag the frame to its destination on the page.

Topic 23 describes frames and the Frame dialog box in more detail.

"Erasing" part of a bitmapped image

The picture window lacks an eraser and other tools for deleting unwanted parts of a bitmapped image, but you can accomplish a similar task with only a little more effort. Mask over unwanted portions of a bitmap by drawing shapes and then using the line width and pattern fill tools to give the shapes no line width and a white fill pattern.

Cropping with the picture window

You might have noticed that the frame Word places around graphics in the document window lacks handles on the top and left sides, making it impossible to crop the top or left portion of a graphic. Fortunately, you can use the picture window to crop the top or left portion of a graphic. Within the picture window, drag the graphic up or to the left as needed to remove the unwanted portions. To restore what you've cropped, reopen the picture window and drag the graphic down or to the right, as needed.

Topic 14
Printing a Document

Overview

Word's basic printing features closely resemble those of any Macintosh program. Using the Print dialog box, you can print multiple copies of a document or only certain pages within a document — or multiple copies of certain pages. You can choose to manually feed paper or to automatically draw paper from your printer's built-in tray or feed mechanism. If you have an Apple ImageWriter or StyleWriter, you can choose between various print-quality options. If your document contains gray-scale images or colors and if you have a monochrome or color PostScript printer, you can specify whether gray-scale or color items be printed as they appear or in black and white (the faster option).

You can jump from one text-entry box to the next by pressing Tab

To print from a certain page through the end of the document, type the starting page number here, leaving the To box blank

To print from the first page through a specific page, type the ending page number here, leaving the From box blank

LaserWriter "HP LaserJet IIISi"		7.0	Print
Copies: 1	Pages: ● All ○ From: [ ] To: [ ]		Cancel
Cover Page:	● No ○ First Page ○ Last Page		
Paper Source:	● Paper Cassette ○ Manual Feed		
Print:	● Black & White ○ Color/Grayscale		
Destination:	● Printer ○ PostScript® File		
Section Range: From: 1	To: 1	☐ Print Selection Only	
☐ Print Hidden Text	☐ Print Next File	☐ Print Back To Front	

The Print dialog box for other types of printers contains slightly different options

Special printing features

Word's Print dialog box also provides special printing capabilities some programs lack, including:

♦ *Back-to-front printing*. By clicking the Print Back to Front check box, you can print a document in reverse page order — from the last page to the first. If your printer delivers pages with the printed side facing up, using this option eliminates the chore of having to reorder the printed pages. (The original Apple LaserWriter and LaserWriter Plus printers are among those that deliver face-up output. The Apple StyleWriter ink jet printer delivers face-up output, too, but unfortunately, Word disables the back-to-front option when printing to the StyleWriter.)

✦ *Printing a selection.* If you want to print a selected portion of a document — even just one word — select what you want to print and choose the Print Selection Only button.

✦ *Printing a section range.* If your document contains multiple sections (created with the Format menu's Section command), you can specify which sections to print. Topic 22 describes how to print a section range.

✦ *Printing hidden text.* If your document contains text formatted in Word's hidden style, you can use the Print Hidden Text button to specify whether you want Word to print the hidden text. You might want to print hidden text if you've used hidden text for comments or annotations, or to proofread index or table of contents entries. (Indexes and tables of contents are covered in Topics 26 and 27.)

✦ *Printing linked documents.* By using the Document dialog box, you can link one document to another and specify that Word number pages sequentially across all of the documents. As Topic 30 describes, you might use this technique when creating a book or manual in which each chapter might be a separate document file. If you've linked a document to another document, the Print dialog box lets you specify whether to print the next file.

Specifying paper size and page orientation

To specify the paper size and page orientation (horizontal or vertical), use the Page Setup command as described in Topic 7.

A reminder about the Chooser

As Topic 7 discusses, if you have different types of printers attached to your Mac — or if you'll be printing a document on a different type of printer than you have — it's important to use the Chooser to select the printer on which you'll print the final version of the document. It's a good idea to select the final printer before extensively formatting a document; otherwise, line endings, page breaks, and other aspects of the document's formatting could change. This is because character widths can vary among different types of printers, and also because some printers can print closer to the edges of the page than others — in printer parlance, they have a larger *printable area.*

(If you're curious, each printer icon in the Chooser window corresponds to a *printer driver,* a program that acts as a middleman between the Mac and your printer. A printer driver teaches the Mac how to communicate with a specific type of printer, and it enables the Mac to display the appropriate Page Setup and Print dialog box options for that printer. Printer drivers are stored in the System Folder on your hard disk; if you're running System 7, they're stored in the Extensions folder, which is located within the System Folder. In the System 7 world, printer drivers are called *Chooser extensions.*)

Other printing techniques

If you need to print several documents, you can print them directly from the Finder by selecting them and choosing Print from the Finder's File menu.

If you've used the Find File command to locate one or more files that meet certain criteria, you can print any number of those files by selecting them (Shift-click each file) and clicking the Print button in the Find File window. For more details on this printing option, see Topic 33.

Step-by-Step

This section contains instructions for printing a document and for printing one or more documents from the Finder.

To print an entire document:

1. Choose Print from the File menu.
   The Print dialog box appears.

2. Choose the desired print options and then click OK or press Return.
   To cancel printing, press Command-period.

To print a range of pages:

1. Choose Print from the File menu.
   The Print dialog box appears.

2. In the From and To boxes, type the page numbers representing the range of pages you want to print.
   See the figure at the beginning of this topic for some keyboard shortcuts.

3. Choose any other print options, and then click OK or press Return.
   To cancel printing, press Command-period.

To print one or more documents from the Finder:

1. Select each document.
   To select more than one document, click the first document, and

then press the Shift key while clicking subsequent documents. You can also select multiple documents by enclosing them within a selection marquee.

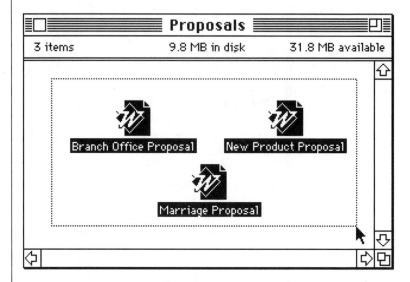

If you use System 7's outline view (available in any text view — By Name, By Size, By Kind, and so on), you can even select and print multiple files that are scattered across different folders.

2. Choose Print from the Finder's File menu.
After a few moments, Word's Print dialog box appears.

3. Choose the desired print options and then click OK or press Return.
The options you specify are applied to all of the documents you selected.

Quick Tips
Page Setup options
Topic 7 discusses the primary options in the Page Setup dialog box — the icons that let you choose between vertical and horizontal page orientation, for example, and the buttons that let you choose the paper size you want. But the Page Setup dialog box contains numerous other options that let you fine-tune the way a document is printed. The following tables summarize the Page Setup options for PostScript printers, the Apple LaserWriter IISC, the Apple Personal LaserWriter NT, the Apple ImageWriter, and the Apple StyleWriter.

PostScript Page Setup options

Option	What it does	Comments
Reduce or Enlarge	Reduces page contents to as little as 25 percent or enlarges them to as much as 400 percent of their normal size	Word adjusts the rulers and margin markers to indicate line breaks and page breaks accurately
Font Substitution	Replaces any occurrences of New York with Times, of Monaco with Courier, and of Geneva with Helvetica	New York, Monaco, and Geneva print poorly and slowly on PostScript printers, so it's best to use this option — or avoid those fonts to begin with unless you have TrueType versions of them
Text Smoothing	Smooths bitmapped fonts, improving their appearance somewhat	It's best to avoid bitmapped fonts in your documents
Graphics Smoothing	Smooths bitmapped graphics on Apple PostScript printers	This option generally doesn't work on non-Apple PostScript printers
Faster Bitmap Printing	Speeds printing of bitmapped graphics	Complex pages may not print properly with this option selected; if a page fails to print, uncheck this option
Fractional Widths	Improves the spacing of proportionally spaced fonts (most fonts are proportionally spaced)	Some fonts can be difficult to read on the screen when this option is checked; if you check this option after creating a document, line and page endings may change
Print PostScript Over Text	Prints any PostScript graphics in the document on top of text or other graphics.	You may need to use this option if you've used items from the PostScript Glossary (see Topic 16)

ImageWriter Page Setup options

Option	What it does	Comments
Tall Adjusted	Corrects the stretched appearance that some graphics may have when printed (for example, circles may appear as ovals)	Use this option if printed circles appear as ovals, for example. Also use to simulate the way lines will break on a PostScript printer
50% Reduction	Prints page contents at half size	Word adjusts margin markers and rulers to accurately indicate line breaks and page endings
No Gaps Between Pages	Word doesn't skip over perforations between pages in fanfold paper	You might use this option when printing continuous-feed mailing labels

StyleWriter Page Setup options

Option	What it does	Comments
Scale	Lets you print page elements at 20, 40, 60, 80, or 100 percent of their actual size	When you choose a scale option other than 100 percent, Word adjusts margin markers and rulers to accurately indicate line breaks and page endings
Fractional Widths	Improves the spacing of proportionally spaced fonts (most fonts are proportionally spaced)	Some fonts can be more difficult to read on the screen when this option is checked; if you check this option after creating a document, line and page endings may change

Personal LaserWriter SC and LS Page Setup options

Option	What it does	Comments
Size	Lets you print page elements at 50, 75, or 100 percent of their actual size	When you choose a scale option other than 100 percent, Word adjusts margin markers and rulers to accurately indicate line breaks and page endings
Exact Bit Images (for LS, called Precision Bitmap Alignment)	Reduces page size by 4 percent, which may improve the printed appearance of some bitmapped (MacPaint-type) graphics	Choosing this option doesn't affect drawings created with Word's Picture window
Text Smoothing (not applicable to LS)	Improves the appearance of fonts that don't have outlines or 4× counterparts in the System Folder	
Fractional Widths	Improves the spacing of proportionally spaced fonts (most fonts are proportionally spaced)	Some fonts can be more difficult to read on the screen when this option is checked; if you check this option after creating a document, line and page endings may change

Don't wait for your printer

Tired of waiting to use your Mac after sending off a document to be printed? Use a *spooler* and you won't have to wait. A spooler is a program that intercepts and stores on disk the data the Mac transmits to a printer. When that's done, the spooler works behind the scenes to send the data to the printer in bursts while you continue to work. A spooler won't speed up your printer — in fact, you'll probably wait a little longer to see your final output — but it will allow you to get back to work while printing takes place. In the Mac world, spooling is often called *background printing,* so named because the spooler talks to the printer in the background, while you continue to work.

The Mac's system software provides background printing for the following printers:

◆ Any PostScript laser printer (examples include the Apple Personal LaserWriter NT and LaserWriter IINT, IINTX, IIf, and IIg; the QMS PS-410, PS-810, and PS-815; the Texas Instruments microLaser; the GCC BLP II, IIs, and BLP Elite)

◆ The Apple StyleWriter (using StyleWriter extension version 1.1 or later; version 1.0 does not support background printing)

◆ The Apple Personal LaserWriter LS and Personal LaserWriter SC

◆ The Apple LaserWriter IISC

To use the background printing option, you must be running MultiFinder or System 7. To determine this, be sure you're at the Finder and then examine your Mac's Apple menu:

◆ If the first command in the Apple menu is About this Macintosh, you're running under System 7.

◆ If the first command in the Apple menu is About the Finder, you're running under a system version prior to 7.0. If the command About MultiFinder appears at the bottom of the Apple menu, you're running under MultiFinder.

If you're using a system version prior to 7.0 and you aren't running under MultiFinder, you can easily activate MultiFinder. (To avoid annoying out-of-memory messages, however, your Mac should have at least 2MB of memory — preferably more. To find out how much memory you have, choose About the Finder or About this Macintosh from the Apple menu when the Finder is active.) Choose Set Startup from the Finder's Special menu, select MultiFinder under the start-up options, and then click OK or press Return. Finally, choose Restart from the Special menu. Your Mac will restart under MultiFinder.

To activate background printing, open the Chooser and select the icon corresponding to your printer. When the Background Printing buttons appear, click On. Finally, close the Chooser.

If you don't have one of the above printers, you can still enjoy the benefits of background printing by buying a commercial spooler such as Fifth Generation Systems's SuperLaserSpool. This program works with the aforementioned printers as well as with the Apple ImageWriter series. It does not work with the GCC PLP series; these printers' design prohibits background printing.

Formatting for a PostScript printer

It's a common scenario: You have a PostScript laser printer at the office or the college library, but your home printer is an ImageWriter. You want to format documents for final output on a PostScript printer, but when you use the Chooser to print your final document, all the line and page endings change.

There are two ways to avoid this problem:

♦ *Copy the LaserWriter printer driver to your hard disk, and then select the driver using the Chooser.* Word will format the document's margins and line endings for the PostScript printer you don't really have. (Be sure you copy the driver to the correct place: In System 7, it must be located in the Extensions folder, within the System Folder. In earlier system versions, the driver must be located in the System Folder. Don't forget to use the Chooser to select the driver after you copy it.)

♦ *Use the ImageWriter driver's Tall Adjusted option (in the Page Setup dialog box).* Choosing Tall Adjusted simulates the spacing you'll get from a PostScript printer — more or less. This second option is less effective than the first.

Part II
Editing and Proofing

Topic 15

Finding and Replacing

Overview

Few features streamline the editing process more than a good set of Find and Replace commands. The most common application of the Find command is to locate a specific section of text. It's faster than manually scrolling through the document.

Type the text you're looking for (up to 255 characters) here. You can also paste text from the Clipboard.

```
☐▐▐▐▐▐▐▐▐▐▐▐▐▐▐▐▐▐▐▐▐ Find ▐▐▐▐▐▐▐▐▐▐▐▐▐▐▐▐▐
Find What:    that is the question         [ Find Next ]
    [ Format ▾ ]
    [ Special ▾ ]                          [ Cancel ]
                                           Search:
    ☐ Match Whole Word Only   ☐ Match Case [ Down  ▾ ]
```

When selected, Word skips over text that occurs within words

When selected, Word skips over text whose capitalization doesn't match what you typed

The Replace command is most often used to locate a text passage and replace it with something else. You might use it to update a product manual if the product's name changes, or to polish your punctuation — changing, for example, each occurrence of a double hyphen (--) into a typesetter's em dash (—).

```
☐▐▐▐▐▐▐▐▐▐▐▐▐▐▐▐▐▐▐ Replace ▐▐▐▐▐▐▐▐▐▐▐▐▐▐
Find What:    --                           [ Find Next ]
    [ Format ▾ ]
    [ Special ▾ ]                          [ Replace ]
                                           [ Replace All ]
Replace With: —                            [ Cancel ]
    [ Format ▾ ]
    [ Special ▾ ]
                                           Search:
    ☐ Match Whole Word Only   ☐ Match Case [ Selection ▾ ]
```

In the Find What and Replace With boxes, you can type up to 255 characters; the text scrolls horizontally as you type. If you have some text on the Clipboard, you can paste it into either box. As described shortly, you can also use a special code to represent the Clipboard's contents in the Replace With box.

Finding and replacing attributes and codes

Word's Find and Replace commands are able to work with more than just text. You can use Find and Replace to locate and change:

+ *Text formatted in a certain way.* You can, for example search for text formatted as 24-point double-spaced Helvetica Bold and change it to single-spaced Times Bold Italic.

+ *Text formatted according to a style sheet.* You can, for example, tell Word to change any text formatted according to a style named Listing and assign a style named BulletList.

+ *Graphics and special, nontext characters such as tabs, footnote references, hard page breaks, and paragraph marks.* Topic 10 described one use for this capability: Removing some or all of a document's hard page breaks so that you can properly repaginate the document after doing major editing.

To specify that Word find and replace formatting attributes and codes, use the ruler and ribbon when the Find or Replace dialog box is open. When you do, the formatting options you choose appear in the Find or Replace dialog box. As an alternative to using the ruler and ribbon when formatting text, you can also use the Format pop-up menu's Paragraph and Character commands to specify the formatting attributes you want to find or replace. In this regard, the Find and Replace dialog boxes work just like Word's main document window: You can use the ruler and ribbon or the Paragraph and Character commands to specify the formatting you want, as shown in the following illustration.

You can use the ruler and ribbon to specify the character and paragraph formatting you want to search for...

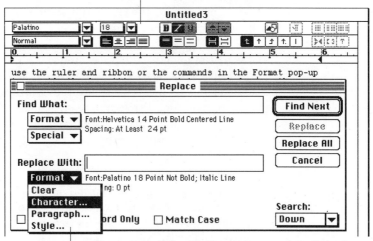

...or choose commands from the Format pop-up menus to display the Character, Paragraph, or Style dialog boxes. Choose Clear to remove formatting attributes from the Find What or Replace With areas.

When you're searching for graphics or codes such as tabs and hard page breaks, you choose the desired code from the Special pop-up menu. When you do, a one- or two-character code appears in the Find What or Replace With text box.

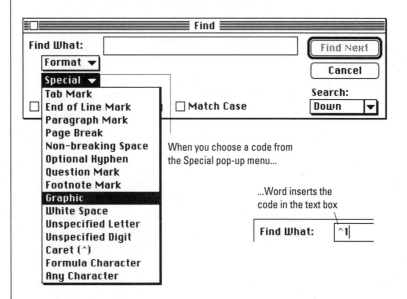

When you choose a code from the Special pop-up menu...

...Word inserts the code in the text box

You can also type these codes instead of choosing them from the Special pop-up menu. (Indeed, earlier versions of Word were able to find and replace the same codes, but *required* you to type them.) As you become familiar with Word, you might prefer to type codes that you've memorized. The Quick Tips section of this topic lists each of the codes Word can find and replace.

If you want to find and replace attributes or codes only — not specific text characters — leave the Find What and Replace With boxes blank. If the Find What box contains text (other than the special codes Word uses for formatting characters), Word assumes you want to find that text. Similarly, if the Replace With box contains text, Word assumes you want to insert that text.

Two ways to replace

You can use the Replace command on a case-by-case basis, approving each replacement before it takes place, or you can tell Word to find and replace everything in one fell swoop. To replace on a case-by-case basis, use the Find Next and Replace buttons in the Replace dialog box (details appear in this topic's Step-by-Step section). To find and replace in one step, use the Replace All button.

If you use Replace on a case-by-case basis, you can undo only the last replacement. If you use the Replace All button, you can undo all of the replacements.

Controlling the search direction

The Find and Replace dialog boxes contain a Search pop-up menu that lets you specify the direction in which Word searches. The following table describes each option's workings.

Search option	How it works
Down	Word searches from the insertion point's position to the end of the document. When it reaches the end of the document, Word asks if searching should continue from the beginning.
Up	Word searches from the insertion point's position to the beginning of the document. When it reaches the beginning, Word asks if searching should continue from the end.
All	Word searches from the insertion point's position to the end of the document, and then jumps to the beginning and continues until it reaches the insertion point again. Word also searches headers, footers, and footnotes.
Selection	Word searches only the selected portion of the document. This option appears only if you've selected something in the document.

The All option is the most versatile, since you often don't know in which direction you want to search. ("If I knew where to search, I wouldn't be searching to begin with.") Unless you specify otherwise, however, Word uses the Down option. Alas, you can't specify a different default direction.

Narrowing the search

The Find and Replace dialog boxes contain two check boxes that let you further refine the search:

✦ *Match Whole Word Only.* When this check box is selected, Word finds only whole words, not sequences of characters within other words. For example, if you search for *of* and select Match Whole Word Only, Word skips over words such as *offer, professional,* and *often.*

✦ *Match Case.* When this check box is selected, Word finds text whose capitalization matches what you typed. If you choose this option and specify *Apple* in the Find What box, Word skips over *apple.* When this check box is unchecked, Word ignores capitalization; in the preceding example, Word would find both occurrences of *apple* — and would even find *ApPlE.*

Wildcards: When any character will do

Sometimes you need to be a bit vague when you're specifying what to search for. For example, say you've written a report containing many occurrences of the words *project* and *product.* You're revising the report, and you want to change each occurrence of either word to *product-design phase.* To do so, use the *wildcard* character — a question mark (?) — to represent the characters that are different in each phrase. In this example, you'd type *pro??ct* in the Find What portion of the Replace dialog box. The wildcard character means "any character."

Word provides other codes that mean "any letter" and "any digit"; they're listed along with all of Word's special codes in this topic's Quick Tips section.

Step-by-Step

This section contains instructions for searching for and replacing text, text attributes, and special codes.

To find specific text regardless of its formatting:

1. **Choose Find from the Edit menu.**

   The Find dialog box appears.

2. **In the Find What box, type the text you want to search for.**

   If any formatting is listed below the Find What box, remove it by choosing Clear from the Format pop-up menu.

3. **Click Find Next or press Return.**
Word searches for the text and selects it if it's found.

To find specific text with specific formatting (for example, the word *Introduction* appearing in 18-point Helvetica Bold):

1. **Choose Find from the Edit menu.**
The Find dialog box appears.

2. **In the Find What box, type the text you want to search for.**

3. **Use the ruler and ribbon or the commands in the Format pop-up menu to specify the formatting of the text you want to search for.**
To remove the formatting descriptions and start over, choose Clear from the Format pop-up menu.

4. **Click Find Next or press Return.**
Word searches for the text and selects it if it's found.

To find any text with specific formatting (for example, any text appearing in 18-point Helvetica Bold):

1. **Choose Find from the Edit menu.**
The Find dialog box appears.

2. **Use the ruler and ribbon or the commands in the Format pop-up menu to specify the formatting of the text you want to search for.**
Leave the Find What box empty.

3. **Click Find Next or press Return.**
Word searches for the formatting and selects the first text containing it.

To find a special code such as a tab, page break, or optional hyphen:

1. **Choose Find from the Edit menu.**
The Find dialog box appears.

2. **Use the Special pop-up menu to choose the desired code or type the code in the Find What box.**
When you choose a code from the Special pop-up menu, Word inserts the characters corresponding to it in the Find What box.

3. **If necessary, use the ruler and ribbon or the commands in the Format pop-up menu to specify the formatting of the code you want to search for.**
You might perform this step if you're searching for a formatted paragraph mark or if you chose the Any Character, Unspecified Letter, Unspecified Digit codes from the Special pop-up menu.

4. Click Find Next or press Return.
Word searches for the code and selects it if it's found.

To find text or a code regardless of its formatting and then delete it:

1. Choose Replace from the Edit menu.
The Replace dialog box appears.

2. In the Find What box, type the text you want to search for or use the Special pop-up menu to specify a code.
Leave the Replace With box empty.

3. Use the Find Next and Replace buttons to search for and delete the text or code on a case-by-case basis. Use the Replace All command to search for and delete all occurrences of the text or code.
You can undo the Replace All command.

To find text and replace it with other text:

1. Choose Replace from the Edit menu.
The Replace dialog box appears.

2. In the Find What box, type the text you want to search for.

3. Click within the Replace With box to move the blinking insertion point, or simply press Tab.

4. In the Replace With box, type the replacement text.

5. Use the Find Next and Replace buttons to search for and delete the text or code on a case-by-case basis. Use the Replace All command to search for and delete all occurrences of the text or code.
You can undo the Replace All command.

To find text and then change its formatting:

1. Choose Replace from the Edit menu.
The Replace dialog box appears.

2. In the Find What box, type the text you want to search for.
If you want to narrow the search to also include formatting information, use the ruler and ribbon or the commands in the Format pop-up menu to specify the formatting you want to search for.

3. Click within the Replace With box to move the blinking insertion point, or simply press Tab.

4. Use the ruler and ribbon or the commands in the Format pop-up menu to specify the formatting you want to apply.
Leave the Replace With text box blank unless you want to also replace the found text with other text.

5. Use the Find Next and Replace buttons to search for and delete the text or code on a case-by-case basis. Use the Replace All command to search for and delete all occurrences of the text or code.

You can undo the Replace All command.

Quick Tips

Keeping Find and Replace close at hand

The Find and Replace dialog boxes are actually windows: You can move them around on the screen and even keep them open while you work in the document window. That latter point is important: If you've just found or replaced something and you anticipate having to do so again shortly, don't close the Find or Replace dialog box; instead, simply click within the document window to activate it. The Find or Replace dialog box stays open but moves behind the document window. When you choose Find or Replace again, the dialog box appears in a flash. You might want to position the Find or Replace dialog box so that part of it is visible beneath the document window. This way, you can activate the dialog box by simply clicking anywhere within the visible portion.

When you close the Find or Replace dialog box, Word saves its position, even if you quit the program. When you choose Find or Replace again, the dialog box appears where it was when you last used it.

Searching for formatting

How specific do you have to be when you're searching for formatting attributes? Depending on the formatting you're looking for and on the formatting present in your document, you may not have to be very specific at all. You simply need to specify enough formatting information for Word to be able to locate the text.

For example, say your document contains only one occurrence of 14-point Times, and that it appears double-spaced and justified. To find that occurrence, you can simply specify 14-point Times in the Find or Replace dialog box — you don't have to specify justification and double spacing. If, on the other hand, your document contains many occurrences of 14-point Times — some justified, some centered — and you want to find only the justified text, then you need to be more specific, specifying not only 14-point Times in the Find or Replace dialog box, but also justification.

Removing a formatting attribute

Sometimes you might search for formatting in order to *remove* a formatting attribute — perhaps you want to change all occurrences of underlined text to italics (a good idea, since underlining is a throwback to the typewriter era). You can't simply specify Underline in the Find What area and Italic in the Replace With area: Doing so would *add* italics to the underlined text, giving you <u>*underlined italics*</u>. Instead, you need to use the ribbon (or the Character command in the Format pop-up menu) to specify that you want to remove the underlining. To do so using the ribbon, click the underline button *twice* to make the Replace With area say No Underline.

Incorrect

Find What:	
Format ▼	Underline
Special ▼	

Replace With:	
Format ▼	Italic
Special ▼	

Correct

Find What:	
Format ▼	Underline
Special ▼	

Replace With:	
Format ▼	No Underline Italic
Special ▼	

Finding and replacing from the keyboard

The Find and Replace dialog boxes provide extensive keyboard shortcuts and let you find and replace without having to take your hands from the keyboard. The following table lists the most useful shortcuts.

Find and Replace keyboard shortcuts

To do this...	Press...
Move the insertion point between the Find What and Replace With text boxes	Tab
Clear any formatting attributes you've specified	Command-F and then Return
Specify character formatting attributes	Command-D
Specify style sheets	Command-F and then S and then Return
Choose the Find Next button	Return or Enter
Choose the Replace button	Command-R
Close the Find or Replace dialog box	Command-period or Esc or Command-W
Choose the Match Whole Word Only option	Command-M
Open the Special pop-up menu	Command-S
Choose a code from the open Special pop-up menu	The first letter of the code's name (or use the arrow keys to select the desired option), and then press Return

Finding or replacing with the Clipboard

I've already mentioned that you can paste the contents of the Clipboard into the Find What or Replace With text boxes. You can also specify the contents of the Clipboard in the Replace With box by choosing Clipboard Contents from the Special pop-up menu or by typing ^c (press Shift-6 to type the caret character). You can use this technique to replace anything with the contents of the Clipboard.

Repeating a search

You can repeat a search without having to reopen or reactivate the Find or Replace dialog box. Simply press the equal sign (=) key on the numeric keypad or type Command-Option-A.

Another way to find formatting

Word provides another way to locate formatting: the Find Formats command. Find Formats lets you search for text whose formatting matches some text that you've selected. For example, if you've selected a heading and you want to find the next occurrence of the same formatting, simply choose Find Formats. Doing so is faster than opening the Find dialog box and then specifying the formatting you want to search for.

There's one catch to using Find Formats: The command isn't in any of Word's menus. To access it, you must use the Commands dialog box, as described in Topic 34.

Word's special formatting codes

The following table describes the special formatting codes Word can find and replace. You can type these codes into the Find What or Replace With boxes yourself (press Shift-6 for the caret character), or have Word insert them by choosing their names from the Special pop-up menu. If you type a code yourself, be sure to type a lowercase character following the caret; for example, ^T will not find a tab code, but ^t will.

Special codes

Name	Code	Description
Tab mark	^t	The code inserted when you press Tab
End-of-line mark	^n	The code inserted when you press Shift-Return
Paragraph mark	^p	The code inserted when you press Return or Enter
Hard page break	^d	The code inserted when you press Shift-Enter or choose Page Break from the Insert menu
Optional hyphen	^-	The code inserted by Word's Hyphenation command
Question mark	^?	A standard question mark (the caret is necessary to differentiate the code from the "any character" wildcard)
Footnote reference mark	^5	The code inserted when you create a footnote
A graphic or empty graphics frame	^1	A graphic pasted into Word or created with the Picture window
Any number and combination of spaces	^w	This code includes tabs, paragraph marks, hard page breaks, word spaces, and section breaks
Any letter	^*	Any alphabetic character
Any single number	^#	Any single digit
Caret	^^	A caret character
Formula character	^\	A formula command character
Any character	?	Any letter, digit, space, or special character
The Clipboard's contents	^c	The contents of the Clipboard (available in Replace With only)

Topic 16

Saving Time with Glossaries

Overview

Word's *glossary* feature allows you to store often-used text and graphics and then recall them with a few keystrokes or mouse clicks. Just a few candidates for glossary entries include:

+ a salutation or closing for business letters

+ your return address

+ standard contractual clauses

+ finger-tangling scientific, medical, or technical terms

+ graphics such as a company logo or ornamental dingbat

+ text with complex formatting, such as borders and shading

+ any word or phrase that you use often

Word also provides a battery of built-in glossary entries that enable you to insert the current date, time, document name, and other information. Word includes several specialized glossaries that let you create special text effects, mathematical equations, and customized date and time formats.

Glossary files

The glossary entries that you create and that Word includes are stored in separate files called *glossary files.* One glossary file can hold any number of glossary entries. When you use Word's Glossary command for the first time during a work session, Word opens a glossary file named Standard Glossary (located in the Word folder). If you add glossary entries during a work session, Word asks you if you want to save changes made to the standard glossary when you quit.

You can create as many glossary files as you like and switch between them by choosing Open from the File menu while the Glossary dialog box is open. You can also add the names of your glossary files and often-used glossary entries to Word's Work menu. You might find it convenient to create separate glossary files for different types of writing tasks — one for business letters, for example, and one for technical reports.

Because Word stores glossary entries separately from your documents, you can move your customized glossaries to another Macintosh by simply copying the glossary files. You might take advantage of this capability to create standard glossaries for everyone in your office, or to copy the glossary entries from one Mac to another.

Glossary entries

A glossary entry can contain any amount of text or graphics — anything from a single character to a lengthy document. You create a glossary entry by first selecting the information you want to store, and then choosing Glossary from the Edit menu. In the Glossary dialog box, type a name for the glossary entry, and then click the Define button.

You can leave the Glossary dialog box open on the screen for fast access

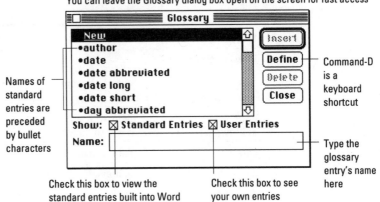

Names of standard entries are preceded by bullet characters

Command-D is a keyboard shortcut

Type the glossary entry's name here

Check this box to view the standard entries built into Word

Check this box to see your own entries

A glossary entry's name can have up to 31 characters. You'll probably want to keep entry names shorter, however, to make it more convenient to summon entries from the keyboard.

Word provides three ways to insert a glossary entry into your document:

◆ You can open the Glossary dialog box, locate and select the entry, and then click Insert.

◆ You can also insert glossary entries from the keyboard: Press Command-Backspace, type part or all of the entry's name, and then press Return.

✦ You can add glossary entry names to Word's menu bar and then choose them.

Regardless of the technique you use, a glossary entry appears at the location of the blinking insertion point. If you've selected something before inserting the glossary entry, the selection is replaced by the entry — just as if you had typed the entry from the keyboard or pasted it from the Clipboard. You can insert a glossary entry into the main body of the document or into a header, footer, table, or footnote. You can't insert a glossary entry when the picture window is open.

You can print the contents of a glossary by choosing Print from the File menu while the Glossary dialog box is open.

Standard entries

Word's standard glossary entries allow you to quickly insert the date and time as well as information about your document. The table below lists the standard glossary entries Word provides. To see the standard glossary entries, select the Standard Entries check box in the Glossary dialog box.

Entry name	Content	Example
Date and time values[1]		
date	date in unabbreviated month, day, year format	December 31, 1991
date abbreviated	date with abbreviated day and month	Sun, Dec 31, 1991
date short	date in mm/dd/yy format	12/31/91
day abbreviated	abbreviated day of week	Mon
day long	spelled-out day of week	Monday
day of month	number corresponding to day of the month	31
month abbreviated	abbreviated name of month	Dec
month long	spelled-out name of month	December
time	current time in hours and minutes	5:05 PM
time with seconds	current time in hours, minutes, and seconds	5:05:01 PM
year long	year in four-digit format	1991
year short	abbreviated year	91

[1]Each date and time entry also has a corresponding printed date and time entry.

Entry name	Content	Example
Document information		
author	Name of author from Summary Info dialog box	Zonker Harris
filename only	name of current document	Letter to Folks
filename with path	name of current document, including enclosing folders and volumes	Hard disk: Documents: Correspondence: Letter to Folks
keywords	keywords listed in Summary Info dialog box	mom home moving free laundry
page number	current page number	1, II, iv, A
print merge	print-merge symbols	« »
section	current section number	2
subject	subject from Summary Info dialog box	Moving in with parents
title	document title from Summary Info dialog box	Moving Home
version	version information from Summary Info dialog box	3a

Step-by-Step

In this section, you'll find instructions for creating, inserting, and deleting glossary entries as well as working with glossary files.

To create a glossary entry:

1. Type the text or create the graphic you want to store.

2. Select the text and/or graphic you want to store.

If you want to store paragraph formatting information along with the entry's text, be sure to include the paragraph mark in the selection. See this topic's Quick Tips section for details.

3. Choose Glossary from the Edit menu.

The Glossary dialog box appears.

4. Type a name for the glossary entry.

5. Click Define.

You can close the Glossary dialog box or simply click within the document window to reactivate it.

To insert a glossary entry with the Glossary command:

1. **Be sure the insertion point is located where you want the entry to appear.**

2. **Choose Glossary from the Edit menu.**
   The Glossary dialog box appears.

3. **In the list of glossary entries, locate the entry you want to insert and then select it.**

4. **Click the Insert button or press Return.**
   You can also simply double-click the desired entry. Whichever technique you use, Word inserts the glossary entry and closes the Glossary dialog box.

To insert a glossary entry with the keyboard:

1. **Be sure the insertion point is located where you want the entry to appear.**

2. **Press Command-Delete (on some keyboards, Command-Backspace).**
   The word "Name" appears in the lower-left corner of the document window.

Type part or all of the glossary entry's name here

3. **Type the name of the glossary entry you want to insert.**
   Shortcut: You can also type just enough of the name for Word to recognize which entry you want. For example, if you have an entry named *salutation* and an entry named *signature*, you can type *sa* for the former and *si* for the latter.

4. **Press Return.**
   Word inserts the entry.

To add a frequently used glossary entry to Word's menu bar:

1. **Choose Glossary from the Edit menu.**
   The Glossary dialog box appears.

Pointer shape when customizing commands

2. **Press Command-Option-equals (the key to the left of the Delete or Backspace key).**
   The mouse pointer turns into a bold plus sign.

3. **In the list of glossary entries, locate the entry you want to insert and then click it once.**

Word adds the glossary entry to the Work menu. Word saves the status of the Work menu when you quit the program, so the entries you add will appear there the next time you start Word.

4. Close the Glossary dialog box.
See Topic 34 for more information on the Work menu, including instructions for removing entries from it.

To edit a glossary entry and save the edited version:

1. Insert the glossary entry into a document.

2. Edit the entry as needed.

3. Select the entry.
Be sure to include the paragraph mark if you want to include paragraph formatting in the entry.

4. Choose Glossary from the Edit menu.
The Glossary dialog box appears.

5. In the list of glossary entries, locate the name of the entry.
As an alternative, you can also type the name in the Name text box.

6. Click the Define button.

To delete a glossary entry:

1. Choose Glossary from the Edit menu.
The Glossary dialog box appears.

2. In the list of glossary entries, select the name of the entry you want to delete.

3. Click the Delete button.
Word asks you to confirm the deletion.

4. Click Yes or press Return.

To switch to a different glossary file:

1. Choose Glossary from the Edit menu.
The Glossary dialog box appears.

2. Choose New from the File menu.
Word asks if you want to delete all nonstandard entries.

3. Click Yes.

This step doesn't delete the nonstandard entries permanently, it simply removes them from the Mac's memory so that they aren't merged with the entries in the glossary you're about to open.

4. Choose Open from the File menu.

The Open dialog box appears.

5. Locate and select the name of the glossary you want to open.

6. Click the Open button or press Return.

Word opens the glossary.

To open a glossary file and merge its entries with those of a currently open glossary file:

1. Choose Glossary from the Edit menu.

The Glossary dialog box appears.

2. Choose Open from the File menu.

The Open dialog box appears.

3. Locate and select the name of the glossary you want to open.

4. Click the Open button or press Return.

Word opens the glossary. If both glossaries contain an entry with the same name, Word uses the contents of the most recently opened glossary for the entry.

To save a glossary:

1. Choose Glossary from the Edit menu.

The Glossary dialog box appears.

2. Choose Save from the File menu.

The Save dialog box appears. Word offers the name Standard Glossary. Use this name if you want your entries to be automatically available the next time you start Word and use the Glossary command.

3. Type a name for the glossary.

4. Click Save or press Return.

Quick Tips

Storing the space following a word

When you select text prior to creating a glossary entry, give some thought to whether or not you want to include a space after the last word in the text. You might want to include the space, since you would probably have to type one anyway. But you may not want to include the space if the glossary entry will often be used at the end of a sentence, or if you anticipate having to add an *s* or an apostrophe and an *s*. In these cases, you'd have to delete the space that Word inserts for you.

Storing formatting in glossary entries

If you're storing one or more paragraphs in a glossary entry and you want to store the paragraph formatting in the entry, remember to include the paragraph mark(s) in the selection when creating the glossary entry. This is important because, as discussed in Topics 5 and 8, Word stores paragraph formatting information in each paragraph's paragraph mark. Remember, too, that a paragraph is any text or graphic followed by a hard carriage return. You can see paragraph marks by choosing Show ¶ from the View menu.

Adding glossary files to the menu bar

Just as you can add individual glossary entries to the Work menu, you can add entire glossaries. To add a glossary file to the Work menu, press Command-Option-equals when the Open Glossary dialog box is open (see the instructions on switching glossary files in this topic's Step-by-Step section) and then click the glossary file you want to add. When you choose a glossary file from the Work menu, Word merges the glossary you choose with the currently open glossary.

Recognizing glossary files at the Finder

A Word glossary file's icon is different from a document's icon:

Document icon   Glossary icon

Memo   Standard Glossary

If you double-click a glossary file, the Finder starts (or activates) Word, and then Word opens the glossary file.

Keeping the Glossary dialog box handy

Like Word's Find and Replace dialog boxes, the Glossary dialog box is actually a window; you can move it around on the screen and keep it open while you work in a document. If you've just worked with the Glossary dialog box and you anticipate having to do so again shortly, don't close the dialog box; instead, simply click within the document window to activate it. The Glossary dialog box stays open but moves behind the document window. To activate the Glossary dialog box, choose Glossary again. You might want to position the Glossary dialog box so that part of it is visible beneath the document window. This way, you can activate the dialog box by simply clicking anywhere within the visible portion.

Copying and pasting with the Glossary dialog box

You can copy and paste the contents of glossary entries by using the Edit menu's Copy and Paste commands while the Glossary dialog box is open. If you select a glossary entry and then choose Copy, the entry's contents are copied to the Clipboard. If you select an entry and then choose Paste, Word replaces the entry's original contents with the contents of the Clipboard.

Sharing glossary files on a network

If you use file server software such as Apple's AppleShare, Sitka's MacTOPS, or the file-sharing options of Apple's System 7, you can store glossary files on a file server, where everyone in the office can access them. However, each user who wants to access a specific glossary file must open it for read-only access (check the Read Only check box in the Open Glossary dialog box). If you're adding glossary files to the Work menu as described earlier in this section, be sure to check the Read Only box when adding the glossary to the Work menu.

Topic 17
Checking Spelling and Grammar

Overview

Can a word processor really check your spelling, grammar, and writing style? Yes and no. Word can scan a document and offer suggestions for words it doesn't recognize. But Word can't guarantee perfectly spelled documents because it can't recognize words in context. To Word, the sentence *Wee mite bee their inn the mourning* contains no spelling errors.

Still, the spelling checker is valuable for finding spelling errors caused by missing or transposed characters and for locating double word occurrences (such as *We went to to the beach)* or incorrect capitalization (such as *FRed).* And by creating and adding words to your own custom dictionaries, you can teach Word to recognize technical terms, names of companies and people, acronyms, and other words not present in Word's dictionary. A session with Word's spelling checker can't replace a careful proofreading job, but it can't hurt.

As for checking grammar and style, Word's Grammar command is able to locate certain types of obvious grammatical errors (such as *my dog are a poodle* or *I didn't never see that before).* And it can flag some problems with style, such as wordy stock phrases (*at this point in time* or *and so on and so forth).*

But all software grammar and style checkers can also give bad advice and miss serious grammatical errors, such as dangling modifiers (*Fresh from the show room, I crashed my new car).* Using the Preferences command to specify that Word look for only certain types of errors can help, but you need to be familiar with grammar to be able to decide which types to look for and which to ignore. In short, grammar and style checkers are only marginally useful.

The Spelling and Grammar commands are available only if their respective files are installed in the Word Commands folder, located within Word's folder; see Appendix A for details on Word's plug-in modules.

Checking spelling

You can check the spelling of an individual word by selecting it and then choosing Spelling from the Tools menu (to save time, use the Command-L keyboard shortcut). If the word is spelled correctly, Word lets you know.

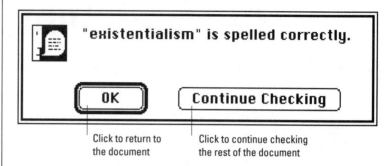

Click to return to   Click to continue checking
the document   the rest of the document

You can check the spelling of a passage of text by selecting the passage and then choosing Spelling. If the selection contains no misspellings, Word notifies you.

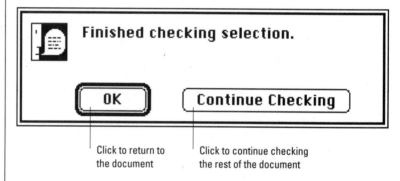

Click to return to   Click to continue checking
the document   the rest of the document

You can also check the spelling of an entire document by choosing Spelling when nothing is selected. If the insertion point isn't at the very beginning of the document when you choose Spelling, Word asks if it should continue checking from the beginning when it reaches the end.

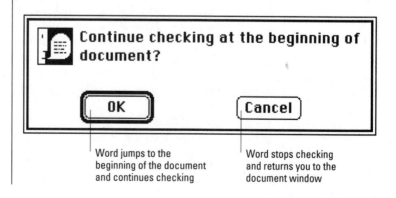

Word jumps to the   Word stops checking
beginning of the document   and returns you to the
and continues checking   document window

When Word encounters a word it doesn't recognize, it attempts to suggest an alternative from its dictionary.

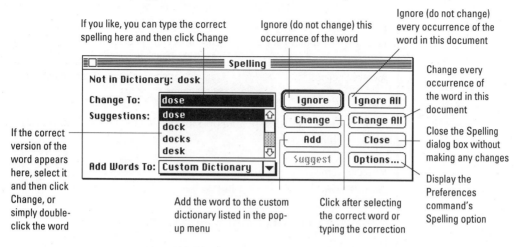

If you like, you can type the correct spelling here and then click Change

Ignore (do not change) this occurrence of the word

Ignore (do not change) every occurrence of the word in this document

Change every occurrence of the word in this document

If the correct version of the word appears here, select it and then click Change, or simply double-click the word

Close the Spelling dialog box without making any changes

Display the Preferences command's Spelling option

Add the word to the custom dictionary listed in the pop-up menu

Click after selecting the correct word or typing the correction

If you're checking a selection or the entire document, Word continues checking after you correct or ignore the suspected misspelling or add it to a custom dictionary.

Custom dictionaries and spelling options

Word can access any number of custom dictionaries containing your own entries. You specify which custom dictionaries you want to use by using the Spelling option of the Preferences command (in the Tools menu).

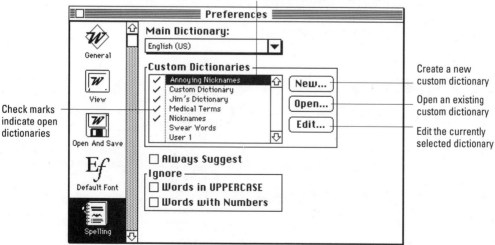

The list shows all dictionaries present in the Word Commands folder or opened using the Open button

Check marks indicate open dictionaries

Create a new custom dictionary

Open an existing custom dictionary

Edit the currently selected dictionary

As the previous illustration shows, the Spelling option also lets you specify spelling checker preferences.

Select this option...	If you want Word to...
Ignore Words in UPPERCASE	skip over all-uppercase words such as NASA, CPU, or FY91
Ignore Words with Numbers	skip over words containing numbers, such as 512K, 100ml, or 35mm
Always Suggest	always attempt to suggest corrections to unrecognized words

You can also access the spelling options by clicking the Options button in the Spelling dialog box.

You can remove words from a custom dictionary by selecting the dictionary and then clicking Edit.

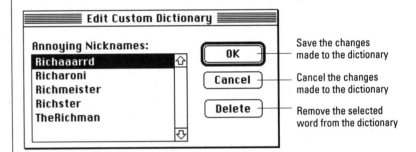

Save the changes made to the dictionary

Cancel the changes made to the dictionary

Remove the selected word from the dictionary

Checking grammar and style

You can use the Grammar command (Tools menu) to check the grammar and style of an entire document or of a selected range of text. When Word encounters a suspect phrase, it displays a dialog box listing the nature of the problem and, in some cases, offering a suggested change.

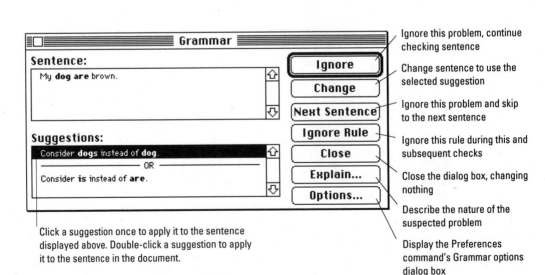

Ignore this problem, continue checking sentence

Change sentence to use the selected suggestion

Ignore this problem and skip to the next sentence

Ignore this rule during this and subsequent checks

Close the dialog box, changing nothing

Describe the nature of the suspected problem

Click a suggestion once to apply it to the sentence displayed above. Double-click a suggestion to apply it to the sentence in the document.

Display the Preferences command's Grammar options dialog box

You can use the Preferences command's Grammar option to fine-tune Word's grammar and style checker to look for only certain types of problems.

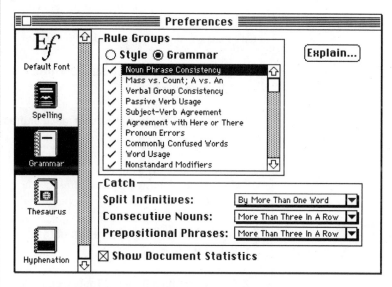

If the Show Document Statistics box is selected, Word calculates and displays information about the text you checked.

Document Statistics

Counts:	
Words	2011
Characters	12222
Paragraphs	122
Sentences	95
Averages:	
Sentences per Paragraph	0
Words per Sentence	21
Characters per Word	4
Readability:	
Passive Sentences	9%
Flesch Reading Ease	56.6
Flesch Grade Level	10.9
Flesch-Kincaid	9.5
Gunning Fog Index	11.9

OK

These are calculated based on the average number of words per sentence and average number of syllables per 100 words

Ease Level	Reading Ease
90–100	Very easy
80–90	Easy
70–80	Fairly easy
60–70	Standard
50–60	Fairly difficult
30–50	Difficult
0–30	Very difficult

Based on overall sentence length and the number of multisyllabic words per sentence

The Readability section is a bit gimmicky, but it may be able to help. For example, if the statistics indicate extensive use of the passive voice (for example, *The dog was walked*) you might want to rewrite certain sentences in the active voice (*We walked the dog*).

Step-by-Step

This section contains instructions for checking the spelling of individual words, text selections, and the entire document. It also describes how to work with custom dictionaries and how to use and customize Word's grammar and style checker.

To check the spelling of a single word:

1. **Select the word.**

2. **Choose Spelling from the Tools menu or press Command-L.**

   If the word is present in Word's dictionary or in any open custom dictionaries, a dialog box appears notifying you that it is spelled correctly and allowing you to continue checking the rest of the document. If the word is not present, the Spelling dialog box appears. See "To correct a misspelling" later in this section.

To check the spelling of a range of text:

1. **Select the text.**

2. **Choose Spelling from the Tools menu or press Command-L.**

   If all the words in the selection are present in Word's dictionary or in any open custom dictionaries, a dialog box appears notifying you that Word has finished checking the selection and allowing you to continue checking the rest of the document. If a word is not present, the Spelling dialog box appears. See "To correct a misspelling" later in this section.

To check the spelling of an entire document:

1. **Be sure nothing is selected.**

   If something is selected, click once anywhere within the document window to deselect it and create a blinking insertion point.

2. **Choose Spelling from the Tools menu.**

   Word checks the document. If it encounters a word not present in Word's dictionary or in any open custom dictionaries, the Spelling dialog box appears. See the next set of instructions in this section. If the insertion point was not at the beginning of the document when you started checking, a dialog box appears asking if you want to continue checking from the beginning of the document. Click OK or press Return to continue checking; click Cancel to stop checking.

To correct a misspelling:

1. **Examine any suggestions Word provides. If one is the correct word, double-click it.**

   Word replaces the misspelled word with the suggestion you selected.

   — or —

1. **Click the misspelled word in the Spelling dialog box.**

   When you point to the misspelled word in the Spelling dialog box, the mouse pointer changes to a down-pointing arrow. The word appears in the Change To box:

   Click the misspelled word to move it to the Change To box, where you can correct it, and then click Change

Spelling

   Not in Dictionary: brwn

   Change To: brawn   Ignore   Ignore All
   Suggestions: brawn   Change   Change All
   brown   Add   Close
   brownie   Suggest   Options...
   (End of Suggestions)

   Add Words To: Jim's Dictionary

2. **Correct the word's spelling in the Change To dialog box.**

3. **Click the Change button.**

   Word replaces the misspelled word with the corrected version.

To add a word to a custom dictionary:

1. **If you've opened more than one custom dictionary using the Preferences command's Spelling option, use the Add Words To pop-up menu to select the dictionary to which you want to add the word.**

2. **Click the Add button in the Spelling dialog box.**

   When you quit Word, it asks if you want to save changes to any dictionaries you modify. Click Yes to save the changes.

To delete one or more words from a custom dictionary:

1. **Choose Preferences from the Tools menu and select the Spelling option.**

   As an alternative, you can also click the Options button in the Spelling dialog box.

2. **Select the custom dictionary from which you want to remove words.**

3. **Click the Edit button.**

   A dialog box appears listing the words in the custom dictionary.

4. **Select the word you want to delete.**

5. **Click the Delete button.**

6. **Repeat steps 4 and 5 as needed.**

7. **Click OK or press Return.**
   Word doesn't actually delete any words until you choose OK. If you change your mind about deleting the words, click the Cancel button.

To check grammar and style of a selection of text:

1. **Select the text you want to check.**

2. **Choose Grammar from the Tools menu.**
   If Word finds no problems with the selection, a dialog box appears notifying you that it has finished checking and allowing you to continue checking the rest of the document. If Word finds a problem, the Grammar dialog box appears. See "To correct a problem with grammar or style" later in this section.

To check grammar and style of the entire document:

1. **Be sure nothing is selected.**
   If something is selected, click once anywhere within the document window to deselect it and create a blinking insertion point.

2. **Choose Grammar from the Tools menu.**
   If Word finds a problem, the Grammar dialog box appears. See the next set of instructions in this section. If Word finds no problems with the document, a dialog box appears notifying you that it has finished checking. If you didn't start checking at the beginning of the document, Word asks if you want to continue checking from the beginning.

To correct a problem with grammar or style:

1. **Examine the problem description in the Grammar dialog box and determine if the problem is genuine.**
   Words that are related to the suspected problem appear in bold.

2. **To accept a suggested correction, double-click the suggestion.**
   — or —
2. **Reactivate the document window by clicking within it and then correct the problem.**

Quick Tips

Sharing dictionaries on a network

If you use file server software such as Apple's AppleShare, Sitka's MacTOPS, or the file-sharing options of Apple's System 7, you can store custom dictionaries on a file server, where everyone in the office can access them. Any number of people can access the same custom dictionaries at the same time.

Only one dictionary named *Custom Dictionary* can be open at a time, however, so you might want to rename the shared dictionary so that each user can open it as well as the Custom Dictionary file on his or her own machine.

Proofread a word before adding it to a custom dictionary

When you're adding a word to a custom dictionary, take an extra second to verify that it's spelled correctly. It's easy to accidentally add a misspelled word to a dictionary — especially if the word is a lengthy one or is unusually spelled — and an inaccurate custom dictionary is worse than no custom dictionary at all.

Create and switch among multiple custom dictionaries

Word's spelling checker runs faster with smaller custom dictionaries, so you might consider creating numerous custom dictionaries and switching among them as needed. If you can categorize the specialized words you use — legal terms, scientific terms, nicknames, gambler's jargon, and so on — do so and create different custom dictionaries for each category. Then use the Preferences command's Spelling option to activate only those custom dictionaries you need for the document at hand.

Adding many words to a custom dictionary

If you want to add a large number of words to a custom dictionary, type the words into a new, untitled document and then check its spelling. When Word trips over each unknown word, click the Add button (or simply press Command-A) to add it to the custom dictionary. Before checking the spelling of the document, use the Preferences command's Spelling option to turn off the Always Suggest option so that Word doesn't spend time looking up each word.

Custom dictionaries and capitalization

When you add a word to a custom dictionary, Word stores the word exactly as it appears in the document. In subsequent spell-checking sessions, Word will recognize the word if it begins with a capital letter or appears in all capitals. It may flag the word as misspelled, however, if the word uses an unusual capitalization scheme that differs from that of the word you originally added. The following table shows examples of the kinds of capitalization schemes that will and will not trip up Word.

If you add...	Word recognizes...	Word doesn't recognize...
LocalTalk	LocalTalk	LOCALTALK, localtalk
NASA	NASA	Nasa, nasa
California	California, CALIFORNIA	california
megadoozy	megadoozy, MEGADOOZY, Megadoozy	meGAdoozy

Topic 18

Using the Thesaurus

Overview

Word's Thesaurus command lets you find synonyms and antonyms for words. (A synonym is a word with the same or similar meaning: *Upright* is a synonym for *good.* An antonym is a word with the opposite meaning: *Bad* is an antonym for *good.)* Word's thesaurus can remind you of the universe of alternatives that exists for common, overused words.

But don't take a thesaurus's suggestions at face value. Word meanings vary, and you could find yourself saying something you didn't mean. The words *aromatic* and *rank* are synonyms for *pungent,* but which one best describes the smell of a bakery?

Often the differences between word meanings aren't as obvious. For example, Word's thesaurus lists *succeed* and *supersede* as synonyms for *replace.* Now consider the sentence, *Robots will replace many factory workers.* Which synonym is more appropriate? If you use *succeed,* you're saying that the replacement of the workers is part of a logical, natural sequence. If you use *supersede,* you're saying that the workers have become obsolete or are inferior to the robots. Consult a dictionary before choosing a synonym or antonym to verify that the word you have in mind means what you want to say.

Using the thesaurus

To find a synonym for a word, select the word and choose Thesaurus from the Tools menu. Word's Thesaurus dialog box appears.

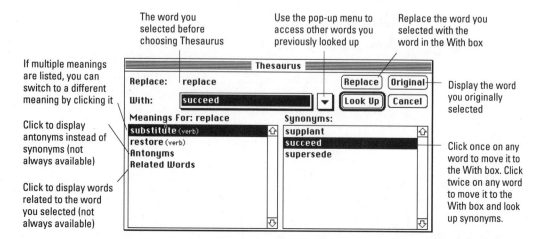

The word you selected before choosing Thesaurus

Use the pop-up menu to access other words you previously looked up

Replace the word you selected with the word in the With box

If multiple meanings are listed, you can switch to a different meaning by clicking it

Click to display antonyms instead of synonyms (not always available)

Click to display words related to the word you selected (not always available)

Display the word you originally selected

Click once on any word to move it to the With box. Click twice on any word to move it to the With box and look up synonyms.

Word also keeps track of the words you look up, listing them in the pop-up menu that appears to the left of the Look Up button. You can use this feature to backtrack to previously found words. You can also type words in the With box and then search for synonyms and antonyms. (Note that the Meanings For box doesn't always list antonyms.)

Step-by-Step

This section contains instructions for using Word's Thesaurus.

To locate synonyms or antonyms for a specific word:
1. **Select the word.**

2. **Choose Thesaurus from the Tools menu.**
   The Thesaurus dialog box appears.

3. **Use the dialog box as described in the following table.**

If...	You can...
The Synonyms box contains a synonym you like	Replace the original word: Click the synonym (it appears in the With box) and then click the Replace button
The word in the With box doesn't have the meaning you want	Select a different meaning from the Meanings For list
The Related Words or Antonyms option appears in the Meanings For list	Click one of the options to display related words or antonyms
You want to locate alternate meanings and synonyms for the word in the With box	Click the Look Up button or press Return. You can also type a word into the With box and then choose Look Up.
You want to revert to the word you originally selected	Click the Original button. You can then click Look Up to display synonyms and meanings for the word.

Quick Tips
Browsing the thesaurus
You can browse Word's thesaurus by typing a letter in the Thesaurus dialog box's With box and then clicking the Look Up button. Word displays an alphabetical list of words beginning with the letter you typed, as shown in the following illustration.

Type a letter in the With box and then press Return or click Look Up

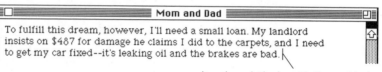

```
╔════════════════════ Thesaurus ════════════════════╗
  Replace:    say                      [ Replace ] [ Original ]

  Not Found: ▐h                    ▼   [ Look Up ] [ Cancel ]

  Alphabetical List:           Synonyms:
  ┌──────────────────────┐▲   ┌──────────────────────┐▲
  │ habiliment           │   │                      │
  │ habit                │   │                      │
  │ habitable            │   │                      │
  │ habitat              │   │                      │
  │ habitation           │▓  │                      │
  │ habitual             │▓  │                      │
  │ habitually           │   │                      │
  │ habituate            │   │                      │
  │ habituated           │▼  │                      │▼
  └──────────────────────┘   └──────────────────────┘
```

Choosing Thesaurus when nothing is selected

If you choose the Thesaurus command without selecting a word, Word looks up the word closest to the insertion point.

```
▣▭══════════════════ Mom and Dad ══════════════════▭▣
  To fulfill this dream, however, I'll need a small loan. My landlord  ▲
  insists on $487 for damage he claims I did to the carpets, and I need
  to get my car fixed--it's leaking oil and the brakes are bad.\
```

Insertion point is closest to the word *bad*...

...so Word selects the word *bad* for you when you choose Thesaurus

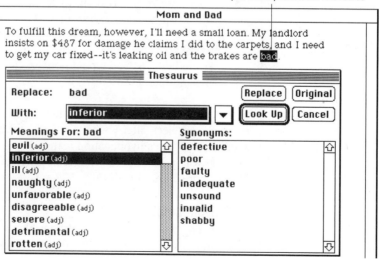

```
═══════════════════════ Mom and Dad ═══════════════════════
  To fulfill this dream, however, I'll need a small loan. My landlord
  insists on $487 for damage he claims I did to the carpets, and I need
  to get my car fixed--it's leaking oil and the brakes are ▓bad▓.

  ╔══════════════════ Thesaurus ══════════════════╗
    Replace:    bad                      [ Replace ] [ Original ]

    With:    ▐inferior                ▼   [ Look Up ] [ Cancel ]

    Meanings For: bad            Synonyms:
    ┌──────────────────────┐▲   ┌──────────────────────┐▲
    │ evil (adj)           │   │ defective            │
    │ inferior (adj)       │   │ poor                 │
    │ ill (adj)            │   │ faulty               │
    │ naughty (adj)        │▓  │ inadequate           │
    │ unfavorable (adj)    │▓  │ unsound              │
    │ disagreeable (adj)   │   │ invalid              │
    │ severe (adj)         │   │ shabby               │
    │ detrimental (adj)    │   │                      │
    │ rotten (adj)         │▼  │                      │▼
    └──────────────────────┘   └──────────────────────┘
```

Keep this in mind if you want to look up synonyms or antonyms as you write. Instead of selecting the last word in the document and then choosing Thesaurus, simply choose Thesaurus. Word will select the last word in the document for you.

Topic 19

Hyphenating Text

Overview

Word provides several features that enable you to control the hyphenation of words at the ends of lines:

✦ *You can automatically hyphenate words using the Hyphenation command in the Tools menu.* The Hyphenation command inserts *optional hyphens.* An optional hyphen appears only when Word breaks a line where the optional hyphen is inserted. Optional hyphens are sometimes called *soft* hyphens; the hyphens you type directly are sometimes called *hard* hyphens.

✦ *You can manually hyphenate a word by typing an optional hyphen.* You might use this technique to accurately hyphenate a word that is hyphenated differently depending on its usage (such as the verb *pro-ject* and the noun *proj-ect).* You type an optional hyphen by pressing Command-hyphen.

✦ *You can type a* nonbreaking hyphen *when you don't want Word to divide a hyphenated word or name, such as Baker-Salmon.* When Word encounters a nonbreaking hyphen, it moves the entire word down to the next line instead of breaking the line after the hyphen. You type a nonbreaking hyphen by pressing Command-tilde (~).

In general, you should use Word's hyphenation feature in the latter stages of a project, after you've copyedited the document. You should avoid using Word's hyphenation feature if you're creating a document that you will import into a publishing program such as Aldus Page-Maker; more about this shortly.

Why hyphenate?

Hyphenating words at the ends of lines allows more text to fit on each line, as shown in the following illustration.

Without hyphenation

> The best time to use the Hyphenate command is after you've finished writing and editing your document but before you fine-tune its page breaks and layout. This way, you won't have to do a lot of rehyphenating if revisions change the document's page breaks.
>
> Another good time to hyphenate is when a document's text takes more space than you want it to. Before resorting to smaller text or wider margins--both of which could adversely affect the document's legibility--hyphenate the document. You may gain enough space to avoid more drastic reformatting.
>
> If you're writing a document that you will import into a publishing program such as Aldus PageMaker, don't use Word's hyphenation feature. Leave hyphenation up to your page-layout program.

With hyphenation

> The best time to use the Hyphenate command is after you've finished writing and editing your document but before you fine-tune its page breaks and layout. This way, you won't have to do a lot of rehyphenating if revisions change the document's page breaks.
>
> Another good time to hyphenate is when a document's text takes more space than you want it to. Before resorting to smaller text or wider margins--both of which could adversely affect the document's legibility--hyphenate the document. You may gain enough space to avoid more drastic reformatting.
>
> If you're writing a document that you will import into a publishing program such as Aldus Page-Maker, don't use Word's hyphenation feature. Leave hyphenation up to your page-layout program.

As the previous illustration shows, hyphenating can also improve the appearance of ragged-right margins by reducing the large variations in line length that often occur in narrow columns.

Hyphenating can also improve the appearance of justified text (text aligned against the left and right margins), since it reduces the amount of space Word must insert between each word.

Without hyphenation

> If you're writing a document that you will import into a publishing program such as Aldus PageMaker, don't use Word's hyphenation feature. Leave hyphenation up to your page-layout program.

With hyphenation

> If you're writing a document that you will import into a publishing program such as Aldus Page-Maker, don't use Word's hyphenation feature. Leave hyphenation up to your page-layout program.

When to hyphenate — and when not to

The best time to use the Hyphenation command is after you've finished writing and editing your document but before you fine-tune its page breaks and layout. This way, you won't have to do a lot of rehyphenating if revisions change the document's line endings.

Another good time to hyphenate is when a document's text takes more space than you want it to. Before resorting to smaller text or wider margins — both of which could adversely affect the document's legibility — hyphenate the document. You may gain enough space to avoid more drastic reformatting.

If you're writing a document that you will import into a publishing program such as Aldus PageMaker, don't use Word's hyphenation feature. Leave hyphenation up to your page-layout program.

Step-by-Step

In this section, you'll find instructions for working with optional hyphens and nonbreaking hyphens, as well as for using Word's Hyphenation command to automatically hyphenate text.

To type an optional hyphen:

1. Position the blinking insertion point at the location where you want the optional hyphen.

2. Press Command-hyphen.

Word inserts the optional hyphen. If the word containing the optional hyphen is at the beginning of a line, Word will divide the word if the portion preceding the optional hyphen will fit on the previous line. If Word doesn't break the word, you will not see the optional hyphen unless you choose Show ¶ from the View menu. When Show ¶ is active, an optional hyphen appears as a hyphen with a dot below it.

Optional hyphens
visible with Show ¶

hy-phen-ation

To delete an optional hyphen:

1. Choose Show ¶ to display invisible characters.

2. Select the optional hyphen you want to delete.

3. Press Delete (on some keyboards, Backspace).

To type a nonbreaking hyphen:

1. Position the blinking insertion point at the location where you want the nonbreaking hyphen.

2. Press Command-tilde (~).

When Show ¶ is off, a nonbreaking hyphen looks like a normal hyphen. When Show ¶ is on, a nonbreaking hyphen appears as a hyphen with a tilde above it, as shown in the following illustration.

Nonbreaking hyphen with Show ¶ on

Zachary·Baker⁒Salmon

Nonbreaking hyphen with Show ¶ off

Zachary Baker‑Salmon

To hyphenate a word based on Word's suggestion:

1. Select the word.

2. Choose Hyphenation from the Tools menu.

The Hyphenation dialog box appears, with possible hyphenation points indicated.

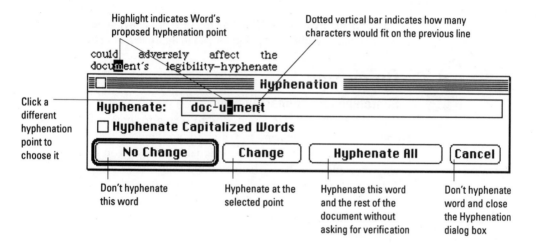

Highlight indicates Word's proposed hyphenation point

Dotted vertical bar indicates how many characters would fit on the previous line

could   adversely   affect   the
document's   legibility–hyphenate

Click a different hyphenation point to choose it

Hyphenate:	doc‑u‑ment

☐ **Hyphenate Capitalized Words**

No Change	**Change**	**Hyphenate All**	**Cancel**

Don't hyphenate this word

Hyphenate at the selected point

Hyphenate this word and the rest of the document without asking for verification

Don't hyphenate word and close the Hyphenation dialog box

3. If you want to hyphenate the word at a point other than the proposed point, choose the desired hyphenation point by clicking it.

4. Click the Change button.

Word inserts an optional hyphen at the hyphenation point you selected.

To automatically hyphenate a selected range of text:

1. Select the text you want to hyphenate.

2. Choose Hyphenation from the Tools menu.

The Hyphenation dialog box appears.

3. **Click the Start Hyphenation button to review and approve each hyphenation as described above.**

— or —

3. **Click the Hyphenate All button to tell Word to hyphenate the selected text without stopping for you to approve each change.**

To automatically hyphenate the entire document:

1. **Be sure no text is selected.**

   Click once anywhere within the document window to deselect anything you may have selected.

2. **Choose Hyphenation from the Tools menu.**

   The Hyphenation dialog box appears.

3. **Click the Start Hyphenation button to review and approve each hyphenation as described above.**

— or —

3. **Click the Hyphenate All button to tell Word to hyphenate the document without stopping for you to approve each change.**

Quick Tips

Searching for optional hyphens

You can use Word's Find command to search for optional hyphens, and the Replace command to search for and remove them. You might want to search for and remove optional hyphens if you've made extensive edits that have changed the document's line breaks. In such cases, the optional hyphens remain, but are invisible unless Show ¶ is active. Editing and moving the insertion point with the arrow keys can be cumbersome when a document contains a large number of optional hyphens.

To search for and remove optional hyphens, choose Replace from the Edit menu. With the insertion point in the Find What box, choose Optional Hyphen from the Special pop-up menu. Leave the Replace With box empty. Finally, to search for and remove all the optional hyphens, click Replace All. To search for and remove optional hyphens on a case-by-case basis, use the Find Next and Replace buttons. For details on the Find and Replace commands, see Topic 15.

Spaces that don't break

Word also lets you type a *nonbreaking space* — a space that won't be used to end a line. You might want to use a nonbreaking space between a person's initials and his or her name — for example, E. B. White. To type a nonbreaking space, press Command-spacebar or Option-spacebar. When Show ¶ is active, a nonbreaking space appears as a space with a tilde above it.

Nonbreaking spaces with Show ¶ on

E.˜B.˜White

Topic 20

Numbering Paragraphs and Lines

Overview

Word lets you automatically number the paragraphs and the lines in a document. You might use Word's paragraph-numbering features when creating:

✦ a step-by-step sequence such as a set of instructions

✦ reports or manuals with numbered sections

✦ tests, questionnaires, or tables of contents

✦ legal documents such as contracts and briefs

If you have to insert or remove steps, sections, questions, chapters, or clauses, you can automatically renumber the paragraphs instead of arduously editing them by hand. The following illustration shows some of the types of documents that can benefit from Word's automatic numbering features. In these examples, the numbers and letters were added by Word.

Tests or questionnaires

1. When did the war of 1812 take place?
   a. 1944
   b. 1776
   c. 1812
2. Who is buried in Grant's Tomb?
   a. Abraham Lincoln
   b. Lou Grant
   c. College Grant

Sequenced instructions

To make tea:
1. Fill kettle with cold water
2. Turn on burner
3. Place kettle on burner
4. Listen for whistle
5. Place tea bag in cup
6. Pour water in cup
7. Let steep one minute

Legal documents

4. TERMS OF ENDEARMENT
   It is hereby agreed upon by both parties that the following shall be considered terms of endearment:
   4.1 Cutesy
   4.2 Love Bug
   4.3 Feral Poodle

Outlines

A. Using Your Program
   1. Backing up disks
      a. copyrights
      b. piracy
   2. Installing software
      a. precautions
      b. version numbers
   3. Starting the program
      a. menus
      b. icons

Paragraph numbering options

To number and renumber paragraphs, you use the Renumber command in the Tools menu. When you choose Renumber, the Renumber dialog box appears.

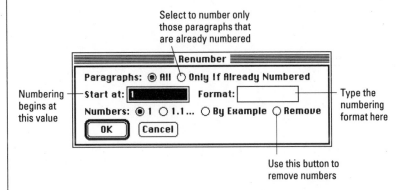

Select to number only those paragraphs that are already numbered

Numbering begins at this value

Type the numbering format here

Use this button to remove numbers

You can number paragraphs using Arabic numerals (1, 2, 3), uppercase or lowercase Roman numerals (i, ii or I, II), and uppercase or lowercase letters (a, b or A, B). As this topic's Step-by-Step section shows, you can mix and match numbering formats within a document by specifying the formats in the Renumber dialog box's Format text box.

You can also choose from a variety of *separator characters.* These are the characters that surround or follow each number and separate it from the text.

Separator character	Example
comma (,)	1,
hyphen (-)	1- or -1-
backslash (\)	1\ or \1\
semicolon (;)	1;
colon (:)	1:
right parenthesis or left and right parentheses	1) or (1)
right bracket or left and right brackets	1] or [1]

Numbering paragraphs in multilevel documents

Legal documents, technical manuals, and scientific papers are often organized according to a hierarchy, and their sections are numbered accordingly, as shown in the following illustration.

Topic 20
Numbering Paragraphs and Lines

```
4. Installing the Program
    4.1 Copying Your Disks
    ━━━━━━━━━━━━━━━
    ━━━━━━━━━━━━━━━
    ━━━━━━━━━━━━━━━

    4.2 Checking Versions
    ━━━━━━━━━━━━━━━
    ━━━━━━━━━━━━━━━
    ━━━━━━━━━━━━━━━
    ━━━━━━━━━━━━━━━
    ━━━━━━━━━━━━━━━
    ━━━━━━━━━━━━━━━
```

You can use the Renumber dialog box's 1.1 option to number paragraphs to show this hierarchy. To do so, you must format the paragraphs in one of the following ways:

✦ *By assigning Word's heading styles to the paragraphs.* (The heading styles are described in Topic 30, and style sheets in general are discussed in Topic 11.)

✦ *By specifying the paragraphs' hierarchy using Word's built-in outliner.* When you promote or demote paragraphs in Word's outliner, Word assigns the appropriate heading styles to the paragraphs. (The outliner is described in Topic 30.)

✦ *By indenting subordinate paragraphs using the Paragraph dialog box or the ruler's indent markers.* An easy way to indent subordinate paragraphs is to use the nested indent keyboard shortcut: Command-Shift-N. (See Topic 5 for details on formatting paragraphs.)

Line numbers

Line numbers are often used in theatrical scripts and legal documents. Word lets you specify where line numbers appear and whether lines should be numbered continuously throughout the document or whether they should begin at 1 on each page or section. You can also choose a numbering increment, such as every third line, and you can choose to suppress line numbers for certain paragraphs.

To number lines, choose Section from the Format menu and then click the Line Numbers button in the Section dialog box. As this topic's Step-by-Step section shows, you can choose from a variety of line-numbering options.

If there's a passage of text whose lines you don't want to number, select the passage and choose Paragraph from the Format menu. In the Para-graph dialog box, select the Suppress Line Numbers check box, and then click OK or press Return.

Word numbers empty paragraphs (that is, paragraph marks that appear on lines by themselves), but it doesn't number lines in tables, headers, footers, or footnotes. Word also doesn't number lines in paragraphs that you've formatted to appear alongside each other using the frame feature (described in Topic 23).

Note that line numbers don't appear on the screen unless you open the Page Preview window.

Paragraphs vs. lines: A reminder

As you work with Word's numbering options, keep in mind the difference between paragraphs and lines: A paragraph is any amount of text or graphic followed by a paragraph mark (a carriage return). A line is one horizontal row of characters that may or may not end with a paragraph mark. The following illustration contains three paragraphs and five lines.

Paragraphs·versus·Lines¶
◆　In·Word,·a·paragraph·is·any·text·or·graphic·that·ends·with·a· paragraph·mark.·A·line·is·a·row·of·characters·that·may·or·may·not· end·with·a·paragraph·mark.¶
◆　Keeping·this·point·in·mind·will·save·you·formatting·migraines.¶

Step-by-Step

This section shows how to number and renumber paragraphs in a variety of formats, and how to number lines.

To number paragraphs:

1. **Select the paragraphs you want to number.**
   If you want to number all the paragraphs in the document, be sure nothing is selected. (Click once anywhere within the document window to deselect anything you may have selected.)

2. **Choose Renumber from the Tools menu.**
   The Renumber dialog box appears.

3. **Specify the numbering format and separator character you want to use.**

```
╔═══════════════════ Renumber ═══════════════════╗
║ Paragraphs: ⦿ All  ○ Only If Already Numbered  ║
║ Start at: 1          Format: (1)                ║
║ Numbers: ⦿ 1  ○ 1.1...  ○ By Example  ○ Remove  ║
║  ┌────────┐  ┌────────┐                         ║
║  │   OK   │  │ Cancel │                         ║
║  └────────┘  └────────┘                         ║
╚═════════════════════════════════════════════════╝
```

This format pro-
duces this result:
(1)
(2)
(3)
and so on

If you don't specify a format or separator, Word uses Arabic numerals and a period, as in these numbered steps.

4. If you want numbering to begin with a number other than 1, type the desired starting number in the Start At box.

If you're using letters or Roman numerals as the numbering format, you should still type a number in the Start At box. For example, if you want to begin numbering at the Roman numeral V, type *5* in the Start At box, not *V*.

5. Click OK or press Return.

Word numbers the paragraphs.

To renumber paragraphs after editing:

1. Select the paragraphs you want to renumber.

If you want to renumber all the paragraphs in the document, be sure nothing is selected.

2. Choose Renumber from the Tools menu.

The Renumber dialog box appears.

3. If you want to change the numbering format or separator character, specify the format and separator character you want to use.

4. Select the Only If Already Numbered button.

5. Click OK or press Return.

Word renumbers the paragraphs.

To remove paragraph numbers:

1. Select the paragraphs whose numbers you want to remove.

If you want to remove numbers from all the paragraphs in the document, be sure nothing is selected.

2. Choose Renumber from the Tools menu.

The Renumber dialog box appears.

3. **Select the Remove button.**

4. **Click OK or press Return.**
Word removes the paragraph numbers.

To number paragraphs of different levels to show their hierarchy:

1. **Format the paragraphs using heading styles, paragraph indents, or Word's outline view.**
See the section "Numbering paragraphs in multilevel documents," earlier in this topic.

2. **Choose Renumber from the Tools menu.**
The Renumber dialog box appears.

3. **Click the 1.1 button.**

4. **If desired, specify the numbering format and separator character you want to use.**
If you don't specify a format or separator, Word uses Arabic numerals separated by a period: *1.1, 1.2, 1.3,* and so on. To use standard outline numbering, type *I.A.1.a.i.*.

```
┌─────────────── Renumber ───────────────┐
│ Paragraphs: ◉ All  ○ Only If Already Numbered
│ Start at: 1          Format: I.A.1.a.i.  ┤──── Type this to
│ Numbers: ◉ 1  ○ 1.1...  ○ By Example  ○ Remove │     indent
│  ┌────────┐  ┌────────┐                          │     paragraphs in
│  │   OK   │  │ Cancel │                          │     standard
│  └────────┘  └────────┘                          │     outline style
└──────────────────────────────────────────┘
```

```
      I. Installing Your Software
         A. Make back ups
                1. remember your license agreement
                     a. back ups are for your own use
                          i. don't give them to your friends
                          ii. don't use them as drink coasters
         B. Check version numbers
                1. you need System 6.0.5 or a later version
                2. check with your dealer
         C. Run the installer
                1. if a problem occurs, call technical support
                     a. note your configuration
```

Paragraphs are indented using the nested indent keyboard shortcut (Command-Shift-N)

If you're creating a questionnaire or a multiple-choice test and you want each question to be preceded by a number and each possible answer to be preceded by a letter, type *1.a.*

To number lines:

1. Choose Section from the Format menu.

The Section dialog box appears.

2. Click the Line Numbers button.

The Line Numbers dialog box appears:

Type *2* to number every other line,
3 to number every third line, and so on

No line numbers

Numbering begins at
one for each page

Numbering begins at
one for each section

Numbering is continuous
throughout the document

Line Numbers

Line Numbers:
Continuous
Off
By Page
By Section
✓Continuous

Count by: 1

From Text: 0 in

OK

Cancel

3. Choose the desired numbering option from the Line Numbers pop-up menu.

The By Page option numbers lines starting with 1 at the top of
each page; By Section numbers lines starting with 1 at the
beginning of each section; Continuous numbers lines sequentially
throughout the document.

4. Optional: In the From Text box, specify the distance from the end of the line number to the begining of the text.

If you don't specify a value, Word positions the number .25 inch
from single-column text and .13 inch from multiple-column text.

5. Click OK or press Return to close the Line Numbers dialog box.

6. Click OK or press Return to close the Section dialog box.

If you want to see the line numbers to check their positioning,
use the Print Preview command in the File menu.

To remove line numbers from certain paragraphs:

1. Select the paragraphs for which you do not want line numbers.

2. Choose Paragraph from the Format menu.

The Paragraph dialog box appears.

3. Select the Suppress Line Numbers check box.

4. Click OK or press Return.

Word removes line numbers from the selected paragraphs.

Quick Tips

Use hanging indents to align runover lines

If you're creating a numbered list of lengthy instructions, you might want to use hanging indents to align runover lines in each numbered instruction.

Hanging indent aligns runover text

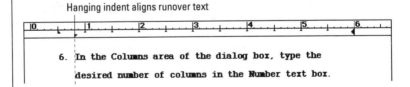

6. In the Columns area of the dialog box, type the desired number of columns in the Number text box.

Topic 5 contains instructions for creating hanging indents.

Another way to selectively number paragraphs

This topic's Step-by-Step section described how to number only certain paragraphs: Select them, and then choose the Renumber command. The problem with this method is that it lets you number only contiguous paragraphs, not paragraphs that are sprinkled throughout a document.

You can be more selective in numbering paragraphs by simply typing a number at the beginning of each paragraph you want numbered. The number you type can be any number — you can even use the same number in each paragraph. Then use the Renumber dialog box's Only If Already Numbered option to renumber the paragraphs.

Because you can use the same number over and over again to mark the paragraphs you want numbered, you might consider creating a glossary entry that inserts a number for you. That way, you can zip through the document and mark each paragraph with only a few keystrokes or mouse clicks. You can also use the Edit menu's Repeat command to enter the number for each paragraph.

Tab characters in numbered paragraphs

Word's Renumber command includes a tab character after each number it adds. You can see this by choosing Show ¶ after numbering some paragraphs, as shown in the following illustration.

Steps align with preset tab stop

```
|0        |1        |2
1.→   Fill·kettle·with·water¶
2.→   Turn·burner·on¶
3.→   Place·kettle·on·burner¶
```

Tabs inserted by Renumber command

If you don't want a tab character — perhaps you want a simple word space instead — you can use the Replace command to replace the tab characters with the desired character. Or "dummy number" each paragraph — type any number along with the character you want to follow it, as described in the previous tip. Then select the By Example button in the Renumber dialog box.

Changing the appearance of line numbers

The appearance of line numbers added with the Section command is controlled by a style sheet named *line number*. You can change the font, size, and style of line numbers by editing this style sheet. For details on editing style sheets, see Topic 11.

An easy way to suppress line numbers

If you need to suppress line numbers frequently, you'll grow tired of opening the Paragraph dialog box to select the Suppress Line Numbers check box. There's an easier way: With the Paragraph dialog box open, press Command-Shift-plus. (The mouse pointer turns into a plus sign.) Next, click on the Suppress Line Numbers check box. (The Mac's menu bar flashes.) Click Cancel to close the Paragraph dialog box. The Format menu now contains a command called No Line Numbers in Paragraph (catchy name, no?). You can choose this command to suppress line numbers in the paragraph containing the insertion point or in a selected range of paragraphs. See Topic 34 for details on customizing Word's menu commands.

Topic 21
Sorting and Calculating

Overview

Sorting information and performing math calculations are tasks you're more likely to associate with database or spreadsheet programs than with a word processor. But Word can do both. Word isn't going to send filing or spreadsheet programs to the breadlines, but its ability to organize information and perform basic calculations is handy. With these features, you can:

✦ Sort a list of names and addresses that you'll use along with Word's print merge feature to create customized form letters or mailing labels

✦ Sort a list of names and phone numbers in a telephone directory

✦ Sort a range of paragraphs numbered using Word's Renumber command (discussed in the previous topic)

✦ Add a column of numbers in a table

✦ Calculate percentage values such as sales tax or discounts

✦ Perform quick calculations without having to switch to a different program

This topic shows how to sort and calculate within paragraphs and within tables created with tabs. For details on sorting and calculating within tables created with Word's Table command, see Topic 25.

Ascending vs. descending sorts

Normally, Word's Sort command sorts in *ascending* order — that is, from A to Z or 0 through 9, as shown in the following illustration.

```
aardvark
bird
cat
chipmunk
deer
dog
horse
poodle
zebra
```

To perform a sort in *descending* order (from Z to A or 9 through 0), press the Shift key before pulling down the Tools menu; doing so causes the Sort command to change to read Sort Descending.

Press Shift before pulling down Tools menu to perform a descending sort

If you find yourself sorting in descending order often, you can add the Sort Descending command to the Tools menu, eliminating having to remember to press Shift. The Quick Tips section of this topic describes how.

What comes before what?

It's obvious that A comes before Z and that 0 precedes 9, but what about the rest of the Mac's characters? Here's the pecking order Word uses when sorting:

◆ Symbols and punctuation marks (% & # * @) come before all other characters

◆ Uppercase letters precede lowercase letters (A comes before a)

◆ Accents and other diacritical characters are ignored (ñ is equal to n)

◆ International characters are sorted according to their position in the English alphabet (for example, ß, which in German represents a double *s,* is sorted as *ss*)

If paragraphs or table rows start with the same character, Word examines subsequent characters to determine which paragraph or row comes first.

Sorting paragraphs

When Word sorts paragraphs, it uses the first word or number in each paragraph to determine that paragraph's position. You must select the paragraphs you want to sort before choosing the Sort command; to sort all the paragraphs in a document, choose Select All from the Edit menu before choosing sort.

Sorting tables created with tab characters

When sorting tables created with tab characters, you can tell Word to sort the table according to the order of a specific column. To do so, select the column by pressing the Option key while dragging across the column.

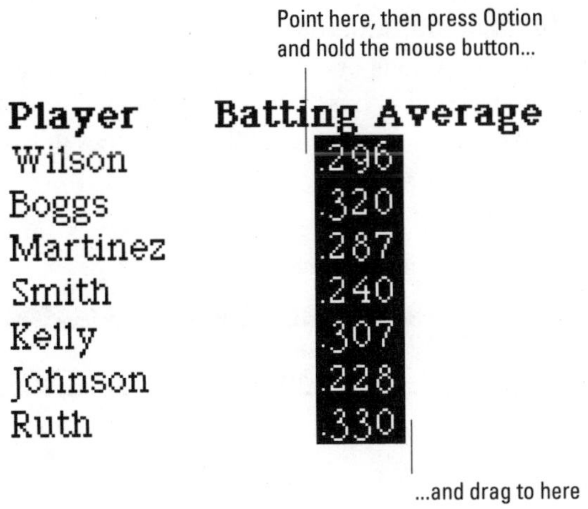

Point here, then press Option and hold the mouse button...

Player	Batting Average
Wilson	.296
Boggs	.320
Martinez	.287
Smith	.240
Kelly	.307
Johnson	.228
Ruth	.330

...and drag to here

After you've selected the column, choose Sort (or Sort Descending), and Word sorts the table according to the column you selected, as shown in the following illustration.

Player	Batting Average
Ruth	.330
Boggs	.320
Kelly	.307
Wilson	.296
Martinez	.287
Smith	.240
Johnson	.228

Saving before sorting

Although you can use the Undo command to reverse the effects of a sort, it's a good idea to save your document before sorting. If you aren't satisfied with the sort, you can close the document without saving changes and then reopen it.

Math calculations

Adding up numbers in Word couldn't be easier: Simply select the numbers and choose Calculate from the Tools menu. You don't need to type plus signs (+), and the numbers can even be separated by text.

Word adds the numbers within the selection...

Sales were $21,093,348 in the first quarter, and $23,348,348 in the second quarter.

44,441,696   Normal

...and displays the total here

To perform multiplication, division, subtraction, or percentage calculations, you do need to type the appropriate symbols:

To...	Use this symbol...	Example
Subtract	- (hyphen)	365-31
Divide	/ (slash)	1500/12
Multiply	* (asterisk)	5*5
Calculate percentage	% (percent sign)	149.87*7%

You can also specify subtraction by enclosing a number within parentheses. This is handy if you're working with financial statements.

```
                        Net Income
First quarter .................... $338
Second quarter ................. 198
Third quarter ................... (110)
Fourth quarter ................. 120
Total ............................ $546
```

Results of calculations go to the Clipboard

When you choose Calculate, Word displays the result of the calculation in the page number area in the lower-left corner of the screen. Word also puts the results on the Mac's Clipboard. You can use the Paste command to paste the results into your document. Note, however, that performing a calculation causes the Clipboard's previous contents to be lost. What's more, you can't restore the Clipboard's contents by choosing Undo. If you have some information on the Clipboard that you don't want to lose, paste it into your document, into the Mac's Scrapbook, or into a new, untitled document before choosing Calculate.

Step-by-Step

This section shows how to sort paragraphs and columns within tables that you've created with tabs, as well as how to perform math calculations. For details on calculating and sorting within tables created with Word's Table command, see Topic 25.

To sort paragraphs:

1. **Select the paragraphs you want to sort.**

2. **Choose Sort from the Tools menu.**
   To sort the paragraphs in descending order, press Shift before pulling down the Tools menu and then choose Sort Descending.

To sort a table according to a specific column:

1. **Select the column by pressing Option and dragging across it.**

2. **Choose Sort from the Tools menu.**
   To sort the table in descending order, press Shift before pulling down the Tools menu and then choose Sort Descending.

To calculate numbers in a paragraph:

1. **Optional: Type math operators for multiplication (*), division (/), or subtraction (-) where appropriate.**
   If you don't perform this step, Word adds the numbers in the paragraph.

2. Select the text containing the numbers.

Word ignores any text that appears between the numbers.

3. Choose Calculate from the Tools menu.

Word calculates the numbers. The result appears in the lower-left corner of the document window and is placed on the Clipboard.

To calculate numbers in the column of a table:

1. Optional: Type math operators for multiplication (*), division (/), or subtraction (-) where appropriate.

If you don't perform this step, Word adds the numbers in the column.

2. Select the column by pressing Option and dragging across it.

3. Choose Calculate from the Tools menu.

Quick Tips

Sorting multiline paragraphs

In Topic 5's Quick Tips section, I mentioned that you can start a new line in Word without starting a new paragraph by pressing Shift-Return instead of Return. Text before and after the new line is considered a single paragraph and its formatting is governed by one paragraph mark. When you press Shift-Return, Word inserts a new-line character. You can use the new-line character to create multiline paragraphs whose lines remain together when you sort.

For example, say you have a list of names and addresses that you want to sort. If you end each line with a carriage return, Word will sort every line independently, yielding useless results, as shown in the following illustration.

Each line ends with   ...yielding worthless
a paragraph mark...   results after sorting

Acton,·Fred¶   98·Fred·Rd.¶
98·Fred·Rd.¶   123·George·Blvd.¶
Joplin,·MO·38937¶   12983·Sam·St.¶
¶   ¶
Jones,·Sam¶   Acton,·Fred¶
12983·Sam·St.¶   Jones,·Sam¶
Pittsburgh,·PA·15222¶   Joplin,·MO·38937¶
¶   ¶
Washington,·George¶   Pittsburgh,·PA·15222¶
123·George·Blvd.¶   Washington,·DC·20098¶
Washington,·DC·20098¶   Washington,·George¶
¶   ¶

To avoid this, use the new-line character to end each line within each address, and then use a carriage return to separate each name and address. This causes Word to keep each address' lines together when sorting:

Lines within each address end with a new line character, allowing correct sorting

Acton, Fred↵
98 Fred Rd.↵
Joplin, MO 38937↵
¶
Jones, Sam↵
12983 Sam St.↵
Pittsburgh, PA 15222↵
¶
Washington, George↵
123 George Blvd.↵
Washington, DC 20098↵
¶

Easier access to the descending sort command

If you sort in descending order often, add the Sort Descending command to the Tools menu. Choose Commands from the Tools menu, and then type *s* to quickly jump to the list of commands beginning with that character. Scroll through the list to locate the Sort Descending command, and then click the Add button. Finally, click Close to close the Commands dialog box. Examine the Tools menu, and you'll see that Word has added the Sort Descending command just below the Sort command.

For more details on customizing Word's menus, see Topic 34.

Controlling the order of calculations

You can control the order in which Word performs calculations by grouping within parentheses expressions you want calculated separately. For example, Word calculates the expression 5 + 10 * 2 as follows: Add 5 to 10 and then multiply the sum by 2, arriving at 30. However, if you type 5 + (10 * 2), Word calculates the expression this way: Multiply 10 by 2, and then add 5, arriving at 25.

If you don't include math operators (* / + -) within the parentheses, Word treats the number within parentheses as a negative number and subtracts it from the total. For example, 5 + (10) equals (5), or -5.

Part III
Advanced Formatting

Topic 22

Changing Formatting with Sections

Overview

You may have encountered the Section command in other topics. It's the command you use to create page numbers that print in the margins, to specify the format of page numbers, and to create different headers or footers for the first page in a document (Topic 9). You also use the Section command to specify line numbers (Topic 20).

Normally, the options you specify with the Section dialog box apply to the entire document. But Word lets you divide a document into any number of *sections,* each of which can have its own page-numbering arrangements, headers and footers, and column arrangements. Here are just a few reasons you might divide a document into multiple sections:

+ *To switch from a one-column format to a two-column format.* By creating sections, you can create a newspaper-style layout, with a headline spanning multiple columns. You can also use sections to control the position of text within multicolumn pages — to specify that a story begin at the top of a column, for example.

+ *To change the contents of headers and footers.* If you're creating a book or manual, you might create a separate section for each chapter so that each chapter can have its own headers and footers, and so that each can begin on a right-hand page.

+ *To change the page-numbering scheme.* If you're creating a book, you might format the front matter (the preface, table of contents, and so forth) to use lowercase roman numerals (i, ii, iii, iv), and then switch to Arabic numerals for the first chapter. Or you might want to begin numbering each chapter with 1, prefacing the page number with the chapter number (for example, 1-1, 1-2 and 2-1, 2-2).

✦ *To activate and deactivate line numbering.* If you're creating a legal document, you might want to create a cover page with no line numbers, and then activate line numbering on the first inside page.

✦ *To change where footnotes appear.* For a book, you might want footnotes to appear at the bottom of each page in one chapter, but to be grouped together at the ends of subsequent chapters.

A section can be any length. In a newsletter, you might have a section that contains just one line — a headline that spans multiple columns.

You may never have to divide a document into separate sections. For example, if you're creating books or manuals, you might prefer to make each chapter a separate file and then link the chapter files as described in Topic 30.

The section break

The key to dividing a document into sections is the *section break.* Just as a page break code tells Word to begin a new page, a section break tells Word to begin a new section.

You insert a section break by choosing Section Break from the Insert menu or by pressing Command-Enter (that's Enter — the large key in the number keypad — not Return). When you're working with the document in the normal view, Word indicates a section break with a double-dotted line.

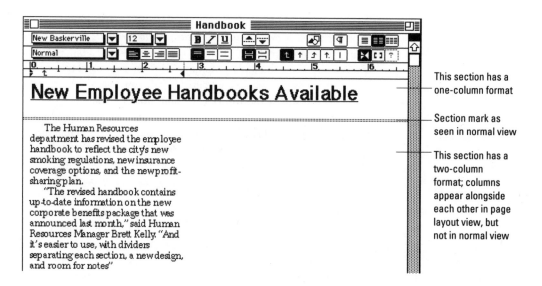

This section has a one-column format

Section mark as seen in normal view

This section has a two-column format; columns appear alongside each other in page layout view, but not in normal view

The double-dotted line that denotes a section break is called a *section mark*. The section mark stores all the section-formatting information for the text that precedes it — just as a paragraph mark stores all the paragraph-formatting information for the text in a paragraph. And as with paragraph marks, if you delete a section mark, the text preceding it takes on the section formatting of the section below it.

When the section mark is deleted, the first section takes on the formatting of the subsequent section — in this case, a two-column format

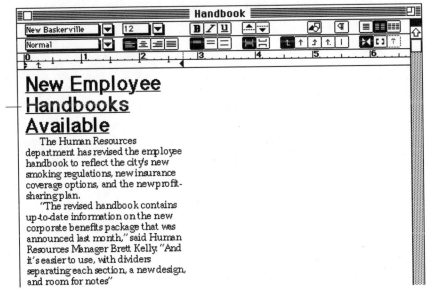

When a document contains more than one section, Word changes the page number display (in the lower-left corner of the document window) to reflect the current page and section number — that is, the page and section containing the insertion point.

Columns appear alongside each other in page layout view; note that section mark doesn't appear

Section number

Page number

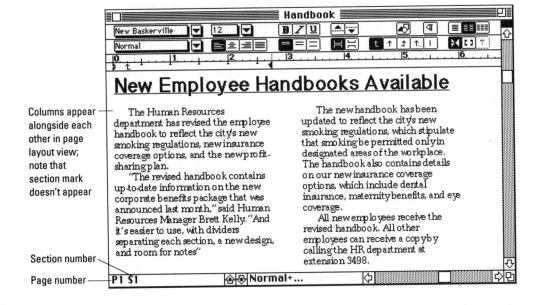

If you open the Header or Footer window in a multisection document, you'll also notice that Word indicates which section the header or footer belongs to.

Section number in
Header window title bar

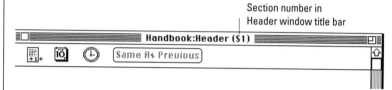

When you're working in page layout view, section marks are visible only when you choose Show ¶ from the View menu.

Creating multiple-column documents

Formatting an entire document to have two or three columns of text on every page is easy — just click on the appropriate column button in the ribbon.

Three columns
Two columns
One column

Clicking either of these buttons has the same effect as choosing Section from the Format menu, and then specifying the desired number of columns in the Section dialog box.

Things get trickier when you want to mix column formats within a document or within a page. To switch between different column arrangements — for example, a one-column heading spanning a three-column page — you need to insert section breaks and then use the Section command to specify the number of columns for each section. This topic's Step-by-Step section shows how.

Note that columns don't appear alongside each other in normal view. To see columns as they'll appear when you print the document, use page layout view or the Print Preview window. Topic 6 describes these viewing options in detail.

Adjusting the width of columns

You can adjust the width of columns by using the ruler's margin scale. When you click on the margin scale button, margin markers appear on the ruler. Drag the markers left or right to adjust column widths, as shown in the following illustration.

Margin scale button

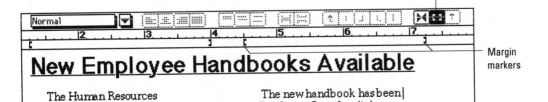

Margin markers

Note that all the columns must have the same width; you can't create newspaper-style columns that have varying widths — for example, a 2-inch column alongside a 6-inch one. When you adjust one column's width using the margin markers, Word adjusts the other columns to match. (You can use the Table command to create unequal columns, however.)

Word separates columns by .5 inch. You can specify a different *gutter width* by choosing Section and then specifying the amount of space you want between columns.

When you're working with a multicolumn document in page layout view, the ruler starts at zero for the column containing the blinking insertion point. If you click in a different column, you'll see the ruler change.

The ruler scale begins at zero for the column containing the selection or insertion point

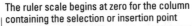

When you move to a different column, the ruler scale changes accordingly

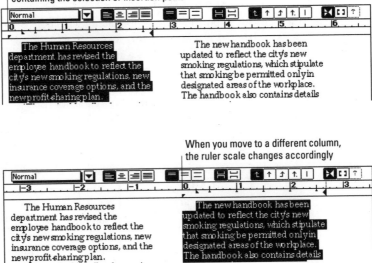

If you know a document will contain multiple columns, consider creating the columns before creating or adjusting paragraph indents. This will allow you to create appropriately sized paragraph indents.

Snaking vs. parallel columns

The column-related information in this topic pertains to *snaking,* or newspaper-style columns, in which text "snakes" from the bottom of one column to the top of the next. Some tasks require *parallel* columns, in which columns of words, numbers, or entire paragraphs appear side-by-side.

Camera	Announcer
Medium close-up of knives	How much would you expect to pay for knives like these? Don't answer yet, because there's more!
Close-up of paring knife cutting through cast iron pipe	You also get this paring knife--so sharp, it can cut through this cast-iron pipe!

To create parallel columns, use Word's tab features (discussed in Topic 8) or Word's table editor (Topic 25). The table editor makes creating parallel columns especially easy.

The section start

An important part of formatting a section is specifying where Word should position the first text or graphic in that section. Should the new section begin on a new page? at the top of a column? Or should it directly follow the preceding section's contents?

You control this aspect of section formatting using the Start pop-up menu in the Section dialog box.

Start pop-up menu

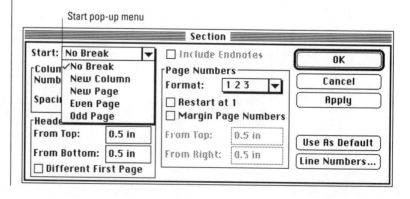

Part III
Advanced Formatting

The following table lists just some of the ways you might use each option.

You might choose...	If you are...
No Break	switching between single-column and multicolumn format on the same page
New Column	working with a multicolumn format and want something (such as a new story in a newsletter) to appear at the top of the next column
New Page	switching between different column, page numbering, or footnoting arrangements on separate pages
Odd Page	creating a book and want the first page of a new chapter to be a right-hand page. If the section break is on a right-hand page, Word leaves the next left-hand page blank.
Even Page	creating a book and want the next section to appear on a left-hand page. If the section break is on a left-hand page, Word leaves the next right-hand page blank.

Step-by-Step

In this section, you'll find instructions for creating multicolumn pages, for mixing column formats within a document and on the same page, for adjusting column widths, and for changing headers and footers and page numbering schemes within a document.

To create a two- or three-column layout for an entire document:

1. Display the ribbon by choosing Ribbon from the View menu.

2. Click the two-column or three-column button.

To create a one-column layout for the first page of a document and a multicolumn layout on subsequent pages:

1. Position the insertion point at the end of the first page of the document.

2. Choose Section Break from the Insert menu or press Command-Enter.
   Word inserts a section break.

3. Be sure the insertion point is located below the section break you just inserted.
   It is, unless you moved it after inserting the section break.

4. Choose Section from the Format menu.

The Section dialog box appears.

5. Choose the New Page option from the Start pop-up menu.

This tells Word to begin the current section on a new page.

6. In the Columns area of the dialog box, type the desired number of columns in the Number text box.

7. Specify any other section formatting you may need.

For example, if you want this section to be numbered beginning with 1, click the Restart at 1 check box.

8. Click OK or press Return.

To switch from a one-column arrangement to another on the same page:

1. Position the insertion point where you want to change column widths.

For example, if you're creating a one-column headline followed by two columns of text, position the insertion point after the headline.

2. Choose Section Break from the Insert menu or press Command-Enter.

Word inserts a section break.

3. Be sure the insertion point is located below the section break you just inserted.

4. Choose Section from the Format menu.

The Section dialog box appears.

5. Be sure the No Break option is selected in the Start pop-up menu.

No Break is the default setting. It tells Word to create a new section, but to position its contents immediately following the preceding section.

6. In the Columns area of the dialog box, type the desired number of columns in the Number text box.

7. Specify any other section formatting you may need.

8. Click OK or press Return.

To break a column:

1. Position the insertion point where you want to break the column.

You might want to use the page layout view to get an accurate picture of how the columns break.

2. Choose Page Break from the Insert menu or press Shift-Enter.

Word breaks the column, forcing text following the column break to the top of the next column.

To insert a page break in a multicolumn section:

1. Position the insertion point where you want the page to break.

2. Choose Section Break from the Insert menu or press Command-Enter.

Word inserts a section break.

3. Be sure the insertion point is located below the section break you just inserted.

4. Choose Section from the Format menu.

The Section dialog box appears.

5. Choose the New Page option from the Start pop-up menu.

This tells Word to start the new section on a new page. Note that the Columns area of the dialog box lists the options that were in effect for the previous section.

6. Click OK or press Return.

To create a new chapter in a book or manual:

1. Position the insertion point at the end of the previous chapter.

2. Choose Section Break from the Insert menu or press Command-Enter.

Word inserts a section break.

3. Be sure the insertion point is located below the section break you just inserted.

4. Choose Section from the Format menu.

The Section dialog box appears.

5. Choose Odd Page from the Start pop-up menu.

This tells Word to begin the new chapter on an odd-numbered (right-hand) page.

6. Specify any other section formatting you may need.

You might, for example, want to begin page numbering at 1 if you are numbering pages with the chapter *and* page number (for example, 1-1, 1-2 and 2-1, 2-2).

7. Click OK or press Return.

8. **Be sure the insertion point is positioned within the new chapter's section.**

9. **Use the Header and Footer commands in the View menu to create new headers and footers for the new chapter.**

To adjust the width of a column:

1. **Be sure the ruler is displayed.**

   If it isn't, choose Ruler from the View menu.

2. **Position the insertion point in the column whose width you want to adjust.**

   You don't have to select the entire column; simply click within it to move the insertion point.

Margin scale
button

3. **Click the ruler's margin scale button.**

   Margin markers appear denoting the columns' widths.

4. **Drag the margin markers left or right as needed to adjust the column's width.**

   Word adjusts the width of all the columns to match.

Quick Tips

Store section marks as glossary entries

As mentioned earlier, the section mark stores all the section-formatting information for the text that precedes it. If you frequently switch between specific section formats, consider storing section marks as glossary entries. This will enable you to insert the section marks that reflect the section formatting you use most often.

To store a section mark as a glossary entry, first select the section mark by clicking once in the selection bar to its left. (If you're in page layout view, switch to normal view first.) Next, choose Glossary from the Edit menu, type a name for the glossary entry, and click Define. See Topic 16 for more details on Word's glossary feature.

The top-down approach to section formatting

If you anticipate using multiple sections in a document, you can save time and trips to the Section dialog box by taking a top-down approach to section formatting. Before creating any sections, choose the Section command and use the Section dialog box to specify the formatting that will apply to all of the document's sections — for example, the page-numbering scheme, or the position of headers and footers.

Subsequently, when you divide the document into sections, the section formatting you specified will be in effect for each section. All you will need to change are the settings that are unique to each section.

Setting defaults

Don't neglect the Use As Default button in the Section dialog box. If you always create documents that use specific section settings, specify those settings and then click Use As Default. Word will apply those settings to new, untitled documents.

Shortcut to the Section dialog box

You can open the Section dialog box by double-clicking a section mark. Any changes you make are applied to the section preceding that section mark.

Controlling column breaks

Word's Keep paragraph options — Keep With Next, Keep Lines Together, and so on — can be useful for controlling where columns break. For example, if you want a newsletter headline to remain with its story, select the Keep With Next option for the headline's paragraph. See Topic 5 for details on Word's Keep options.

Multicolumn selection bars in page layout view

When you're working with a multicolumn document in page layout view, there are selection bars to the left of each column.

You can select lines and paragraphs by clicking in the appropriate column's selection bar.

Sections and the Go To command

You can use the Go To command (Edit menu) to jump to a specific section. In the Go To dialog box, simply type *s* followed by the section number. For example, to go to the first page of section 2, type *s2*. To go to a specific page within a section, type *p* and the page number, followed by **s** and the section number. For example, type *p4s3* to go to page four of section three.

When a document contains more than one section, you can also use the Print dialog box to print a specific section or range of sections.

Topic 23
Positioning Items with Frames

Overview

Word lets you insert text or graphics within a *frame* that you can drag around on the page until it's positioned where you want it. A frame is an invisible box that holds text or graphics. If the frame is positioned within a page's margins, the text outside the frame flows around a frame like water in a stream flows around a rock. Graphic designers call this text-flowing effect a *runaround*. (The other effect is called "a rock in a stream.")

You might use frames to position:

◆ a graphic so that adjacent text runs around it

◆ a paragraph so that it prints in the margin

◆ a graphic or a table so that it spans two or more columns of text

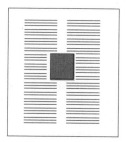

Graphic positioned between columns, with text flowing around it

Paragraphs formatted to print in the margin

Graphic formatted to straddle two columns

You can specify that a framed item always appear in the same place on a page, or that it be positioned relative to the margin or a specific column. With the latter approach, when you adjust the margin or column, the frame moves along with it.

Jim Heid's Word Companion, the disk set (sold separately) that complements this book, includes several template documents that illustrate various ways to use frames; see the order page at the back of this book for details.

Word displays framed items in position in the page layout view only. In normal view, a framed item appears in the order in which you entered its contents in the document. For example, say you frame a paragraph that originally appeared in the middle of a page and then you drag it to the top of the page. In page layout view, the framed paragraph will appear at the top of the page, but in normal view, the framed paragraph will appear in the middle of the page — where it was when you originally typed it.

Creating frames

Word has two Frame commands — one in the Insert menu and one in the Format menu. Creating a frame involves selecting the item you want to position, and then choosing one of the Frame commands. Which command should you use? That depends on what you're framing:

♦ *To position tables, graphics, and other items with a fixed, predetermined width, use the Frame command in the Insert menu.* This command creates a frame whose width matches the item you've selected.

Select the graphic (or other fixed-width item) and then choose Frame from the Insert menu...

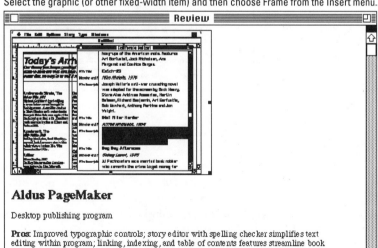

...Word creates a frame whose width matches the width of the item, and opens the Print Preview window, where you can adjust the frame's position

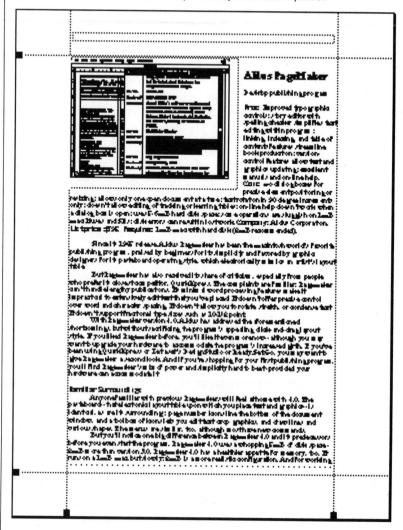

♦ *To position multiple lines of text, use the Frame command in the Format menu.* Choosing *this* Frame command displays a dialog box that enables you to specify the width of the frame. Lines of text that are inside the frame are broken to fit within the frame's boundaries.

Before choosing Frame from the Format menu:
the selected text runs the full width of the margin

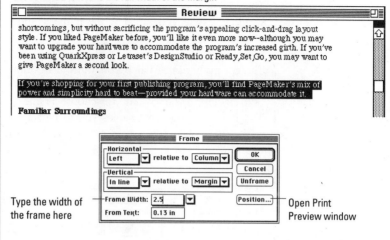

Type the width of
the frame here

Open Print
Preview window

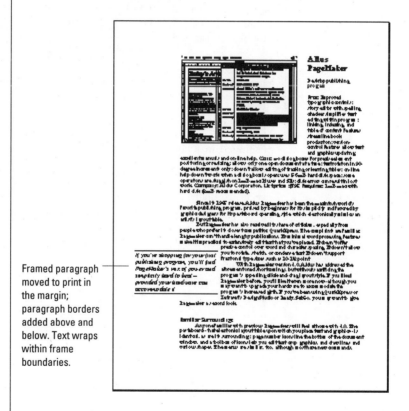

Framed paragraph
moved to print in
the margin;
paragraph borders
added above and
below. Text wraps
within frame
boundaries.

You can also use the Format menu's Frame command to adjust the
size and position of frames created using the Insert menu's Frame
command. This topic's Step-by-Step section shows how.

Fine-tuning the position of a frame

The easiest way to position a frame is to use the Print Preview window, where you can drag the frame to the desired spot on a page. (Topic 6 describes Print Preview in detail.)

There may be times when you want to be more precise, however. You can fine-tune the position of any frame by using the Frame dialog box, which appears when you choose Frame from the Format menu. The Frame dialog box enables you to type measurements that describe the frame's location from the margin or the left and top edges of the page, and the distance between the frame and adjacent text.

This frame's left edge will be 2 inches from the left edge of the page

This frame's top will be 5 inches from the top edge of the page

Not available when frame width is set to Auto

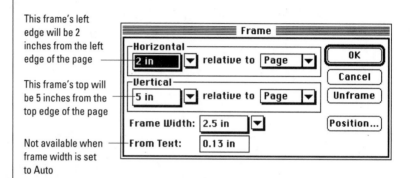

You can also use the Frame dialog box to specify that the frame be positioned in relation to a specific part of the page. You can specify that a frame be:

◆ horizontally centered within the page size, within a column, or within the margins, as shown in the following illustration.

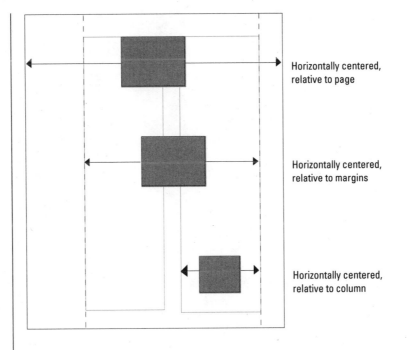

Horizontally centered, relative to page

Horizontally centered, relative to margins

Horizontally centered, relative to column

✦ vertically centered within the page size or within the margins.

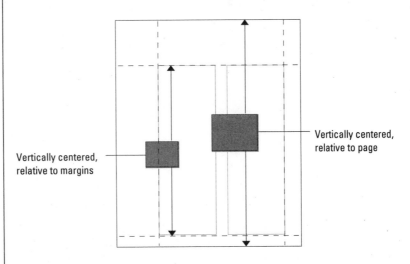

Vertically centered, relative to page

Vertically centered, relative to margins

✦ aligned left or right against a margin, column, or page boundary, as shown in the following illustration.

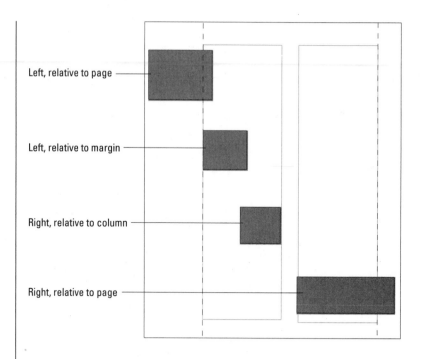

Left, relative to page

Left, relative to margin

Right, relative to column

Right, relative to page

♦ vertically aligned with a specific paragraph of text.

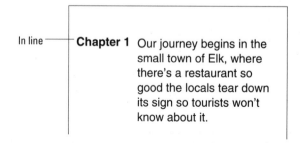

In line

Chapter 1 Our journey begins in the small town of Elk, where there's a restaurant so good the locals tear down its sign so tourists won't know about it.

The last option is useful if you want to position a heading or graphic adjacent to a specific paragraph. If the paragraph moves up or down during editing or reformatting, the frame moves along with it. This lets you position a heading or graphic next to the text it refers to — and ensures that the heading or graphic will remain adjacent to that text even after editing or reformatting.

Using the ruler in frames

You can use the ruler to control paragraph indents within a frame. If you're framing a paragraph, it's a good idea to first remove any paragraph indents you may have created for that paragraph. That way, the paragraph's text will align with the left edge of the frame, as shown in the following illustration.

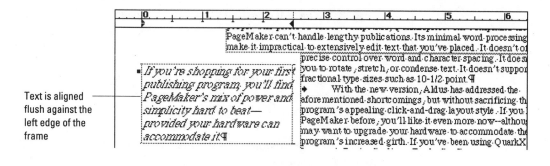

Text is aligned flush against the left edge of the frame

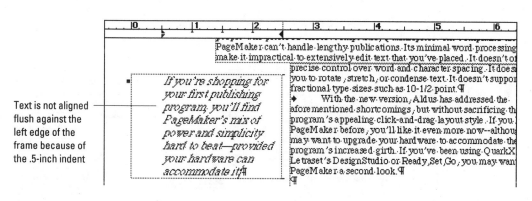

Text is not aligned flush against the left edge of the frame because of the .5-inch indent

Once you've framed a paragraph, you can use the ruler to create a first-line indent or a hanging indent. As the preceding illustration shows, when the insertion point is within the framed paragraph, the ruler's zero point is at the left edge of the frame.

Step-by-Step

In this section, you'll find instructions for framing text and graphics, for positioning frames, and for removing frames. You'll also find instructions for using frames to create two specific effects: a heading or caption in the margin, and a *drop cap* — a large capital letter that begins a paragraph.

To enclose a paragraph within a frame that will be the same width as the document or column margins:

1. Select the paragraph.

You can select a paragraph by double-clicking the selection bar to the left of the paragraph or by triple-clicking anywhere on the paragraph.

2. Choose Frame from the Insert menu.

Word creates the frame and displays the Print Preview window.

3. **Drag the frame to the desired location on the page.**

You can use the Print Preview window's magnifying glass tool to zoom in on the page for a closer look.

4. **Click the Close button to return to the document window.**

You can see the framed paragraph in position by switching to page layout view.

To frame a paragraph and specify a width for the frame:

1. **Select the paragraph.**

2. **Choose Frame from the Format menu.**

The Frame dialog box appears.

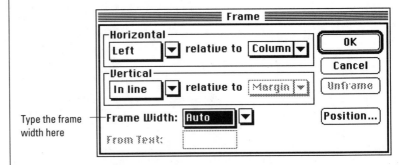

Type the frame width here

3. **In the Frame Width box, type a measurement for the frame.**

4. **Specify any other positioning options you want.**

See "Fine-tuning the position of a frame" in this topic's Overview section for details.

5. **If you want to position the frame using the Print Preview window, click the Position button. Otherwise, click OK or press Return.**

To frame a graphic:

1. **Select the graphic.**

2. **Choose Frame from the Insert menu.**

Word creates a frame that's the same width as the graphic and displays the Print Preview window.

3. **Drag the frame to the desired location on the page.**

You can use the Print Preview window's magnifying glass tool to zoom in on the page for a closer look.

4. Click the Close button to return to the document window.

You can see the framed graphic in position by switching to page layout view.

To adjust an existing frame's position using the Print Preview window:

1. Choose Print Preview from the File menu.

The Print Preview window appears.

2. Be sure the margin icon is selected.

If it isn't, select it by clicking it once.

3. If necessary, scroll to the page containing the frame whose position you want to adjust.

You can scroll using the Print Preview window's scroll bar or the keyboard's Page Up and Page Down keys.

4. Point to the frame you want to move, and then press and hold down the mouse button.

In the Print Preview window, when the mouse pointer is over a frame, it turns from an arrow into a crosshair (+).

5. Drag the frame to the desired position on the page.

As you drag, the top of the Print Preview window shows the distance from the top-left corner of the frame to the top-left corner of the page. When you release the mouse button, Word reformats the page to reflect the frame's new location.

To format a heading to appear in the margin:

1. Type the heading and then press Return so that the heading is in its own paragraph.

2. Select the heading.

Be sure to include the paragraph mark.

3. Choose Frame from the Format menu.

The Frame dialog box appears.

4. Be sure the In Line option is selected in the Vertical pop-up menu.

This option formats the frame so that it stays adjacent to the paragraph that follows it.

5. In the Frame Width box, type a width for the frame.

Be sure that the width you specify will allow the frame to fit in the margin without encroaching on the main text. For example, if you have a 1.5-inch left margin, give the frame a width of less than 1.5 inches — try 1 inch for starters.

6. In the Horizontal section of the dialog box, change the pop-up menus to read "Left relative to Page."

7. Click OK or press Return.

If you want to fine-tune the frame's position or preview it, click the Position button before clicking OK or pressing Return.

To create a drop cap for a paragraph:

1. Select the first character in the paragraph.

2. Format the character in the desired font and size.

Drop caps often appear in 24- or 36-point type.

3. With the character still selected, choose Frame from the Insert menu.

The Print Preview window appears. If the Frame dialog box appears, you selected the Format menu's Frame command. Click Cancel, and then choose Frame from the Insert menu.

4. Drag the drop cap character down slightly so that its top aligns with the top of the paragraph's first line.

You might need to use the Print Preview window's magnifying glass tool to zoom in on the page to check your positioning.

5. Click Close to close the Print Preview window, or Page Layout to close the window and activate page layout view.

In page layout view, the drop cap appears in position. But there's too much space between it and the adjacent text.

O nce upon a time, there were writers who couldn't begin a story without using the phrase "once upon a time."

You'll fix that in the next step.

6. With the character still selected, choose Frame from the Format menu.

The Frame dialog box appears.

7. In the From Text box, type *0* (zero).

This tells Word to add no extra space after the drop cap and the adjacent text.

8. Click OK or press Return.

Word closes up the space between the drop cap and the adjacent text.

O nce upon a time, there were writers who couldn't begin a story without using the phrase "once upon a time."

Depending on the font, size, and style you're using for the drop cap and the paragraph text, you may need to add a bit of space after the drop cap. If so, repeat steps 6–8, substituting a small value such as .03 or .05 in Step 7.

To unframe a paragraph or graphic:

1. Select the contents of the frame.

To unframe only some of the frame's contents, select only the items you want to unframe.

2. Choose Frame from the Format menu.

The Frame dialog box appears.

3. Click the Unframe button.

Word removes the selected items from the frame and restores them to their original position in the document.

Quick Tips

Frames can be part of styles

If you often use a similar type of framed item — for example, a drop cap, a heading in the margin, a graphic spanning two columns — you can define the frame as part of a Word style sheet. This allows you to quickly frame other items by simply applying the style, with no time-consuming trips to the Frame dialog box or the Print Preview window.

To specify a style for a framed heading in the margin, for example, first format one heading to appear in the margin as described in this topic's Step-by-Step section. Next, with the insertion point within the framed heading, choose Style from the Format menu. When the Style dialog box appears, type a name for the style and then click Define. Finally, close the Style dialog box. You can now format a paragraph as a framed margin head by placing the insertion point within the paragraph and then applying the style's name using the ruler's Style pop-up menu or the Style dialog box. (For details on defining and applying styles, see Topic 11.)

If you use drop caps frequently, you might also want to create a style that produces them. The steps are similar to those just described, except that you select the drop cap before defining the style. Before applying the style to the first character in a paragraph, press Return after the character so that the character is in its own paragraph.

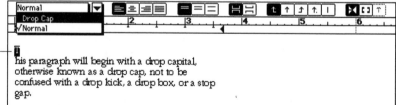

Press Return after the first character to put it in its own paragraph, and then select the character and apply the style

Moving a framed item to a different page

You can drag a frame around on a page, but you can't drag it to another page. To move a framed item to a different page, select the framed item, choose Cut from the Edit menu, and then scroll to the desired page. Finally, click where you want the item to appear, and then choose Paste from the Edit menu. As an alternative to cutting and pasting, you can also use the move-to keyboard shortcut or the drag-and-drop technique, both described in Topic 3.

Creating a tricky layout? Frame everything

If you're creating a single-page document with a fancy layout — for example, a restaurant menu or a poster — consider placing every paragraph and graphic on the page within its own frame. This approach lets you use Word as you would use a desktop publishing program, clicking and dragging page elements in the Print Preview window until you're satisfied with the layout.

A shortcut to the Frame dialog box

If you activate Show ¶ for a document containing frames, you'll notice a small black bullet adjacent to framed paragraphs. This isn't the bullet character (•) that you get when you press Option-8; it's a *paragraph properties mark* — a symbol Word displays to indicate that the paragraph has special formatting attributes that may not show up unless you print the document or view it in the Print Preview window.

Paragraph properties mark

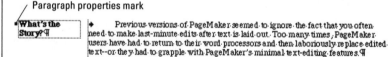

You can display the Frame dialog box by double-clicking the paragraph properties mark.

Stay within the printable area

Keep in mind that most printers — particularly laser printers — can't print to the very edge of the page. If you're positioning frames in the margins, be sure to stay within your printer's printable area. If you'll be printing to a laser printer, don't position anything closer than .25 inch to the edge of the page.

Use a frame to vertically center a one-page document

Although frames are most useful when creating complex layouts, you can also use them to solve a formatting problem common in simple documents: how to vertically center the text in a one-page document such as a business letter or memo. Simply select all the text, and then choose Frame from the Format menu. When the Frame dialog box appears, configure the Vertical pop-up menus to read "center relative to page." Word will place equal amounts of space above and below the text.

Topic 24

Working with Tables

Overview

If you've ever struggled to create a table using a typewriter's or word processor's tab features, you'll love Word's built-in table editor. The table editor enables you to create an on-screen grid made up of *cells* that can contain text or graphics. You can use the table editor to:

♦ *Create tables without having to struggle with tabs.* The table editor is especially useful for creating tables containing multiline entries in each column, since text wraps within each cell as you type.

Virus Name	Nature of Infection	Symptoms	Comments
ANTI, ANTI-B, ANTI-ange	Infects applications only (including the Finder), not other system files or documents.	Nondestructive but may cause crashes due to its poor programming.	Disinfected applications aren't identical to original, but generally still run. Best approach is to replace infected application with an uninfected copy from its master disk.
CDEF	Infects DeskTop file only, not system files, programs, or documents.	Slows performance. AppleShare server performance slows significantly.	You can remove this virus from an infected disk by rebuilding its DeskTop file: Press Command and Option while inserting the disk. For hard disks, restart and hold down Command and Option until rebuild dialog box appears. To avoid infecting an AppleShare server, do not grant "make changes" privilege to the server's root directory (desktop level).
Frankie	Infects applications, not documents or system files. Infects only Atari computers containing certain Mac emulator hardware.	Draws bomb icon, displays, "Frankie says: No more piracy," then crashes.	Very rare. Doesn't infect genuine Macs. Doesn't spread under MultiFinder.

◆ *Format a graphic so that it appears along with its caption.*

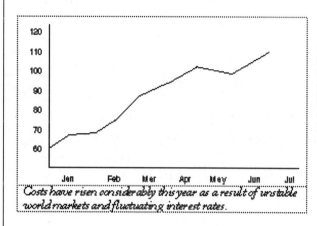

A one-column table containing two rows: The graphic is in the top row; the caption is in the bottom row

Costs have risen considerably this year as a result of unstable world markets and fluctuating interest rates.

After placing a graphic and its caption within a table, you can frame the table using the techniques described in the previous topic, and then drag the framed table to the desired position on a page.

◆ *Format paragraphs to appear side-by-side.*

English	German
Do not attempt to clean the exterior with chemical solvents; this may damage the finish.	Benutzen Sie ein weiches, trockenes Tuch, um das Gerät zu säubern.
When moving the instrument, be sure to unplug the AC wall plug and all other connecting cables.	Vor dem Transport, alle Anschlußkabel und Stecker ziehen.

If you use a spreadsheet program such as Microsoft Excel, some aspects of Word's table editor will seem familiar, although you'll need to learn new techniques for resizing and selecting the table's horizontal rows and vertical columns. It's worth noting that you can paste a completed table into a spreadsheet program and retain its row-and-column arrangement. You can also paste spreadsheet data into a Word document and then use Word's table-editing features to reformat the data.

Once you've created a table, you can add borders and shading to all or only some of its cells. You can also enclose the table within a frame and then use the Print Preview window to move the framed table around on the page. Instructions for adding borders and shading appear in the next topic. Details on frames appear in Topic 23.

Table basics

You create a new, empty table by choosing Table from the Insert menu. Word displays a dialog box that lets you specify how many horizontal rows and vertical columns you want.

Columns run vertically

Rows run horizontally

Word calculates this value by dividing the space between the page margins by the number of columns you type

Insert Table

Number of Columns: 2
Number of Rows: 2
Column Width: 3 in

OK
Cancel
Format...

Convert From
○ Paragraphs   ○ Comma Delimited
○ Tab Delimited   ○ Side by Side Only

Generally, don't worry about typing a specific number of rows; Word adds new rows automatically as you work with a table. To avoid extensive reformatting, though, you should try to accurately estimate how many columns you'll need. (If you have trouble remembering the difference between rows and columns, remember that a row of houses runs horizontally, while the columns of a building run up and down.)

Word sets the width of each column based on the size of your page margins and the number of columns you want. For example, if the margins are 6 inches apart and you specify 3 columns, each column will be 2 inches wide. You can easily change the column widths after creating the table.

After you click the Table dialog box's OK button, Word inserts an empty table containing the number of rows and columns you specified.

Insertion point in upper-left cell

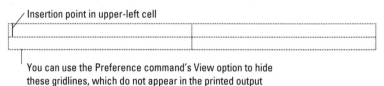

You can use the Preference command's View option to hide these gridlines, which do not appear in the printed output

You can enter text or insert a graphic in a specific cell by first clicking within that cell. You can also move from one cell to the next cell by pressing the Tab key, and to the previous cell by pressing Shift-Tab. If you press Tab when the insertion point is in the last cell in the table (the bottom-right cell), Word inserts a new row for you. (You can add new columns using the Format menu's Table Layout command; this topic's Step-by-Step section shows how.)

You can format text within cells using Word's standard paragraph-formatting tools: the ruler and the Format menu's Paragraph command. Text can be centered, aligned left, aligned right, or justified within table cells, and you can change its line spacing. You can also define and apply styles for the contents of cells. See Topic 5 for details on Word's paragraph formatting options, and Topic 11 for details on style sheets.

Selecting rows, columns, and cells

You can select text within a cell using Word's standard selection techniques: Drag to select a range of characters, double-click to select words, and triple-click to select paragraphs. (If a cell contains only one paragraph, triple-clicking selects the entire cell.)

Word also provides some selection techniques that deal specifically with tables. You'll use these techniques when formatting, cutting, and reorganizing rows and columns.

♦ Each cell has an invisible *cell selection bar* to its left. The cell selection bar works much like the selection bar that exists to the left of a paragraph: When the mouse pointer is within the selection bar, it changes to a right-pointing arrow.

What You Say	What I Say
tomayto	tomahto
potayto	potahto

Use the cell-selection bar to select cells

To select a cell, click once within its selection bar. If you double-click, Word selects the entire row containing the cell.

♦ Each row has an invisible *row selection bar* to its left. When the mouse pointer is within the row selection bar, it changes to a right-pointing arrow.

What You Say	What I Say
tomayto	tomahto
potayto	potahto

Double-click the row selection bar to select a row

To select a row, double-click its row selection bar.

✦ Each column has an invisible *column selection bar* above it. When the mouse pointer is within the column selection bar, it changes to a down-pointing arrow.

What You Say	What I Say ↓
tomayto	tomahto
potayto	potahto

To select a column, click once within its column selection bar. You can also select an entire column by pressing Option and clicking anywhere within the column. Option-clicking is often easier and faster than using the column selection bar, since it doesn't require you to scroll to the top of the table.

You can also select a range of adjoining cells by dragging across them.

Click here...

Frankie	Infects applications, not documents or system files. Infects only Atari computers containing certain Mac emulator hardware.	Draws bomb icon, displays, "Frankie says: No more piracy," then crashes.	Very rare. Doesn't infect genuine Macs. Doesn't spread under MultiFinder.
INIT 29	Infects any file (document or application) containing resources. Spreads only via applications and System files.	Its poor coding may cause printing problems, INIT conflicts, and MultiFinder crashes. If you insert a locked floppy disk, a dialog box appears saying the disk needs repairs. Normally, this dialog box doesn't appear with locked disks.	INIT 29 can spread very rapidly because it infects unlocked floppies as soon as they are inserted.
MDEF (strains A, B, and C; also called Garfield)	Infects applications, various system files, and documents.	System crashes. On Macs using CE Software's Vaccine, MDEF-A causes menus to work only in infected applications.	Often infects DeskTop, DA Handler, and Finder files. Strains B and C attempt to bypass watchdog INITs.

...and then drag to here

Finally, you can select an entire table by pressing Option and then double-clicking within the table.

Adjusting cell and column widths with the ruler

You can change the width of a single cell or of an entire column by using the ruler or the Table Cells command in the Format menu. The ruler lets you adjust cell widths with the mouse and immediately see the results.

Table scale button

To adjust cell or column widths with the ruler, you use the *table scale,* which is active when you click the table scale button. When the table scale is active, T-shaped *column markers* denote each column's width, as shown in the following illustration.

Column markers indicate the width
of each column or selected cell(s)

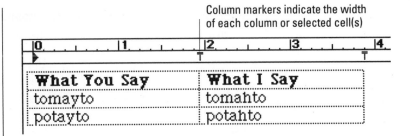

You can change the width of an individual cell by selecting the cell
(or simply clicking within it to create a blinking insertion point), and
then dragging the cell's column marker. You can change the width of
an entire column by selecting the column and then dragging the
column marker.

Normally, when you resize a cell or column, the width of other cells
or columns remains the same. As a result, the total width of the table
increases or decreases.

Before resizing column 1 — table width is 4 inches

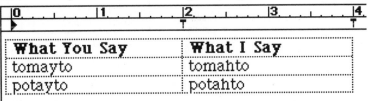

After resizing column 1 — table width is 3.5 inches

If you want to resize a cell or column without changing the table's
overall width, press the Shift key while dragging the column marker.
With this approach, Word adjusts the size of adjacent cells to maintain
the table's overall width.

Column 1 resized while pressing the Shift key — Word adjusts
the width of column 2 to maintain the original table width

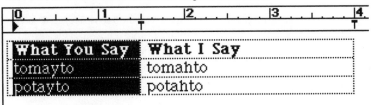

Formatting a table with the Table Cells command

The Format menu's Table Cells command lets you specify:

✦ precise values for cell and column widths

✦ that one or more rows of the table be indented from the document's left margin

✦ the amount of space between columns

✦ the alignment of one or more rows relative to the document's left and right margins

When you choose the Table Cells command, the Table Cells dialog box appears.

Controls row height

Controls space between columns

Indents selected row(s) from left margin

Left-aligns, centers, or right-aligns table within the page margins

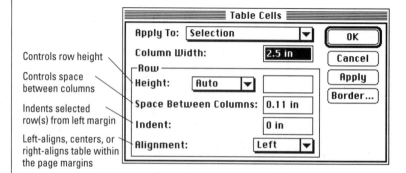

The options you specify in this dialog box apply to the cells that you selected before choosing the command. As the following table shows, you can also use the dialog box's Apply To pop-up menu to apply your changes in other ways.

Ways to apply Table Cells options

To apply formatting to...	Select this option...
Only those cells you selected before choosing the command	Selection
The column(s) containing the selected cell(s)	Entire Columns Selected
The row(s) containing the selected cell(s)	Entire Rows Selected
The entire table	Each Cell in Table

These options are handy if you forget to select the appropriate cells, rows, or columns before choosing the Table Cells command. Instead of having to close the Table Cells dialog box, reselect the appropriate parts of the table, and then choose the Table Cells command again, simply choose the desired options from the Apply To pop-up menu.

If you want to apply your changes to the table without closing the Table Cells dialog box, click the Apply button instead of clicking OK or pressing Return. This lets you experiment with different formatting options without having to choose the Table Cells command over and over again.

Adjusting the height of rows

When you need to adjust the height of one or more rows, use the Table Cells command. Normally, Word sets the height of a row to accommodate the largest item in that row.

Word increases row height to accommodate the largest item in the row

What YOU Say	What I Say
tomayto	tomahto
potayto	potahto

You can specify a precise row height by typing the value in the Row Height box in the Table Cells dialog box.

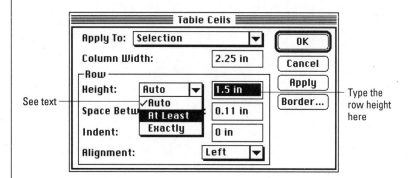

See text ←

Type the row height here →

Note that the Height pop-up menu lets you specify an exact row height or a minimum row height. If you choose Exactly, Word will not increase the row height to accommodate a larger font or graphic. If you choose At Least, Word will increase the row height if necessary.

You can also adjust the line spacing between rows by choosing the Paragraph command and specifying how much extra space you want before or after each paragraph. See Topic 5 for details on the Paragraph command and its dialog box.

Changing the layout of a table

When you want to change a table's cell, row, and column layout, use the Format menu's Table Layout command. With this command, you can:

✦ insert or delete cells, rows, or columns

✦ merge two or more cells into a single cell — for example, to create a heading that spans multiple columns

✦ split a merged cell into two or more cells

This topic's Step-by-Step section shows how to perform these jobs.

Converting text into a table

You can convert a table created with tabs into a cell-based table. You might use this feature to convert a tab-based table that was created in a different word processor or by the Copy Table command available in many telecommunications programs. Simply select the table and then choose Text to Table from the Insert menu as described in this topic's Step-by-Step section.

You can also use the Text to Table command to create a table from a series of paragraphs containing *tab-* or *comma-delimited* items — that is, items that are separated by tabs or commas. Many database programs can create tab- or comma-delimited text files. In a tab-delimited text file, the fields in each record are separated by tabs, and each record is separated by a carriage return. In a comma-delimited text file, the fields in each record are separated by commas, and each record is separated by a carriage return.

Comma-delimited text

Fred,Smith,123 Smith Street,Smithtown,PA,12983
Joe,Shmoe,1500 W. Joe Blvd.,Joeville,MO,93876

Tab-delimited text

Fred✦Smith✦ 123·Smith·Street✦ Smithtown✦PA✦ 12983¶
Joe✦ Shmoe✦ 1500·W.·Joe·Blvd.✦ Joeville✦ MO✦ 93876¶

This topic's Step-by-Step section shows how to convert tab- or comma-delimited text into tables.

Step-by-Step

This section contains instructions for creating tables, changing the size of columns and rows, inserting and deleting columns and rows, merging and splitting table cells, and converting comma- or tab-delimited text into a table.

To create a new table:

1. Position the insertion point where you want the table.

2. Choose Table from the Insert menu.

The Insert Table dialog box appears.

3. **In the Number of Columns box, type the number of columns you want.**

   Word automatically updates the value in the Column Width box to reflect the number of columns you've specified.

4. **Optional: In the Number of Rows box, type the number of rows you want.**

   This step is optional because Word will insert new rows for you as you add to the table. Still, you might perform this step if you want to create an empty table of a specific size to see how it will fit into the page layout.

5. **Click OK or press Return.**

   Word inserts an empty table. If you click the Format button instead of clicking OK or pressing Return, the Table Formats dialog box appears. This dialog box is described in "Formatting a table with the Table Cells command," in this topic's Overview section.

To change the width of one or more columns using the ruler and the mouse:

1. **If the ruler isn't visible, display it by choosing Ruler from the View menu.**

2. **Click the ruler's table scale button.**

   It's the T-shaped button at the far-right side of the ruler.

3. **Select the column(s) you want to resize by clicking the column selection bar(s) once.**

   The selection bar is the invisible area at the top of each column; when the pointer is in the selection bar, its shape changes to a down-pointing arrow.

4. **Drag the T-shaped column markers on the ruler left or right. Press the Shift key while dragging if you don't want to change the table's overall width.**

   As you drag, Word displays the column's width in the bottom-left corner of the document window. When you release the mouse button, Word resizes the column(s) and, if necessary, adjusts line breaks within cells.

To resize one or more columns using the Table Cells command:

1. **Select the column(s) you want to resize by clicking the column selection bar(s) once.**

   When the pointer is in the selection bar, its shape changes to a down-pointing arrow.

2. Choose Table Cells from the Format menu.

The Table Cells dialog box appears. The Apply To pop-up menu's Entire Columns Selected option is active. If you want to apply your changes to all the columns in the table, choose the Each Cell in Table option.

3. Type the desired width in the Column Width box.

4. To apply your changes without closing the dialog box, click Apply. Otherwise, click OK or press Return.

Word resizes the column(s) and, if necessary, adjusts line breaks within cells.

To change the height of a row:

1. Select the row(s) by double-clicking the selection bar to the left of the row(s).

When the mouse pointer is in the selection bar, it turns into a right-pointing arrow. Be sure to double-click; if you click once, you'll select only the first cell in the row.

2. Choose Table Cells from the Format menu.

The Table Cells dialog box appears. The Apply To pop-up menu's Entire Rows Selected option is selected. If you want to apply your changes to all the rows in the table, choose the Each Cell in Table option.

3. Type the desired row height, in points, in the Height box.

If you want to specify the height in inches, type *in* after the value. To specify the height in centimeters, type *cm* after the value.

4. Choose the desired height-control option from the Height pop-up menu.

If you choose Exactly, Word won't increase the row height to accommodate a larger font or graphic. If you choose At Least, Word will increase the row height if necessary.

5. To apply your changes without closing the dialog box, click Apply. Otherwise, click OK or press Return.

Word resizes the row(s).

To insert a column:

1. Position the insertion point in the column to the right of where you want the new column.

For example, to insert a column between columns 2 and 3 in the following illustration, you would position the insertion point in column 3, as shown in the following illustration.

Position the insertion point here...

1	2	3	4
	March	February	January
Western	150	160	2439
Eastern	309	384	398

...to insert a column here

Note that you don't have to select the entire column (although you can — the end result is the same).

2. Choose Table Layout from the Format menu.

The Table Layout dialog box appears.

3. Select the Column option.

4. Click the Insert button.

Word inserts a new column and shifts to the right the columns to its right. If you want to insert another column, choose Repeat Insert Columns from the Edit menu.

To delete a column:

1. Select the column you want to delete by clicking its column selection bar.

As an alternative to selecting the entire column, you can simply position the insertion point within one of the column's cells.

2. Choose Table Layout from the Format menu.

The Table Layout dialog box appears.

3. Be sure the Column option is selected.

If you didn't select the entire column, the Selection option is selected; click the Column option to select it, otherwise you'll delete only the cell containing the insertion point.

4. Click the Delete button.

Word deletes the column.

To insert a row:

1. Select the row below where you want the new row to be inserted by double-clicking its selection bar.

For example, to insert a row between Western and Eastern in the following illustration, you would select the Eastern row.

1	2	3	4
	March	February	January
Western	150	160	2439
Eastern	309	384	398

Select this row...   ...to insert a row here

2. Choose Table Layout from the Format menu.

The Table Layout dialog box appears.

3. Be sure the Row option is selected.

4. Click the Insert button.

Word inserts the row.

To delete a row:

1. Select the row you want to delete by double-clicking its selection bar.

2. Choose Table Layout from the Format menu.

The Table Layout dialog box appears.

3. Be sure the Row option is selected.

4. Click the Delete button.

Word deletes the row.

To combine two or more cells into a single cell:

1. Select the cells you want to combine by dragging across them.

The cells must be in the same row; you can't combine cells from different rows.

2. Choose Table Layout from the Format menu.

The Table Layout dialog box appears.

3. Click the Merge Cells button.

Word creates a single cell that is the same width as the cells you selected. The single cell contains the contents of the cells you merged, with each entry in its own paragraph.

Before merging

What You Say	What I Say
tomayto	tomahto
potayto	potahto

After merging

What You Say	What I Say
tomayto	tomahto
potayto	
potahto	

If, in the future, you need to split the cell back into multiple cells, you can do so by selecting the merged single cell, choosing Table Layout, and clicking the Split Cell button.

To convert comma- or tab-delimited text into a table:

1. Select the comma- or tab-delimited text.

Be sure to select the delimited text correctly: Include each line's paragraph mark, and don't include any paragraphs above or below the delimited lines. If you don't select the text correctly, Word may not be able to determine the appropriate number of columns to insert. The easiest way to ensure that you select each line correctly is to select it by clicking the selection bar to the left of the text.

2. Choose Text to Table from the Insert menu.

The Insert Table dialog box appears.

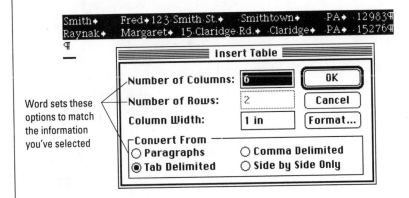

Word sets these options to match the information you've selected

3. Click OK or press Return.

Word creates a table and inserts each delimited entry into its appropriate cell.

Quick Tips

Working with the ruler in tables

When working with tables, you can put Word's ruler to work in a number of ways. As this topic's Step-by-Step section shows, you can use the table scale button to change the width of certain cells or entire columns. But you can also use the indent scale to indent text from the cell's left edge and to create hanging indents and first-line indents.

The ruler's zero point is at the left edge of a cell. If the ruler is displayed and the indent scale is selected, you'll see the zero point change as you move from one cell to the next.

Other ways to insert columns and cells

This topic's Step-by-Step section shows that you can insert one column by selecting a column and then using the Table Layout dialog box. Here are a couple of variations on the column-insertion theme:

◆ *You can insert a specific number of columns by selecting that many columns before choosing the Table Layout command.* For example, to insert two columns, select two columns and then choose Table Layout.

◆ *You can insert one or more cells and specify that adjacent cells be shifted to the right or shifted down.* To insert four cells, select four cells and then choose Table Layout. Finally, specify how adjacent cells should be shifted. The following illustration shows the effects of a horizontal and vertical shift.

Original table

		Sales Results		
	April	February	January
Western	150	160	2439
Eastern	309	384	398

Insert cells, shift horizontally

		Sales Results				
	April			February	January
Western	150			160	2439
Eastern	309	384	398		

Insert cells, shift vertically

		Sales Results		
	April		
Western	150		
Eastern	309	February	January
		160	2439
		384	398

Customizing menus for tables

If you work with tables extensively, you probably get tired of making trips to the Table Layout dialog box to insert and delete rows and columns and to shift cells horizontally or vertically. You can cut down on those trips by customizing Word's menus to include table layout commands. Choose Commands from the Tools menu, and then scroll through the list of commands. As the following table shows, Word provides numerous table-related commands.

Table-editing commands

Command name...	What it does...
Cell Borders...	Adds borders and shading to selected cell(s); see Topic 25
Delete Cells, Shift Left	Deletes selected cell(s), shifting adjacent cell(s) to the left
Delete Cells, Shift Up	Deletes selected cell(s), shifting adjacent cell(s) up
Delete Columns	Deletes selected column(s)
Delete Rows	Deletes selected row(s)
Insert ¶ Above Row	Adds a blank paragraph above the selected row
Insert Cells Down	Inserts new cells, shifting adjacent cells down
Insert Cells Right	Inserts new cells, shifting adjacent cells right
Insert Rows	Inserts as many new rows as you've selected
Merge Cells	Combines selected cells into one cell of the same overall width
Split Cell	Splits a merged cell back into separate cells
Show Table Grid Lines	Shows or hides the nonprinting dotted grid lines that surround each cell
TLBR Single Cell Border	Adds a border to the top, left, bottom, and right edges of the selected cell(s); see Topic 25.
TLBRVH Single Cell Border	Same as above, but also adds vertical and horizontal column borders; see Topic 25

By adding these commands to Word's menus, you can turn Word into a lean, mean table-editing machine. After adding the commands, use the Commands dialog box's Save As button to save your table-oriented menus in a settings file — perhaps one called Table Settings. Then, when you feel a table-editing session coming on, open the Table Settings file. When you've finished editing the table, use the Commands dialog box to open your standard settings file. (See Topic 34 for details on settings files and customizing Word's menus.)

Jim Heid's Word Companion, the disk set (sold separately) that complements this guide, contains several settings files, including one designed for creating and editing tables. See the order form at the back of this book for details.

Topic 24
Working with Tables

Keyboard shortcuts for inserting and deleting rows

Word provides keyboard shortcuts for inserting and deleting rows.

To do this...	Press...
Delete a selected row or series of rows	Command-Control-X
Insert a row or series of rows	Command-Control-V

Note that Macintosh Plus keyboards do not have Control keys.

You can also use the Commands dialog box to add keyboard shortcuts for the table-editing commands listed in the previous tip. See Topic 34 for details.

Changing the order of a table's columns

At times, you might need to change the order of columns in a table. In the following example, you might prefer to have the three months listed in chronological order rather than in alphabetical order.

1	2	3	4
	March	February	January
Western	150	160	2439
Eastern	309	384	398

To change the order of the columns in a table, you need to insert columns and then cut and paste the existing columns until they're in the correct order. To rearrange the columns in the preceding illustration, you might use the following routine.

1. **Select the March column and then insert a new column using the Table Layout command.**
   This makes room for the January column.

2. **Select the January column and then choose Cut.**
   This puts the January column on the Clipboard.

3. **Select the empty second column and then choose Paste.**
   The January column is now in the correct spot.

4. **Select the March column and then choose Cut.**
   This puts the March column on the Clipboard.

5. **Select the blank column where the January column used to be and then paste.**
   The columns are now in the correct order, but an extra column exists between January and February.

6. Select the extra column and then delete it using the Table Layout command.

As these steps show, significantly reorganizing the columns in a table can require an odyssey of cutting, pasting, inserting, and deleting. For this reason, try to plan the order of your table's columns ahead of time.

Changing the order of a table's rows

Fortunately, changing the order of rows in a table is a breeze. Simply activate Word's outline view, and then drag the rows up or down as needed.

When you're working in outline view, you can also use the keyboard to move a row up or down:

To move a row...	Press...
Up	Option-Up arrow
Down	Option-Down arrow

The Format menu's Table Cells and Table Layout commands are not available in outline view; to format table cells or change the table's layout, you need to be in the normal or page layout views. See Topic 29 for details on Word's outline view, and Topic 6 for details on switching between views.

Sorting a table

You can also reorganize the rows in a table by using the Sort command in the Tools menu. First, select the column you want Word to use for sorting, and then choose Sort. Word sorts the table's rows according to the column you selected.

To sort in descending order — from Z to A, for example — press the Shift key and then choose Sort Descending from the Tools menu. For details on Word's Sort command, see Topic 21.

Inserting a paragraph before a row

You've inserted a table at the beginning of a document, and then realize you need to add text above the table. You scroll to the top of the table, and find that you can't move the insertion point above the upper-left cell in the table. What to do? You could cut the table, insert the new text, and then paste the table, but there's an easier way: the cleverly named Insert ¶ Before Row command. This command inserts a blank paragraph before the selected row. (If you've selected several rows, the new paragraph is inserted before the topmost row.) Word assigns the style Normal to the blank paragraph.

You can add the Insert ¶ Before Row command to Word's menus, or simply use its keyboard shortcut: Command-Option-spacebar. If you use this command when the insertion point is in the middle of a table, Word splits the table and inserts the blank paragraph between the row containing the insertion point and the row above it.

Before inserting paragraph

1	2	3	4
	April	February	January
Western	150	160	2439
Eastern	309	384	398

After inserting paragraph

1	2	3	4
	April	February	January
Western	150	160	2439
Eastern	309	384	398

New paragraph

If you use CE Software's QuicKeys2 keyboard-enhancement utility, you can't use the Command-Option-spacebar sequence to issue the Insert ¶ Before Row command, since this key sequence displays QuicKeys2's quick reference screen. Either use Word's Commands command to assign a different key sequence to the Insert ¶ Before Row command, or use QuicKeys2 to redefine the key sequence for the quick reference card.

Converting a table into text

Just as you can convert text into a table, you can convert a table into text. You might want to do this in order to move the contents of a table:

✦ into a word processor or publishing program that doesn't provide its own table editor or that doesn't support Word's tables

✦ into a spreadsheet program other than Microsoft Excel

✦ into a database manager such as Claris FileMaker Pro

To convert a table into text, first select the table (the easiest way to do that is to press the Option key while double-clicking within the table). Next, choose Table to Text from the Insert menu to display the Table to Text dialog box.

Each cell becomes a paragraph

Each row becomes a paragraph; cells within each row are separated by tabs

Each row becomes a paragraph; cells within each row are separated by commas

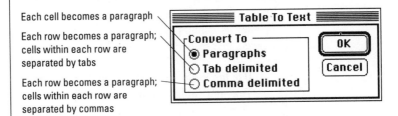

Choose the desired option and then click OK. Word removes the table's cells, but retains their contents, and separates each item with a paragraph mark, comma, or tab character, depending on the option you chose in the Table to Text dialog box.

Importing a table into Aldus PageMaker or QuarkXPress

You can import a table into Aldus PageMaker 4.0, but you must precede the table with a code that tells PageMaker to treat the table as tab-delimited text. To insert this code, perform the following steps:

1. Insert a new line before the table.

If necessary, use the Insert ¶ Before Row command described earlier in this section.

2. Type an uppercase *T* in the new line.

3. Save the Word document.

4. Import the file using PageMaker's Place command.

You can import a table into QuarkXPress without having to perform the preceding steps. Simply use QuarkXPress's Get Text command as you normally would.

When you import a table into PageMaker or QuarkXPress 3.1, each cell is imported as a left-aligned tab stop. To determine the spacing between tabs, PageMaker takes into account the column width and space between column settings that you specified in Word. Neither PageMaker nor QuarkXPress imports borders, shading, or row height formatting. (QuarkXPress, however, does import shading and borders for paragraphs; see the next topic's Quick Tips section for details.)

Exporting a table as a graphic

If you're moving a table into a different program and you want to retain all of a table's formatting, including borders and shading, you can do so by converting the table into a graphic, copying the graphic, and then pasting the graphic into the second program. You won't be able to use the second program to edit the table's text, change its font, or alter its column widths, however, so be sure the table appears as desired before performing the following steps.

1. Use the Preferences command's View option to turn off the Hidden Text and Table Gridlines options.

These steps effectively take a snapshot of the table as it appears on the screen, and you don't want hidden text or gridlines getting in the picture.

2. Select the entire table by pressing the Option key and then double-clicking anywhere within the table.

3. Press Command-Option-D.

As Topic 13 describes, this key sequence copies the selection to the Clipboard as a graphic.

4. Switch to the second program and choose Paste.

As an alternative, you can paste the "graphic table" into the Scrapbook. You can then open the Scrapbook in the second program, choose Copy, and then choose Paste.

Topic 25
Adding Borders and Shading

Overview

Graphic designers frequently use lines, or *rules*, to separate the columns or the rows in a table, as well as to emphasize graphics, captions, or key text passages.

In-margin subheads formatted with a thick top border

=== Top-Bordered Subheads ===

Selecting Rows, Columns, and Cells	You can select text within a cell using Word's standard selection techniques: drag to select a range of characters, double-click to select words, and triple-click to select paragraphs. (If a cell contains only one paragraph, triple-clicking selects the entire cell.)
	Word also provides some selection techniques that deal specifically with tables. You'll use these techniques when formatting, cutting, and reorganizing rows and columns.
	• Each cell has an invisible *cell selection bar* to its left. The cell selection bar works much like the selection bar that exists to the left of a paragraph: when the mouse pointer is within the selection bar, it changes to a right-pointing arrow.

Top, left, bottom, right table borders; top and bottom row borders

Frankie	Infects applications, not documents or system files. Infects only Atari computers containing certain Mac emulator hardware.	Draws bomb icon, displays, "Frankie says: No more piracy," then crashes.	Very rare. Doesn't infect genuine Macs. Doesn't spread under MultiFinder.
INIT 29	Infects any file (document or application) containing resources. Spreads only via applications and System files.	Its poor coding may cause printing problems, INIT conflicts, and MultiFinder crashes. If you insert a locked floppy disk, a dialog box appears saying the disk needs repairs. Normally, this dialog box doesn't appear with locked disks.	INIT 29 can spread very rapidly because it infects unlocked floppies as soon as they are inserted.
MDEF (strains A, B, and C; also called Garfield)	Infects applications, various system files, and documents.	System crashes. On Macs using CE Software's Vaccine, MDEF-A causes menus to work only in infected applications.	Often infects DeskTop, DA Handler, and Finder files. Strains B and C attempt to bypass watchdog INITs.

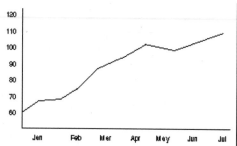

Double right table border separating a table containing
a graphic and caption from an adjacent column

Costs have risen considerably this year as a result of unstable world markets and fluctuating interest rates.

In March, costs began to rise at a faster rate as a result of unstable world markets and fluctuating interest rates. By reducing materials costs in our Fredericksville manufacturing plant and at the Wilson Research Facility, however, we were able to reverse the trend in April.

In mid-May, the Milford facility opened; costs relating to the opening were $103,398.

The Format menu's Border command lets you create these effects. If you've worked with publishing programs such as Aldus PageMaker or with drawing programs such as Claris's MacDraw series, you're probably used to drawing rules, boxes, and borders with the mouse. Word's border feature works differently; it automatically draws the lines for you, based on the paragraphs you've selected and on the border options you choose. For example, instead of drawing a box around a paragraph, you select the paragraph, choose Border, and then choose the box border style from the Border dialog box.

Specify the width of the border's lines here

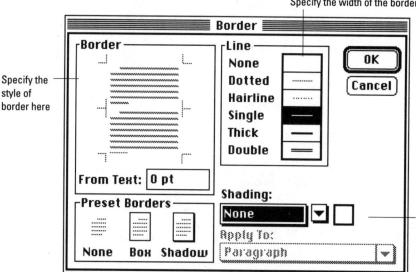

Specify the style of border here

Use these controls to shade the selected paragraph or table cells

By creating, resizing, and formatting table cells and then applying borders to them, you can even create complex forms.

This is a blank paragraph shaded 50 percent

Applicant Information

This paragraph has a top border

Do you purchase or recommend the purchase of any of the following?

Check all that apply

This is a four-column, four-row table

☐ Lawn care equipment   ☐ Wrenches
☐ Gardening supplies   ☐ Screwdrivers
☐ Electrical supplies   ☐ Power tools
☐ Plumbing supplies   ☐ Kitchen supplies

These columns are narrow and have borders

How many employees does your company have?

Check one

☐ 1-50   ☐ 100-200
☐ 51-99   ☐ More than 200

You can apply borders to any or all of the four sides of a paragraph or table cell — its left, top, right, and bottom edges — in any combination.

In some ways, working with borders isn't as straightforward as drawing lines with a mouse — the Border dialog box can be a bit confusing at first, and mastering it requires some practice. But Word's approach to borders and rules also has advantages: You don't have to worry about lines not being straight or the right length, the borders and lines stay with their text during editing or reformatting, and you can create style sheets that apply borders quickly and automatically.

Shading

Graphic artists also use shades of gray, called *screens,* to emphasize portions of a document or highlight every other row in a table to make the table easier to read.

Description	Index	Color	Height	Width	Depth	Weight	Collect
Widget	349	Red	35	24	39	34.56	Yes
Gizmo	387	Blue	39	88	73	4.56	No
Thingy	388	Green	2	4	9	4.35	No
Whatzit	338	Brown	9	8	6	9.98	Yes
Whatever	987	Red	98	77	6	533.24	Yes
Thingy	388	Green	2	4	9	4.35	No
Whatzit	338	Brown	9	8	6	9.98	Yes

Topic 25
Adding Borders and Shading

Word's shading features let you create these effects. Using the Border dialog box, you can apply shading in ten-percent increments or in any degree you specify.

Like Word's line spacing controls, borders and shading work at the paragraph level — they apply to an entire paragraph or table cell. This means you can't create a border for an individual word within a paragraph, nor shade a single word within a paragraph. But there's also a positive side to having borders and shading as paragraph attributes: You can define a style sheet that incorporates them and then apply them quickly throughout a document.

Borders and shading can't guarantee readable or professional-looking documents; if you go overboard with either effect, you'll decrease legibility and make the document look tacky. This topic's Quick Tips section contains some advice for applying borders and shading.

Applying borders

Applying a border requires two basic steps:

◆ Select what you want to apply the border to — a paragraph or a series of paragraphs, or a table cell, a series of cells, a series of rows and columns, or an entire table.

◆ Choose Border from the Format menu and then use the Border dialog box to specify the kind of border you want. You can also apply shading at this step if you like.

The Border dialog box lets you create a simple box or a shadowed box with a single mouse click. For creating other border arrangements — a line above a paragraph, for example — you need to use the *border sample,* the small preview page in the Border dialog box, as shown in the following illustration.

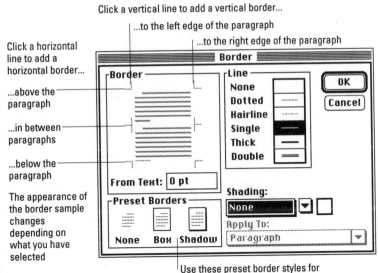

Click a vertical line to add a vertical border...

...to the left edge of the paragraph

...to the right edge of the paragraph

Click a horizontal line to add a horizontal border...

...above the paragraph

...in between paragraphs

...below the paragraph

The appearance of the border sample changes depending on what you have selected

Use these preset border styles for a boxed or shadowed paragraph

The Line area of the Border dialog box lets you choose from several line styles. The following table describes the styles.

Line styles

Line Style	Description
Dotted	1-point dots with 1 point of space between them
Hairline	The narrowest line your printer can produce; appears as a 1-point line on the screen, and prints as a 1-point line on non-PostScript printers
Single	1 point wide
Thick	2 points wide
Double	Two 1-point lines with 2 points of space between them

Adjusting the space between a border and adjacent text

Word adds 2 points of spacing between a border and the text adjacent to it. You can increase this amount by typing the desired spacing in the From Text box. Word adds the value you type to the 2 points it provides automatically, so if you want 8 points of space between the border and the text, for example, type 6 in the From Text box. You can add up to 31 points of extra space. (There are 72 points in an inch.)

If you want to change the spacing between a border and its adjacent text, be sure the border is selected in the border sample before typing a value in the From Text box. Otherwise, Word will ignore the value you type. A selected border has diamond-shaped handles on each side.

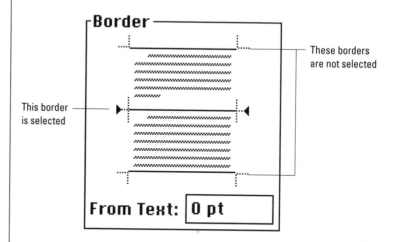

If you find yourself wondering why Word isn't changing a border even though you keep typing various values in the From Text box, chances are you forgot to select the border in the border sample.

Controlling how borders are applied in tables

When you select any part of a table and choose the Border command, you'll notice the Apply To pop-up menu gives you options that let you specify what part of the table you want to add borders to. The following table describes the Apply To options that deal with table cells.

Ways to apply borders to table cells

To apply borders to...	Select this option...
Only the cell(s) you selected before choosing Cells, the Borders command	Selected Cell (or Selected if you selected more than one cell)
The column(s) containing the selected cell(s)	Entire Columns Selected
The row(s) containing the selected cell(s)	Entire Rows Selected
The entire table	Each Cell in Table
All paragraphs in the selected cell(s)	Paragraph

Other ways to control how borders are applied

If you've selected more than one item that can have borders — for example, a graphic, a table, and a paragraph or two — the Border dialog box's Apply To pop-up menu includes additional options.

Ways to apply borders in a mixed selection

To apply borders to...	Select this option...
A graphic	Picture
The outer edges of a table	Table

Removing borders

You can also use the Borders command to remove one or more borders. First, select the bordered item and then choose Borders. Then, to remove all borders, click the None option in the Preset Borders area. If you want to remove only certain borders, first click the None option in the Line area, and then, in the border sample, click the borders you want to remove.

Step-by-Step

This section shows how to create several types of borders for paragraphs, and how to shade paragraphs or table cells. For details on creating various border arrangements for tables, see this topic's Quick Tips section.

To create a box around a paragraph:

1. **Select the paragraph or click within it to create a blinking insertion point.**

2. **Choose Border from the Format menu.**
   The Border dialog box appears.

3. **Click the Box option in the Preset Borders area.**

4. **Optional: Choose the desired line style in the Line area.**
   If you don't perform this step, Word uses a single-line (1-point) style.

5. **Optional: Type the desired space in the From Text area.**
   If you don't perform this step, Word puts 2 points of space between the border and adjacent text. If you type a value, Word adds it to the 2 points it uses automatically. Typing 4, for example, produces a total of 6 points of space.

6. Click OK or press Return.
Word creates a box around the selected paragraph.

To create a vertical line between two columns of text:

1. Select all the paragraphs in the rightmost column of text.

2. Choose Border from the Format menu.
The Border dialog box appears.

3. Click the border sample, as shown in the following illustration.

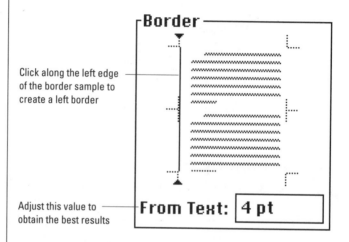

Click along the left edge of the border sample to create a left border

Adjust this value to obtain the best results

4. Optional: Choose the desired line style in the Line area.
If you don't perform this step, Word uses a single-line (1-point) style.

5. Optional: With the border in the border sample selected, type the desired space in the From Text area.
If you don't perform this step, Word puts 2 points of space between the border and adjacent text.

6. Click OK or press Return.
Word creates a line between the two columns, as shown in the following illustration.

Employee News

Our athletic shoe division took a step toward the twenty-first century this month when it purchased a robot to assist with manufacturing.

The robot threads shoelaces into track shoes at an astounding rate of speed. Human co-workers report that the robot is pleasant to work with and "doesn't complain much." In fact, the robot doesn't talk at all.

Nicknamed "TongueTied" by his co-workers, the 5' 6" tall robot was originally programmed to whistle as he worked. Fellow workers

Autographs, anyone?

TongueTied, our company robot, seems to have a competitive side to him. As a publicity gimmick, marketing entered him in a nation-wide computer games contest last week. Along with 1,200 kids, ages 9 to 14, TongueTied competed for top scores on arcade computer games. TongueTied rolled away with not only top honors, but the world-record score for all three games.

Although all prizes went to the humans, the company sponsoring the contest

newfound celebrity status. Marketing director Veronique Caspary announced in a televised press conference yesterday that TongueTied will soon begin autographing each pair of high-tech track shoes that he laces.

Will celebrity status change our mild-mannered TongueTied? He already lost a day of work while he practiced signing his name. Programmers say his natural writing is "rather flamboyant." They're trying to tone it down to fit on the side of a shoe.

To shade one or more paragraphs of text:

1. Select the paragraph(s).

2. Choose Border from the Format menu.

The Border dialog box appears.

3. Choose the desired shading percentage from the Shading pop-up menu, or type the amount in the Shading box.

See this topic's Quick Tips section for tips on which shading percentages to use for your printer.

4. Click OK or press Return.

Word shades the selected paragraph(s).

To shade every other row or column in a table:

1. Select the first row or column of the table.

To select a row, double-click the selection bar to the left of the row. To select a column, press Option and click within the column.

2. Choose Border from the Format menu.

The Border dialog box appears.

3. Choose the desired shading percentage from the Shading pop-up menu, or type the amount in the Shading box.

See this topic's Quick Tips section for tips on which shading percentages to use for your printer.

4. Click OK or press Return.

Word shades the selected row or column.

5. Select the third row or column of the table.

Topic 25
Adding Borders and Shading

6. Choose Repeat Border from the Edit menu or press Command-Y.
Word shades the selected row or column.

7. Continue selecting odd-numbered rows or columns (the fifth, seventh, ninth, and so on) until you reach the end of the table.
The fastest way to shade alternate rows or columns is to press Command-Y with one hand and select using the mouse with the other.

To remove shading from one or more paragraphs or table rows or columns:

1. Select the paragraph(s), row(s), or column(s).
To select a paragraph or row, double-click the invisible selection bar to its left. To select a column, press Option and click within the column.

2. Choose Border from the Format menu.
The Border dialog box appears.

3. Choose None from the Shading pop-up menu.
You can also type *none* in the Shading box.

4. Click OK or press Return.

Quick Tips

Shading guidelines

The ideal percentage of shading to use depends on two factors:

◆ *Your printer's resolution.* The higher the resolution of a printer, the lighter a given shade will appear. An Apple ImageWriter II can produce only about 144 dots per inch, while a LaserWriter can produce 300, and an imagesetter, over 1000. Because shading involves turning on a certain percentage of dots per inch, a ten-percent gray shade printed on an ImageWriter will be much darker than a ten-percent gray printed on a LaserWriter, and the LaserWriter's ten-percent gray will be darker than an imagesetter's. For this reason, it's important to choose shading percentages based on the printer you'll use to print the final version of a document. For 300-dpi laser printers, start with 15- or 20-percent gray and then tweak the shading as needed. If you're using a dot-matrix printer such as an ImageWriter, use the percentages that are multiples of 12.5 — 12.5, 25, 37.5, 50, 62.5, 75, and 87.5.

✦ *The text you're shading*. Smaller type sizes can break up and become difficult to read when shading is applied to them. Sans-serif typefaces such as Helvetica, Avant Garde, and Futura stand up to shading better than serif typefaces such as Times, Century Schoolbook, and Palatino.

Creating borders for tables

You can create a wide variety of border schemes for tables and their cells. A horizontal line between each row of a table can make a wide table easier to read by separating and guiding the eyes across each line. A vertical line between each column can separate parallel paragraphs nicely.

The table below shows how to configure the Border dialog box's border sample to create various border schemes. Before choosing Border, be sure to select the entire table. (The quickest way to do so is to press Option while double-clicking within the table.)

Table border arrangements

To...	Configure the border sample like this...
Enclose a table within a box and create a horizontal line between each row	
Create a vertical line between each column of a table	
Create a horizontal line between each row of a table	

(continued on next page)

To...	Configure the border sample like this...
Enclose a table within a box	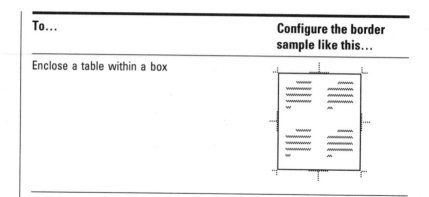

Creating reverse type

You can use the Border dialog box's shading option to format a paragraph or part of a table in *reverse type* — white type on a black background. Here's how:

1. **Select the paragraph or table cell, column, or row.**

2. **Choose Character from the Format menu.**
   The Character dialog box appears.

3. **Choose White from the Color pop-up menu.**
   This tells Word to format the selected characters in white.

4. **Click OK or press Return.**
   The text seems to disappear — that's because it's now white text on a white background. You'll fix this in the next steps. In the meantime, don't deselect the text.

5. **Choose Border from the Format menu.**
   The Border dialog box appears.

6. **Choose 100% from the Shading pop-up menu.**
   You can also type *100* in the Shading box.

7. **Click OK or press Return.**
   Word shades the paragraph or cell to black, allowing the white text to appear.

White text, 100-percent paragraph shading

Word shades the entire width of the paragraph margins

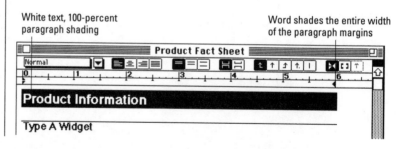

Vertically centering text within borders or shades

As the preceding illustration shows, depending on the type size and line spacing you use, reverse text may not be vertically centered within the black area. You may encounter a similar problem if you format a paragraph to have a border above and below it. You can fix both problems by formatting the paragraph's text as superscript text. Because Word raises superscript text above the baseline, the text will move up within the shaded or bordered area. Here's how:

1. **With the text selected, choose Character from the Format menu.**
   The Character dialog box appears.

2. **Click the Superscript button.**

3. **In the By box, type a value between 1 and 5.**
   You may need to experiment with this value to get the best results for the text you're formatting.

4. **Click the Apply button.**
   This applies the superscript formatting to the text without closing the Character dialog box. You can examine the results and adjust the superscript amount if necessary.

5. **When the text appears vertically centered, click OK or Close.**
   If you're formatting a heading or other short line as reversed type, see the next tip for details on formatting the line so that you don't have a black bar running the full width of the page or column.

Changing the width of borders and shading

Borders and shading always run the full width of the selected paragraph or table cell. If you want to format a heading or short line as reversed type, use the ruler's margin scale to decrease the width of that line so that you don't have a black bar extending all the way across the line.

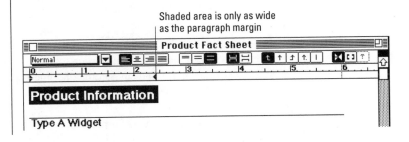

Shaded area is only as wide as the paragraph margin

You might also want to use this technique if you're creating a border above or below a heading. Simply change the heading paragraph's right margin so that it accommodates the heading's text.

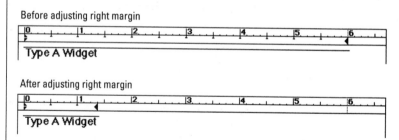

Before adjusting right margin

Type A Widget

After adjusting right margin

Type A Widget

Creating change bars with borders

Some word processors allow you to apply vertical *change bars* to text as you edit it. If you're circulating copies of a document for approval and revisions, you can use change bars to show readers what information has changed since the last revision, eliminating the need for them to reread the entire document every time. Word doesn't provide an automatic change bar feature, but you can use a left paragraph border to indicate paragraphs that have changed.

A left paragraph border indicates this paragraph has changed since the last revision

```
image replaces the existing image or is blended with it. For
blends, you can further specify that overlapping areas be
lightened or darkened.
     Another useful correction aid is a histogram, a bar
chart that shows the distribution of gray shades in the image
(see "Better Grays"). As you gain experience with image
processing, you'll be able to determine the degree of
correction an image needs by looking at its histogram.
     Fixing some contrast problems doesn't require fiddling
with gray maps or histograms. Simply choose your program's
```

By adding a left-border command to Word's menus (see the next tip), you can apply change bars to a paragraph quickly, and without having to use the Border dialog box.

Adding border schemes to Word's menus

If you frequently use a certain border scheme, you can add it to Word's Format menu and save yourself some trips to the Border dialog box. Here's how:

1. Choose Border from the Format menu.

The Border dialog box appears.

2. Specify the desired border arrangement.

3. Press Command-Option-equals.

The mouse pointer turns into a plus sign (+).

4. Click on the gray lines of sample text in the border sample or on the currently selected line style.

The menu bar flashes and the pointer reverts to its normal shape.

5. Click OK or Cancel.

If you examine the Format menu, you'll see a new command that describes the border arrangement you chose.

These border settings...

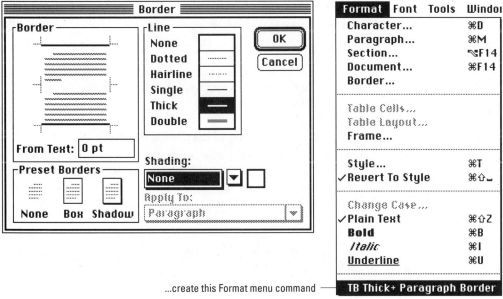

...create this Format menu command — TB Thick+ Paragraph Border

You can also add shading percentages to the Format menu: With the Border dialog box open, press Command-Option-equals, and then choose the desired shading value from the Shading pop-up menu.

See Topic 34 for more details on customizing Word's menus.

Paragraph borders vs. cell borders

You can create borders for table cells or for the paragraphs within the cells. What's the difference? If you create borders for the cells, the borders will touch; if you create borders for the cell's paragraphs, they won't touch, as shown in the following illustration.

Paragraph borders created using the Border button in the Paragraph dialog box

Check one

- [ ] 1–10
- [ ] 11–20
- [ ] 41–50

- [ ] 21–30
- [ ] 31–40
- [ ] more than 50

Borders created using the Border command

Check one

- [ ] 1–10
- [ ] 11–20
- [ ] 41–50

- [ ] 21–30
- [ ] 31–40
- [ ] more than 50

To create a border for a paragraph within a cell, choose Paragraph from the Format menu, and then click the Border button in the Paragraph dialog box.

Adding line spacing around horizontal borders

When you create horizontal borders between paragraphs or table rows, Word uses the current paragraph spacing setting to determine where to draw the horizontal borders. If you want to add more space between a paragraph or row and the border below it, select the paragraph or row and then choose Paragraph from the Format menu. In the Spacing area, type a value in the After box. To add more space between a paragraph or row and the border above it, type a value in the Before box.

No extra space before or after rows

ANTI, ANTI-B, ANTI-ange	Infects applications only (including the Finder), not other system files or documents.	Nondestructive but may cause crashes due to its poor programming.	Disinfected applications aren't identical to original, but generally still run. Best approach is to replace infected application with an uninfected copy from its master disk.
CDEF	Infects DeskTop file only, not system files, programs, or documents.	Slows performance. AppleShare server performance slows significantly.	You can remove this virus from an infected disk by rebuilding its DeskTop file: Press Command and Option while inserting the disk. For hard disks, restart and hold down Command and Option until rebuild dialog box appears. To avoid infecting an AppleShare server, do not grant "make changes" privilege to the server's root directory (desktop level).
Frankie	Infects applications, not documents or system files. Infects only Atari computers containing certain Mac emulator hardware.	Draws bomb icon, displays, "Frankie says: No more piracy," then crashes.	Very rare. Doesn't infect genuine Macs. Doesn't spread under MultiFinder.

4 points space added before and after rows using Paragraph command

ANTI, ANTI-B, ANTI-ange	Infects applications only (including the Finder), not other system files or documents.	Nondestructive but may cause crashes due to its poor programming.	Disinfected applications aren't identical to original, but generally still run. Best approach is to replace infected application with an uninfected copy from its master disk.
CDEF	Infects DeskTop file only, not system files, programs, or documents.	Slows performance. AppleShare server performance slows significantly.	You can remove this virus from an infected disk by rebuilding its DeskTop file: Press Command and Option while inserting the disk. For hard disks, restart and hold down Command and Option until rebuild dialog box appears. To avoid infecting an AppleShare server, do not grant "make changes" privilege to the server's root directory (desktop level).
Frankie	Infects applications, not documents or system files. Infects only Atari computers containing certain Mac emulator hardware.	Draws bomb icon, displays, "Frankie says: No more piracy," then crashes.	Very rare. Doesn't infect genuine Macs. Doesn't spread under MultiFinder.

Borders and desktop publishing programs

If you're creating a document that you'll import into a desktop publishing program, should you bother creating borders and adding shading in Word? It depends. Both PageMaker and QuarkXPress can import top and bottom paragraph borders, turning them into paragraph rules. You can modify the resulting rules in PageMaker by clicking the Rules button in PageMaker's Paragraph dialog box. In QuarkXPress, you can modify paragraph rules by choosing Rules from QuarkXPress's Edit menu.

Both PageMaker and QuarkXPress ignore shading as well as borders located on the left or right edges of a paragraph.

Topic 26

Creating a Table of Contents

Overview

Books, manuals, and lengthy reports often begin with a table of contents that lists the page number upon which each chapter or section begins. Word can create and update tables of contents automatically.

Or at least semiautomatically. Word will compile a table of contents for you, and it will update a table of contents when editing or refor-matting alters your document's page breaks. But first, you must indicate which items you want included in the table of contents. You can do this in either of two ways:

♦ *By applying Word's built-in heading styles to chapter titles and section headings.* When you create a document using Word's outline view, Word automatically applies these styles to the headings in the outline. (The outline view is discussed in Topic 29.) Because an outline uses a hierarchical format to show the relationship between the sections in the document, its headings translate nicely into a multilevel table of contents, as shown in the following illustration.

This outline...

- Chapter 1–Printers
    - Some History
    - Types of Printers
        - Laser Printers
        - Dot Matrix Printers
        - Ink Jet Printers
        - Color Printers
    - Shopping for Printers
        - How to Find the Best Price
        - Buying Supplies
        - Recycling Toner Cartridges
- Chapter 2–Paper
    - How to Choose Paper
    - Paper Details
        - The Wire Side versus the Felt Side
        - Paper Finishes

♦ *By inserting a code, called a* contents code, *at the beginning of each chapter or section whose name you want to include in the table of contents.* When you tell Word to create or update the table of contents, it repaginates the document, looks for contents codes, and then gathers and formats their text.

Working with contents codes requires a bit more effort than using heading levels, but it allows for more flexibility in formatting a table of contents.

Coding table-of-contents entries

Word's table-of-contents codes make use of that unusual character-formatting style, hidden text. To indicate that you want a chapter or section title to appear in your document's table of contents, you surround it with the contents code.

Denotes beginning of
contents entry

Denotes end of
contents entry

```
..c..Chapter 1-Laser Printers.:.
```

The contents code will not appear on your screen unless you use the Preference command's View option to have Word show hidden text.

You insert a contents code by selecting the text you want to include in the table of contents, and then choosing TOC Entry from the Insert menu. Each entry can contain up to 252 characters.

You can indicate a section within a chapter by including a number within its table-of-contents code. When Word creates the table of contents, it indents these subordinate sections to show that they're part of a larger section.

These codes...

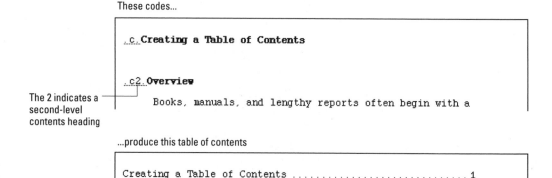

```
..c..Creating a Table of Contents


..c2..Overview
     Books, manuals, and lengthy reports often begin with a
```

The 2 indicates a second-level contents heading

...produce this table of contents

```
Creating a Table of Contents ............................ 1
    Overview .......................................... 1
```

You can indicate up to nine levels within a table of contents.

Page numbers in the table of contents

In most cases you'll want Word to include page numbers for the entries in the table of contents — after all, that's probably why you're creating the table of contents in the first place. But there may be times when you will want to suppress page numbers for some or all of the entries. For example, you might want to have page numbers for the sections within a chapter, but no page number for the chapter title itself, as shown in the following illustration.

You can tell Word to suppress the page number for a single item by including a colon (:), formatted as hidden text, after the item's name.

.·.c.·.Topic 26--Creating a Table of Contents:·.

Colon character formatted
as hidden text

If you want to include a colon or a semicolon (which marks the end of a contents entry) in the entry itself, you need to enclose the entire entry's text within single quotes (') that are formatted as hidden text. This topic's Step-by-Step section contains more details.

If you will be importing your document into a desktop publishing program where you'll change its formatting extensively, you probably won't want to include any page numbers at all. By suppressing the page numbers, you can create a list of the document's headings and sections, and then import that list into the publishing program. You can then use the publishing program to add page numbers after you've finalized the publication's appearance.

You can suppress page numbers for every item in the table of contents by unchecking the Show Page Numbers option in the Table of Contents dialog box.

Generating the table of contents

To create a table of contents after you've applied heading styles or coded the entries, choose Table of Contents from the Insert menu. The Table of Contents dialog box appears.

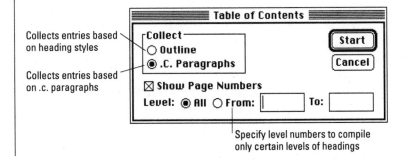

Collects entries based on heading styles

Collects entries based on .c. paragraphs

Specify level numbers to compile only certain levels of headings

When you click OK in the dialog box, Word repaginates the document to ensure that its page numbers are accurate; the page numbers themselves are determined by the starting page number you specified in the Section dialog box. Word then generates the table of contents, inserting it in its own section at the beginning of the document. (See Topic 22 for details on Word's ability to divide a document into sections.) Word places the table of contents in its own section so that you can apply a different page-numbering scheme to it — such as lowercase Roman numerals (i, ii, iii).

Word doesn't include text in headers, footers, or footnotes in a table of contents.

If you've linked numerous documents together using Word's File Series button (in the Document dialog box), you can compile a table of contents whose entries span the entire group of documents. Be sure the insertion point is in the first document of the series, and then choose Table of Contents. For details on linking documents, see Topic 31.

Formatting and editing a table of contents

Word automatically formats a table of contents using up to nine standard (built-in) styles named *toc 1, toc 2,* and so on, through *toc 9,* each for its own level in the table of contents. Each style is based on the Normal style, but has successively larger left-margin indents to show up to nine levels of headings. Each style also has tab stops that allow Word to draw a row of leader dots across the line to the page number, which is aligned against the right margin.

You can reformat a table of contents by using the Format menu's Styles command to alter the style definitions. (Topic 11 describes Word's style sheet features.)

You can also reformat a table of contents as you would format any text — by using the ruler and ribbon and the Font and Format menus.

You can edit the entries in a table of contents using any or all of Word's text-editing features.

Step-by-Step

This section contains instructions for inserting and modifying table-of-contents codes and for creating and updating tables of contents.

To insert a table-of-contents code:

1. Select the text that you want included in the table of contents.

A single table-of-contents entry can contain up to 252 characters.

2. **Choose TOC Entry from the Insert menu.**

Word inserts the .c. table-of-contents code, formatted as hidden text. If the Hidden Text box is checked in the Preferences command's View option, you can see the code.

To change the level of a contents entry by editing its contents code:

1. **Be sure the Hidden Text box is checked in the Preferences command's View option.**

You can't edit a code if you can't see it.

2. **Click the I-beam pointer after the *c* in the contents code.**

The blinking insertion point must be between the *c* and the period that follows it.

3. **Type a number between 2 and 9 to indicate the level of the table-of-contents entry.**

The entry .c1. is the same as the entry .c. — both refer to a first-level table-of-contents entry.

To suppress the page number for a specific entry:

1. **If you haven't already, type the entry's text and then format it as a contents entry by selecting it and choosing TOC Entry from the Insert menu.**

2. **After the text of the entry, type a colon (:).**

3. **Format the colon as hidden text.**

Select the colon, choose Character from the Format menu, and check the Hidden box. Or simply use the keyboard shortcut for hidden text: Command-Shift-X.

To include a semicolon or colon in a table-of-contents entry:

1. **If you haven't already, type the entry's text and then format it as a contents entry by selecting it and choosing TOC Entry from the Insert menu.**

2. **Enclose the entire text — including the colon or semicolon — within single quote marks.**

Press the key to the left of the Return key for a single quote mark. The quote mark can be a typewriter-style quote (straight up and down) or a typographer's curly quote obtained through Word's smart quotes feature.

Topic 26
Creating a Table of Contents

3. **Format both quote marks as hidden text.**

Select one, press Command-Shift-X, and then select the other and press Command-Shift-X.

To compile or update a table of contents:

1. **Choose Table of Contents from the Insert menu.**

The Table of Contents dialog box appears.

2. **Select the .c. Paragraphs or Outline option, depending on how you've formatted your contents entries.**

3. **If you don't want to include page numbers in the table of contents, uncheck the Show Page Numbers check box.**

4. **If you want to include only certain levels of entries in the table of contents, type the entry values in the From and To boxes.**

For example, to collect levels 1 through 3, type 1 in the From box and 3 in the To box. To collect only level 2 entries, type 2 in both boxes.

5. **Click Start or press Return.**

If the document already contains a table of contents, Word asks if you want to replace the existing one. If you're updating an existing table of contents, click Yes. Word compiles the table of contents and inserts it, in its own section, at the beginning of the document.

Quick Tips

Creating multiple lists in a document

Books and technical manuals often contain lists of illustrations, tables, or figures as well as a standard table of contents. You can create multiple lists by using a different set of heading or table-of-contents levels for each type of list. For example, you might use:

✦ levels 1 through 4 for the main table-of-contents entries

✦ level 5 for the list of figures

✦ level 6 for the list of tables

Then, to compile each list:

1. **Choose Table of Contents from the Insert menu.**

2. **Type the appropriate level number(s) in the Table of Contents dialog box.**

To compile the list of figures using the values in the preceding example, you would type 5 in the From and To boxes.

3. Click Start or press Return.

Word compiles the list that corresponds to the levels you specified.

4. Choose Table of Contents again.

5. Type the appropriate level number(s) in the Table of Contents dialog box.

6. Click Start or press Return.

7. When Word asks if you want to replace the existing table of contents, click No.

8. Repeat these steps for each list you want to create.

When you use this technique, be sure to compile the main table of contents last. This way, you can include the other lists in the main table of contents. And because Word always inserts a list at the very beginning of the document, the main table of contents will appear first in the document.

Notes about .c. contents codes

Here are a few subtle points to note about .c. contents codes:

✦ A contents code doesn't actually have to end with a hidden-text semicolon (;). If the semicolon is missing, Word includes the entire paragraph (or its first 252 characters) in the table of contents.

✦ You can create a contents entry for a paragraph or section that doesn't have its own heading in the document. Simply type the entry, insert the contents code, and then format the whole shebang — including the text you typed — as hidden text.

✦ You can include only part of a paragraph's text in a table of contents by placing a hidden-text semicolon after the portion you want to include. For example, in the following illustration, only the text "Once upon a time" will be included in the table of contents.

Codes mark the beginning
and end of the contents entry

.c.Once upon a time; all stories began with the phrase "once upon a time."

If you create a contents entry by selecting existing text and then choosing TOC Entry, Word adds the end-of-entry semicolon for you.

Tables of contents and Aldus PageMaker

The Aldus PageMaker desktop publishing program provides its own automatic table-of-contents features. PageMaker can import table-of-contents entries that you format using Word's outline heading styles or .c. contents codes. However, PageMaker ignores end-of-entry semicolons; PageMaker always includes an entire paragraph as a table-of-contents entry.

Topic 27
Creating an Index

Overview

A good index is at least as important as a good table of contents.
Word provides indexing features that enable you to mark words,
phrases, or sections that you want listed in the index. You can then
compile the index, which Word inserts in a separate section at the end
of the document.

Word lets you create as ambitious an index as you want. You can
create simple indexes that have only one level of entry.

> birds 14, 15, 38
> cats 18, 36-49
> dogs 16, 18-36

You can also create complex indexes that have multilevel entries,
page ranges, and cross-references.

> Birds
> > ducks, 38
> > hawks, 14
> > hummingbirds ,15
>
> Cats
> > *see also specific breeds*
> > breeds of, 36-49
> > personalities of, 18
>
> Dogs
> > *see also specific breeds*
> > breeds of, 18-36
> > introduction to, 16

Word's indexing features are similar to its table-of-contents features. If
you've created tables of contents using Word's Table of Contents
command, you have a head start in learning how to create indexes.

Still, there's an art to creating an effective index. The choice of words you include, the number of cross-references to other index entries, and the total number of entries work together to determine an index's usefulness. In this topic's Quick Tips section, you'll find some tips for creating an index and a list of books that can help you learn more.

Inserting index entry codes

You indicate an index entry by surrounding it with an *index code,* a series of hidden-text characters. If you've used the Preferences command's View option to specify that Word show hidden text on the screen, you can see the index codes.

This text appears in the index and will print in the main part of the document

```
   • By applying Word's built-in .i.heading styles;. to
chapter titles and section headings. When you create a
document using Word's outline view, Word automatically
applies these styles to the headings in the outline. (The
outline view is discussed in Topic 30.) .i.outline:format
of;.Because an outline uses a hierarchical format to show the
relationship between the sections in the document, its
headings translate nicely into a multi-level table of
contents.
```

This text will appear in the index only; it will not print in the main part of the document

```
heading styles 1
outline
   format of 1
```

As the preceding illustration shows, you can format an index entry's text itself in hidden text so that it appears in the index, but not in the main part of the document. This enables you to create additional references to a section of text, to capitalize main entries, and to include a range of page numbers in the index instead of a single page number.

To mark an existing word or phrase as an index entry, simply select it and choose Index Entry from the Insert menu. Word surrounds the text you selected with the index code and the end-of-entry code, as shown in the following illustration.

Before choosing Index Entry

built-in █heading styles█ to chapter

After choosing Index Entry

built-in .i.heading styles; to

You may want to create an entry that appears in the index, but not in the main part of the document. For example, you might want an index entry for a person to be in last name – first name format in the index, but in first name–last name format in the main part of the document. You can create an entry that doesn't print in the main part of the document by formatting the entire entry as hidden text. First, choose Index Entry without first selecting any text. Word inserts an index code and end-of-entry code, and positions the blinking insertion point between the two.

After choosing Index Entry with no selection

Topic 30.) .i.;Because an

Insertion point positioned between
index and end-of-entry codes

You can then type the entry, which is automatically formatted in the hidden-text style.

Compiling the index

After you've inserted index entries, you can compile the index by choosing Index from the Insert menu. The Index dialog box appears.

Birds
   ducks, 38
   hawks, 14
   hummingbirds,15   Birds: ducks 38; hawks 14; hummingbirds 15

Index

Format: ● Nested
      ○ Run-in

Index Characters:
  ● All
  ○ From: ☐ To: ☐

Start

Cancel

As the illustration shows, you can specify that Word compile an index for all characters or for a specific range of characters. You might use the latter option when compiling a large index that would be too time-consuming to compile in one fell swoop. Word can also run out of memory when compiling large indexes; by compiling an index in two or more separate passes, you can work around this problem.

When you click OK in the Index dialog box, Word repaginates the document to ensure that its page numbers are accurate; the page numbers themselves are determined by the starting page number you specified in the Section dialog box. Word then generates the index, inserting it in its own section at the end of the document. (See Topic 22 for details on Word's ability to divide a document into sections.) Because the index is in its own section, you can apply different formatting to it — for example, you can format it to appear in two columns.

If you've linked numerous documents together using Word's File Series button (in the Document dialog box), you can compile an index whose entries span the entire group of documents. Be sure the insertion point is in the last document of the series, and then choose the Index command. For details on linking documents, see Topic 30.

Formatting and editing an index

Word automatically formats an index using up to seven standard (built-in) styles named *index 1, index 2,* and so on, through *index 7,* each for its own level in the index. Each style is based on the Normal style, but has successively larger left-margin indents to show up to seven levels of index entry.

You can reformat an index by using the Format menu's Styles command to alter the style definitions. (Topic 11 describes Word's style sheet features.)

You can also reformat an index as you would format any text — by using the ruler and ribbon and the Font and Format menus.

In addition, you can also edit the entries in an index using Word's standard text-editing features. If you anticipate having to update the index, however, it's better to indicate formatting such as italics and bold as part of the index entry; that way, you won't have to reformat the index when you update it. The following section describes how to indicate character formatting as part of the index entry.

Special formatting for index entries

By including other characters within an index code, you can add additional information to your index as well as fine-tune its appearance.

✦ You can create subentries — entries related to a larger category — by typing the main entry and the subentry, and then separating the two with a colon character (:). When you compile the index, Word lists subentries in alphabetical order beneath the main entry:

This index code... ——— `.i.Dogs:breeds of;`

...produces this entry ——— Dogs

breeds of 1

✦ You can indicate a range of pages in an entry by creating two separate entry codes: one at the beginning of the passage and one at the end. In the first entry, type an opening parenthesis — (— between the *i* and the second period of the entry code. In the second entry, type a closing parenthesis between the *i* and the second period of the entry code.

Place this entry code at the beginning of ——— `.i(.Dogs;`
the passage (in this example, page 16)

Place this entry code at the end of the ——— `.i).Dogs;`
passage (in this example, page 36)

Sample result ——————————— Dogs 16-36

✦ You can tell Word to format a page number or cross-reference in italics or bold by typing an *i* (for italics) or a *b* (for bold) between the *i* and the second period of the entry code. You can format a page number or cross-reference in italics *and* bold by including both characters, as shown in the following illustration.

This index entry code... —— ¡b¡.Best.pets.#see.Dogs;

...produces this result —— Best pets, *see Dogs*

✦ You can suppress an entry's page number by including two colon characters (::) after the entry's text.

¡.Dogs::

✦ You can include a comma or other character between the entry and the page number by typing the comma or other character after the entry's text.

¡.Dogs.;

If you want to include a colon or a semicolon (which marks the end of a contents entry) in the index entry itself, you need to enclose the entire entry within single quotes (') that are formatted as hidden text. This topic's Step-by-Step section contains more details.

Step-by-Step

In this section, you'll find instructions for inserting and typing index entries and for compiling and updating indexes.

To mark existing text as an index entry:

1. Select the text.

An index entry can contain up to 252 characters.

2. Choose Index Entry from the Insert menu.

Word surrounds the selected text with an index code, formatted as hidden text. If the Hidden Text box is checked in the Preferences command's View option, you can see the code. If you like, you can add formatting characters to the entry; see "Special formatting for index entries," in this topic's Overview section.

To create an index entry that will not print in the main part of the document:

1. With nothing selected, choose Index Entry from the Insert menu.

Word inserts the index and end-of-entry codes, formatted as hidden text, and positions the blinking insertion point between them.

2. Type the text for the entry.

You can include formatting characters in the entry; see "Special formatting for index entries," in this topic's Overview section. The text is automatically formatted as hidden text.

To include a semicolon or colon in an index entry:

1. If you haven't already, type the entry's text and then format it as an index entry by selecting it and choosing Index Entry from the Insert menu.

2. Surround the text — including the colon or semicolon — within single quote marks.

Press the key to the left of the Return key for a single quote mark. The quote mark can be a typewriter-style quote (straight up and down) or a typographer's curly quote obtained through Word's smart quotes feature or the Mac's own finger-twisting key sequence.

3. Format both quote marks as hidden text.

Select one, press Command-Shift-X, and then select the other and press Command-Shift-X.

To compile or update an index:

1. Choose Index from the Insert menu.

The Index dialog box appears.

2. Choose the Nested or Run-In option as desired.

The Nested option places each entry on its own line, indenting subentries; the Run-In option places subentries on the same line as the main entry.

3. Optional: Specify the range of characters you want to include in the index.

You might want to compile a large index in several passes to avoid out-of-memory problems; see this topic's Overview section for details.

4. Click Start or press Return.

If the document already contains an index, Word asks if you want to replace the existing one. If you're updating an existing index, click Yes. Word compiles the index and inserts it, in its own section, at the end of the document. You can cancel the Index command by pressing Command-period.

Quick Tips

Indexing tips

Here are a few tips for creating effective indexes.

♦ *Plan the index before making entries.* Consider the broad concepts as well as the details your readers will be searching for.

♦ *Use cross-references to describe each topic in as many ways as you can.* For example, you might use Creeks, Brooks, and Streams as cross-references for a main entry called Rivers.

♦ *Arrange entries logically, with the significant word first.* You may need to invert words to bring the important word to the key position. For example, instead of the entry "Abraham Lincoln," use "Lincoln, Abraham." Similarly, instead of "Signing of treaty," use "Treaty, signing of."

♦ *Use multilevel entries to group related entries.* The topic called Rivers, for example, might be nested within a larger topic called Bodies of Water. Multilevel entries can also make an index more useful by providing the specifics that a reader needs to find the appropriate passage.

Poor	Good
Macintosh, 12, 15, 17–21, 35	Macintosh
	Steve Jobs and, 12
	IBM PC versus, 15
	choosing, 17–21
	learning to use, 35

As the preceding example shows, if subentries require *with, and, versus,* and so on, change the word order so that the key word appears first in the subentry.

There's far more to creating an effective index than I've described here. For more background on the art of indexing, see *Words into Type* (Prentice-Hall) and *The Chicago Manual of Style* (University of Chicago Press).

Indexes and Aldus PageMaker

The Aldus PageMaker desktop publishing program has excellent indexing features. PageMaker can also import Word's index entries. Because it's often more efficient to edit text in a word processor than in a publishing program, you might want to use Word to add index entries to a document, and then import the document into PageMaker and use its indexing commands to generate the actual index after you've completed the publication and finalized its page breaks.

PageMaker handles index entries with page ranges (created using parentheses) differently than Word, however. PageMaker imports these entries as two individual page references separated by a comma. For example, if your Word document contains a start-entry code — .i(. — on page 1 and an end-entry code — .i). — on page 5, Page-Maker will create an entry that reads *Topic 1,5* instead of *Topic 1–5*.

Also, PageMaker supports only up to three total levels (a main level and up to two subordinate levels), not seven.

Topic 28

Creating Footnotes

Overview

Footnotes are comments, explanations, or notes of reference usually located below the main text on a page[1]. Footnotes can also appear at the end of a chapter or book, in which case they're called *endnotes*. Within the main text, one or more superior, or superscript, characters — usually a number — reference the footnote.

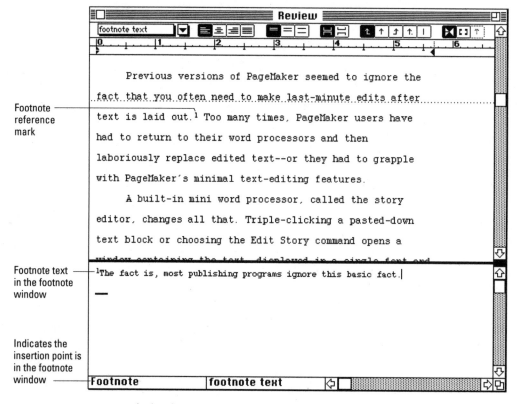

Footnote reference mark

> Previous versions of PageMaker seemed to ignore the fact that you often need to make last-minute edits after text is laid out.[1] Too many times, PageMaker users have had to return to their word processors and then laboriously replace edited text--or they had to grapple with PageMaker's minimal text-editing features.
>
> A built-in mini word processor, called the story editor, changes all that. Triple-clicking a pasted-down text block or choosing the Edit Story command opens a window containing the text displayed in a single font and

Footnote text in the footnote window

[1]The fact is, most publishing programs ignore this basic fact.

Indicates the insertion point is in the footnote window

Footnote   footnote text

[1] Like this one!

Word makes it easy to create footnotes and control where they appear. If editing or reformatting alters the document's page breaks, Word moves footnotes so that they remain on the same page as their references. You can use any character or combination of characters (up to ten) to reference a footnote. Better still, have Word automatically number the references for you as you create footnotes. If you insert or delete footnotes, Word renumbers the footnotes accordingly.

You can customize the appearance of footnotes and their references by altering Word's standard (built-in) footnote style sheets. You can create a customized footnote *separator,* which separates the footnote from the body text on the printed page. You can also create a *continuation notice* for footnotes that span more than one page.

Footnotes can include text, graphics, and tables. Don't insert table-of-contents or index entries in footnotes, however; Word ignores the contents of footnotes (as well as headers and footers) when compiling indexes or tables of contents.

Creating a footnote

To create a footnote, you must be working in normal or page layout view; you can't create a footnote in outline view. To switch to normal or page layout view, choose Normal or Page Layout from the View menu.

You use the Insert menu's Footnote command to create a new footnote. When you choose Footnote — or press its Command-E keyboard equivalent — the Footnote dialog box appears.

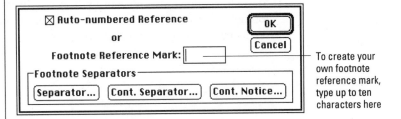

To create your own footnote reference mark, type up to ten characters here

If you're allowing Word to number footnotes for you, simply press Return. (Indeed, if you press Command-E and then Return, you can create an automatically numbered footnote without taking your hands away from the keyboard.) Otherwise, type the footnote reference (up to ten characters) and then press Return.

If you're working in normal view, the document window splits in two after you click OK in the Footnote dialog box. The fledgling footnote and the blinking insertion point appear in the bottom part of the window, as shown in the following illustration.

```
┌─────────────────────────────────────────────────────┐
│ ▣ ▤▤▤▤▤▤▤▤▤▤▤ Untitled2 ▤▤▤▤▤▤▤▤▤▤▤ ▣              │
├─────────────────────────────────────────────────────┤
│                                                  ⇧   │
│  sent the results of the survey to the Food and Drug Administration.[1] │
│  ─                                                   │
│                                                      │
│                                                      │
│                                                      │
│                                                  ⇩   │
│  1│                                              ⇧   │
│                                                      │
│  ─                                                   │
│                                                  ⇩   │
│ Footnote        footnote text      ⇦▯▨▨▨▨▨▨▨  ⇨▯   │
└─────────────────────────────────────────────────────┘
```

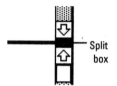

Split box

After you create the footnote, you can close the footnote window by double-clicking its split box or dragging it to the bottom of the document window. You can also click within the upper part of the window to return to the main body text, leaving the footnote window open for fast access.

If you close the footnote window and then need to reopen it to edit or reformat the footnote's entry, press Shift and then double-click the split box. Doing so opens the footnote window, which shows the footnotes on the current page.

Creating footnotes in page layout view

If you're working in page layout view when you click OK in the Footnote dialog box, the document window doesn't split to show the footnote window. Instead, Word moves the insertion point to the new footnote, which appears where it will appear when you print the document, as shown in the following illustration.

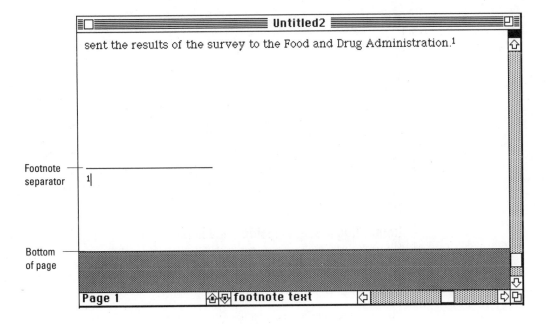

Footnote separator

Bottom of page

Formatting footnotes

The appearance of footnote references is controlled by a standard style called *footnote reference*. The footnote reference style is based on the Normal style, but with 9-point superscript text. The formatting of the footnote text itself is controlled by a standard style called *footnote text*. It's also based on the Normal style, but with the type size changed to 10 point.

You can reformat footnote references or text by using the Format menu's Style command to alter the appropriate style definition. If you want your changes to apply to the footnotes in new documents you create, click the Use As Default button in the Style dialog box. (Topic 11 describes Word's style sheet features in detail.)

If you redefine the appearance of the footnote reference style in a document that already contains footnote reference marks, Word doesn't update the appearance of the existing footnote reference marks. For this reason, if you want to redefine the appearance of the footnote reference style, try to do so before creating any footnotes.

You can apply any other style in your document to footnote text; you can't apply a different style to a footnote reference, however. Footnote references always use the style named *footnote reference*. Note that you can redefine the appearance of the footnote reference style.

You can reformat a footnote reference or text by using the ruler and ribbon and the Font and Format menus. To ensure a consistent appearance across all your document's footnotes, however, it's better to alter the footnote text or footnote reference styles.

Deleting and moving a footnote

Deleting a footnote is a cinch: Simply select the footnote reference in the main text and then press Delete (on some keyboards, Backspace). If the footnote was part of an automatically numbered series, Word renumbers the surviving footnotes accordingly.

You *can't* delete a footnote by deleting its text in the footnote window.

You can move a footnote to a different page by moving its reference to that page. Use the Cut and Paste commands or Word's drag-and-drop text-editing feature to move the reference. (See Topic 3 for details on moving text.)

Controlling footnote position and numbering

Normally, Word places a footnote at the bottom of the page containing its reference. On multiple-column pages, footnotes appear below each column.

You can use the Format menu's Document command to control where footnotes print as well as to control footnote numbering.

Start numbering at 1 for each page

To start numbering at a value other than 1, type the value here

```
┌──────────────── Document ────────────────┐
│ ┌─Margins────────────────────────┐        │
│ │ Left:  [1.25 in]  Top:  [1 in]  [At Least ▼] │  [    OK    ] │
│ │ Right: [1.25 in]  Bottom: [1 in] [At Least ▼] │ [  Cancel  ] │
│ │ Gutter: [0 in]    ☐ Mirror Even/Odd │ [Use As Default] │
│ └────────────────────────────────┘  [File Series...] │
│ ┌─Footnotes──────────────────────┐        │
│ │ Position: [Bottom of Page  ▼]   ☒ Widow Control │
│ │ ○ Restart Each Page             ☐ Print Hidden Text │
│ │ ◉ Number From: [1]              ☐ Even/Odd Headers │
│ │                          Default Tab Stops: [0.5 in] │
│ └────────────────────────────────┘        │
└───────────────────────────────────────────┘
```

The following table describes each option in the Position pop-up menu.

Footnote position options

To position footnotes...	Select this option...
At the bottom of the page, regardless of how much text is on the page	Bottom of Page
Below the last line of text on the page	Below Text
At the end of the current section	End of Section
At the end of the document	End of Document

If you're working in page layout view, Word always scrolls to the appropriate location when you create a new footnote — even if you specify that footnotes appear at the end of the document. This is another potential drawback of using page view: You'll do a lot more scrolling when working with footnotes.

Creating a custom separator

Word's standard footnote separator — a single line — is adequate for most tasks. Still, you might want to jazz up a document with a custom separator — perhaps a double horizontal rule. You can create a custom separator by clicking the Separator button in the Footnote dialog box. Doing so displays the footnote separator window.

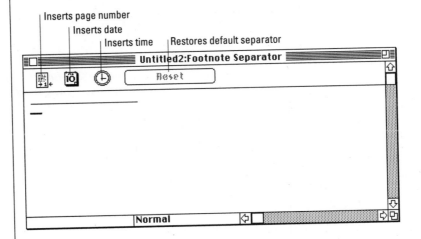

Inserts page number
Inserts date
Inserts time   Restores default separator

As the preceding illustration shows, the footnote separator window is virtually identical to Word's header and footer windows. Like them, the footnote separator window can contain text, graphics, and tables. And like them, the footnote separator window provides icons that allow you to insert the time, date, and page number into the separator. You can also display the ruler and ribbon for the separator. Clearly, you can create some pretty sophisticated footnote separators.

But don't go overboard. The footnote portion of a page isn't supposed to scream for attention; it's supposed to sit there unobtrusively and not distract the reader from the main text.

After you create a custom separator, close the separator window. If you're in page layout view, you can scroll to a page containing a footnote to see the new separator. If you're in normal view, you can see the new separator by opening the footnote window for a page containing a footnote.

It's worth noting that Word's line separator will not print on letter-quality printers such as daisy wheel printers. If you use such a printer, change the separator to one that's made up of characters your printer can produce, such as a row of hyphens (-) or underline characters (_).

Creating a continuation notice

If you have lengthy footnotes or a large number of small ones, they may not fit on the bottom of one page. For those cases, you can use the Footnote dialog box's Cont. Notice button to create a continuation notice that tells readers the footnotes continue on the next page.

When you click the Cont. Notice button, a continuation notice window opens. Like the footnote separator, header, and footer windows, the continuation notice window can contain text, graphics, and tables. Chances are, however, that you'll simply want a line of text saying *Continued on page xx.*

You can also create a customized *continuation separator,* which separates the footnote text from the continuation notice. Click the Footnote dialog box's Cont. Separator button to open the continuation separator window, which works just like the standard separator window described earlier.

Step-by-Step

This section describes how to create a footnote, edit an existing footnote's text, delete a footnote, copy a footnote, modify the footnote reference and footnote text styles, and control the positioning and numbering of footnotes.

To create a footnote:

1. **Be sure you're in normal or page layout view.**
   You can't create a footnote in outline view.

2. **Be sure the blinking insertion point is positioned where you want the footnote's reference.**

3. **Choose Footnote from the Insert menu or press Command-E.**
   The Footnote dialog box appears.

4. **Optional: Type the footnote reference (up to ten characters) in the Footnote Reference Mark box.**
   If you don't type a footnote reference, Word automatically numbers the footnote for you.

5. **Click OK or press Return.**
   Word creates the footnote and its reference, and moves the insertion point to the beginning of the footnote.

6. Type the footnote's text.

Footnotes can also contain tables and graphics. You can also paste items from the Clipboard.

7. Return to the main portion of the document. If you're working in normal view, you can close the footnote window by double-clicking the split box that divides the vertical scroll bar.

The easiest way to return to the main text is to use Word's Go Back keyboard shortcut: the 0 key on the number keypad. Otherwise, use the mouse to return to the main text. For more details, see "Creating a footnote" and "Creating a footnote in page layout view" in this topic's Overview section.

To edit or reformat an existing footnote while working in normal view:

1. Double-click the footnote's reference in the main text.

The document window splits to show the footnote in the footnote window.

2. Edit or reformat the footnote as desired.

3. Close the footnote window by double-clicking the split box that divides the vertical scroll bar.

You can also use the Command-Option-S keyboard shortcut.

To edit or reformat a footnote when working in page layout view:

1. Scroll until you can see the footnote.

If you've used the Document dialog box to specify that footnotes appear at the end of the document, you'll need to scroll to the end of the document. As an alternative to scrolling, you can open the footnote in the footnote window by following the previous set of steps.

2. Edit or reformat the footnote as desired.

To delete a footnote:

1. Select its reference in the main text.

2. Press Delete (on some keyboards, Backspace).

Word deletes the reference and the footnote.

To copy a footnote:

1. Select its reference mark in the main text.

Don't select the footnote text in the footnote window; this would copy only the text itself.

2. Choose Copy from the Edit menu or press Command-C.

The footnote is now on the Clipboard. You can paste it elsewhere by moving the insertion point and then choosing Paste from the Edit menu (or pressing Command-V).

To modify the footnote reference or footnote text style:

1. Choose Style from the Format menu.

2. Be sure the All Styles button in the Show area is selected.

If the Document Styles button is selected, Word shows only those styles that you've defined for the document; standard (built-in) styles don't appear.

3. In the styles list, select the style named *footnote reference* or *footnote text*.

The footnote reference style controls the formatting of the reference marks; the footnote text style controls the formatting of the text within footnotes.

4. Use the ruler and ribbon or the Format and Font menus to make the desired formatting changes.

5. Click the Define button.

6. If you want Word to use the redefined style in all new, untitled documents you create, click the Use As Default button.

If you click Use As Default, Word asks if you want to add the style to the default style sheet. Click Yes.

7. Click Close to close the Style dialog box.

If you click OK, Word applies the style to the paragraph containing the insertion point. You can restore the paragraph's previous formatting by choosing Undo.

To specify the position and numbering of footnotes:

1. Choose Document from the Format menu.

The Document dialog box appears.

2. Choose the desired option from the Position pop-up menu.

The options are described in this topic's Overview section.

3. Specify the desired numbering option.

If you select the Restart Each Page option, Word begins numbering at 1 on each page. If you select Restart Each Section, Word begins numbering at 1 in each section. The Restart Each Section option is available only if you choose End of Section from the Position pop-up menu. If you choose End of Document from the Position pop-up menu, you can't specify that Word restart numbering at 1.

Quick Tips

Numbering footnotes in linked documents

If you link documents using the Document dialog box's File Series button, you need to tell Word where to begin numbering each document's footnotes. For example, if the first document in a three-document series contains five footnotes, you need to open the second document and use Word's Document command to specify that its footnote numbering begin at 6. If the second document contains four footnotes, you need to open the third document and specify that its footnote numbering begin at 10.

You can avoid this chore by merging the documents using Word's INCLUDE print merge statement. When you combine multiple documents using INCLUDE, Word keeps track of footnote numbering across the documents.

For details on print merging, see Topic 31. For details on linking documents using the File Series button, see Topic 30.

Reusing a footnote

If you want to reuse a specific footnote repeatedly, save the footnote's reference mark as a glossary entry. You can then insert the footnote as often as you like. See Topic 16 for details on Word's glossary feature.

Exporting footnotes

Here are a few notes regarding footnotes and files:

+ If you save a document containing footnotes as a text-only file, Word retains the footnote reference marks and each footnote's text. The footnote text is placed at the end of the text-only file.

+ If you save a document containing footnotes as a MacWrite or MacWrite II file, Word groups the footnotes at the end of the document and places a hard page break between them and the main text.

+ If you save a document containing footnotes as a Word for DOS, Word for Windows, or WordPerfect file, Word exports the footnotes as footnotes. You can open the file in those programs and use their footnote features to work with the footnotes.

How do other programs treat Word documents containing footnotes? Aldus PageMaker and QuarkXPress retain footnote reference marks and footnote contents, but group the footnotes together at the end of the document. Frame Technology's FrameMaker imports the footnotes as footnotes.

Topic 29
Creating an Outline

Overview

With Word's outline view, you can develop outlines to flesh out the structure of a document. You can drag your ideas around, rearranging your document's furnishings until everything is just so.

You don't have to use tabs or paragraph indents to create an outline. You can indent headings by simply dragging them to the right. You can change the order of headings and paragraphs by dragging them up or down.

Word's outline view lets you write and reorganize not only headings and subheadings, but also your document's main text. You don't have to develop an outline in one document window, and then write the finished document in another. A document can grow from a skeletal outline of topics and subtopics to a formatted finished product — in one window. And you can switch between outline, normal, and page layout views at any time.

Use the outline bar to rearrange headings and control the appearance of the outline

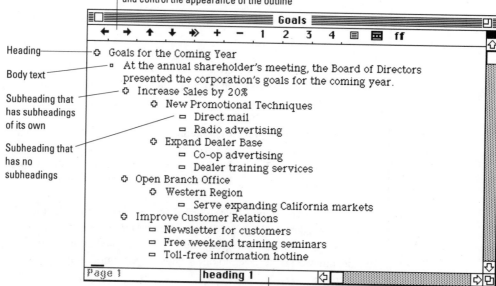

Nine standard styles — heading 1 through heading 9 — control the formatting of headings

As mentioned in Topic 6, you can even mix and match views within one document window: Split the document window by double-clicking the split box above the vertical scroll bar, and then choose the desired view for each of the window's two panes.

Word's outline view isn't just for outlines. You can use it to create to-do lists and to plan presentations and create overhead transparencies. You can use it to change the order of paragraphs or the rows in a table. You can use it any time you want to step back and look at the big picture of how a document is organized.

Outlining on a computer

There are four concepts behind electronic outlining:

* *Demote and promote.* These have nothing to do with office politics (at least not where outlining is concerned). Instead, they refer to the process of specifying a heading's pecking order in relation to the heading above it. When you want to indicate that Heading B is subordinate to Heading A, for example, you *demote* Heading B.

Before demoting

▢ Heading A
▢ Heading B

After demoting

✛ Heading A
   ▢ Heading B

* *Expand and collapse.* When you're fleshing out an outline and working with a large number of subhead levels and maybe even paragraphs, you might want to step back for the big picture every now and then. You can, by *collapsing* one or more topics to show only certain heading levels.

Expanded heading:
subheadings are visible

✛ Heading A
   ▢ Heading B

Collapsed heading:
subheads are hidden

✛ Heading A

Gray line indicates
collapsed heading

When you want to zoom in on the details, you can *expand* a topic. You can collapse and expand topics selectively and in varying degrees. For example, you might collapse one topic to show only its main heading, another topic to show two levels of subheads, and another to show every level.

The outline bar

Your control center for working with outlines is the *outline bar*, which appears at the top of the screen when you're working in outline view. (To switch to outline view, choose Outline from the View menu.) By clicking the outline bar's icons, you can promote and demote headings, move headings up and down, control the level of detail you see, and control the way the outline is displayed and printed.

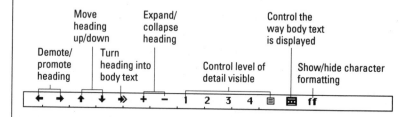

Creating an outline

To create an outline, switch to outline view and begin typing headings. In outline view, each heading is preceded by an outlined plus or minus sign. A plus sign indicates that the heading has subheadings. A minus sign means the heading has no subheadings. When you press Return after creating a heading, Word creates another heading at the same level.

Before pressing Return

○ The Main Point
  ▫ Introduction|

After pressing Return

○ The Main Point
  ▫ Introduction
  ▫ |

New heading created
at the same level

You can change a heading's level — promote or demote it — by dragging it left or right.

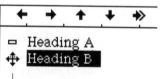

Point to the plus or minus
sign before the heading...

Dotted vertical bar moves as
you drag and aligns with the
tick marks in the outline bar

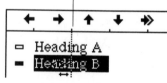

...drag to the right to demote,
or to the left to promote

You can move a heading up or down by dragging it.

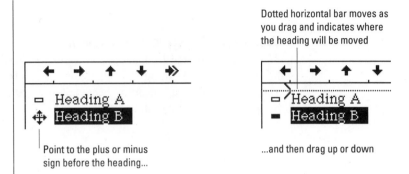

Dotted horizontal bar moves as you drag and indicates where the heading will be moved

Point to the plus or minus sign before the heading...

...and then drag up or down

When you promote or demote a heading or move it up or down, its subheadings move along with it, even if you've collapsed the heading. A main heading can have up to eight subheading levels.

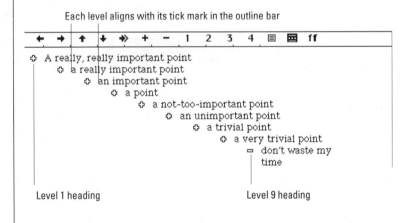

Each level aligns with its tick mark in the outline bar

Level 1 heading

Level 9 heading

You collapse a heading by double-clicking its plus sign. You can also expand and collapse the entire outline to show a specific level of heading by clicking the heading number in the outline bar.

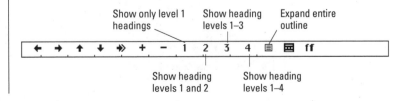

Show only level 1 headings

Show heading levels 1–3

Expand entire outline

Show heading levels 1 and 2

Show heading levels 1–4

You can also use the keyboard to promote and demote headings and move them up or down. This topic's Step-by-Step section shows how; all of Word's keyboard shortcuts for outlining are listed in this topic's Quick Tips section.

Working with body text in outline view

As mentioned earlier in this topic, you can write and edit not only headings and subheadings in outline view, but also entire paragraphs. You can specify that a heading become body text by clicking the body text icon in the outline bar.

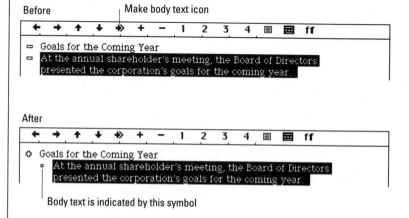

Another icon in the outline bar lets you control how body text is shown in outline view. You can choose to view entire paragraphs, or only the first line of each paragraph.

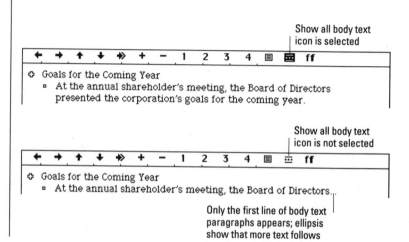

Formatting in outline view

When you promote or demote a heading, Word works behind the scenes applying a heading style. Word contains nine standard (built-in) styles that it assigns to heading levels. (The specific formatting behind each style is listed in this topic's Quick Tips section.) You can redefine the appearance of any heading style using the Style command. This topic's Step-by-Step section shows how.

When working in outline view, you can format characters, but not paragraphs — for example, you can switch from 12-point Courier to 18-point Times, but you can't switch from single spacing to double spacing. When you consider that outline view always shows your document as single spaced with no paragraph indents, this limitation makes sense. Accordingly, you can display Word's ribbon in outline view, but not its ruler.

For those times when you don't want to view an outline in its fully formatted glory, click the character formatting icon at the rightmost end of the outline bar. When this icon is not selected, Word shows the entire outline in one font, size, and style, and you can't format characters.

Selecting text in outline view

When you're working in outline view, you can select text using Word's standard text-selection techniques — dragging across text, double-clicking to select by the word, clicking the selection bar, and so on. When you drag across text, be sure you don't begin dragging by pointing to the plus or minus sign that precedes the heading. If you do, you'll drag the heading itself left or right.

Step-by-Step

This section shows how to promote, demote, expand, and collapse headings using the mouse and keyboard, how to turn a heading into body text, how to alter the heading styles Word uses, and how to number an outline using a standard outline numbering format. Each set of instructions assumes you're working in outline view; if you aren't, choose Outline from the View menu or press Command-Option-O.

To demote a heading using the mouse:

1. Point to the plus or minus sign that precedes the heading.
The mouse pointer turns into a four-sided arrow.

2. Press and hold down the mouse button.
Word selects the heading and any subheadings and body text that belong to it.

3. While still pressing the mouse button, drag to the right.

As you drag, a vertical dotted bar moves along with the mouse pointer.

4. When the vertical dotted bar is located at the desired heading level, release the mouse button.

Word demotes the heading and any subheadings and body text.

To demote a heading using the keyboard:

1. Position the insertion point within the heading you want to demote.

You don't have to select the entire heading.

2. Press Option-right arrow.

Word demotes the heading and any subheadings and body text.

To promote a heading using the mouse:

1. Point to the plus or minus sign that precedes the heading.

The mouse pointer turns into a four-sided arrow.

2. Press and hold down the mouse button.

Word selects the heading and any subheadings and body text that belong to it.

3. While still pressing the mouse button, drag to the left.

As you drag, a vertical dotted bar moves along with the mouse pointer.

4. When the vertical dotted bar is located at the desired heading level, release the mouse button.

Word promotes the heading and any subheadings and body text.

To promote a heading using the keyboard:

1. Position the insertion point within the heading you want to promote.

You don't have to select the entire heading.

2. Press Option-left arrow.

Word promotes the heading and any subheadings and body text. If there were headings at the same level below the heading you promoted, they become subheadings for that heading.

To expand or collapse a heading:

1. Double-click the plus sign that precedes the heading.

If the heading was expanded, Word collapses it. If it was collapsed, Word expands it. If the heading is preceded by a minus sign, it doesn't have any subheadings and therefore can't be expanded or collapsed.

To move a heading up or down using the mouse:

1. Point to the plus or minus sign that precedes the heading.

The mouse pointer turns into a four-sided arrow.

2. Press and hold down the mouse button.

Word selects the heading and any subheadings and body text that belong to it.

3. While still pressing the mouse button, drag up or down.

As you drag, a horizontal dotted bar moves along with the mouse pointer.

4. When the horizontal dotted bar is located at the desired heading level, release the mouse button.

Word moves the heading and any subheadings and body text.

To move a heading up or down using the keyboard:

1. Position the insertion point within the heading you want to move.

You don't have to select the entire heading.

2. Press Option-up arrow to move the heading up, or Option-down arrow to move it down.

The heading and any subheadings and body text move up or down but retain their levels.

To turn a heading into body text:

1. Position the insertion point within the heading.

You don't have to select the entire heading.

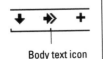

Body text icon

2. Click the body text icon in the outline bar.

Word turns the heading into body text.

To modify the styles Word uses to format headings:

1. If necessary, switch out of outline view and into normal or page layout view.

You can't modify styles in outline view.

2. Choose Style from the Format menu.

3. In the Show area, be sure the All Styles button is selected.

If the Document Styles button is selected, Word shows only those styles that you've defined for the document; standard (built-in) styles don't appear.

4. In the styles list, select the heading style you want to modify.

The heading styles are named *heading 1, heading 2, heading 3,* and so on, through *heading 9.*

Topic 29
Creating an Outline

5. Use the ruler and the ribbon or the Format and Font menus to make the desired formatting changes.

6. Click the Define button.

7. Optional: If you want Word to use the redefined style in all new, untitled documents you create, click the Use As Default button.
   If you click Use As Default, Word asks if you want to add the style to the default style sheet. Click Yes.

8. Click Close to close the Style dialog box.
   If you click OK, Word applies the style to the heading or paragraph containing the insertion point. If this isn't what you want, you can restore the paragraph's previous formatting by choosing Undo.

To number an outline using standard outline numbering:

1. In outline view, choose Renumber from the Tools menu.
   The Renumber dialog box appears.

2. Select the 1.1 button.

3. In the Format box, type I.A.1.a.i.

4. Click OK or press Return.
   Word renumbers the outline. If the results aren't what you want, you can remove the numbering by immediately choosing Undo from the Edit menu.

Quick Tips

Undo and outlines

If you move, promote, or demote a heading and aren't happy with the results, choose Undo immediately (or press Command-Z) and Word will restore the heading to its previous location or level.

Using outline view to create presentation materials

You can use outline view to create overhead transparencies or other presentation aids in which each main heading appears on its own page (or transparency), with its subheadings grouped below it, as shown in the following illustration.

As seen in outline view with formatting turned off

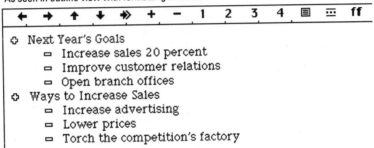

To achieve the formatting shown in the preceding illustration, first use the File menu's Page Setup command to change to wide orientation. Next, modify the styles that Word applies to headings as follows:

Style name	Formatting
heading 1	36-point Helvetica Bold, page break before, framed (centered vertically relative to page)
heading 2	36-point Helvetica Bold, 1-inch paragraph indent, framed (centered vertically relative to page)

By adding the Page Break Before paragraph-formatting option to the *heading 1* style, you tell Word to place each main heading on its own page. By framing both heading styles and specifying that they be vertically centered relative to the page, you tell Word to vertically center each visual's text. (Details on Word's framing features appear in Topic 23.)

A template for this combination of styles is included with Jim Heid's Word Companion, the disk set (sold separately) that complements this book. See the order page at the back of this book for details.

Using outline view to move paragraphs

Even if you don't use outline view to create outlines, it's handy for reorganizing paragraphs in a large document. Click the show first line icon in the outline bar so that only the first line of each paragraph appears. This way, you can see more paragraphs at once and you won't have to drag long distances to move paragraphs.

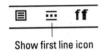

Show first line icon

Inside Word's heading styles

Word's heading styles — *heading 1* through *heading 9*— control the formatting of the headings you create. The following table lists each style's default formatting. All of the styles are based on the Normal style.

Default heading style formats

Style	Formatting
heading 1	Font: Helvetica, bold underline, space before 12 pt
heading 2	Font: Helvetica, bold, space before 6 pt
heading 3	Bold, indent: left 0.25 in.
heading 4	Underline, indent: left 0.25 in.
heading 5	Font: 10 point, bold, indent: left 0.5 in.
heading 6	Font: 10 point, underline, indent: left 0.5 in.
heading 7	Font: 10 point, italic, indent: left 0.5 in.
heading 8	Font: 10 point, italic, indent: left 0.5 in.
heading 9	Font: 10 point, italic, indent: left 0.5 in.

Personally, I think these default heading styles are tacky. The heading 1, heading 4, and heading 6 styles use underlining, which is a throwback to the typewriter era and should generally be avoided. One of the first things I did when starting out with Word 5 was to redefine the heading styles to match my tastes. If you're not into bold underlined Helvetica headings, you might want to do the same.

Headings and tables of contents

Remember that you can use Word's Table of Contents command (Insert menu) to generate a table of contents based on the headings in an outline. See Topic 26 for details on the Table of Contents command.

Topic 30

Creating a Long Document

Overview

According to Microsoft, a single Word document can contain up to 16 million characters. That's over 2.6 million words, or nearly 11,000 double-spaced pages. That's a *long* document, and if you ever create one like it, write and let me know — if the asylum gives you pencils.

When you're creating large publications, it's best to divide the project into a number of smaller documents of about 20 to 30 pages each. Word runs faster when you work with smaller documents. Smaller documents are also infinitely easier to scroll through and to back up.

Word lets you *connect* any number of small documents to form a tome. Imagine a series of connected documents as a train: Each car — each document — is connected to the next.

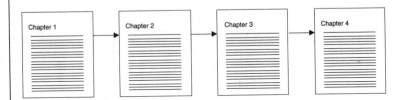

When you connect documents, Word can:

✦ number their pages continuously — if Document 1 has 20 pages, Word begins numbering Document 2 at 21 (unless you say otherwise)

✦ compile an index and table of contents that spans all the documents

✦ print the entire series of documents with one Print command instead of making you open and print each one in turn

For reasons known only to Microsoft, Word can't automatically number footnotes consecutively across connected documents. In this topic's Step-by-Step section, I'll describe the techniques required to accurately number footnotes across connected documents. In the Quick Tips section, I'll describe another method of printing multiple documents that *does* allow for automatic footnote numbering.

Connecting documents with the Document command

To connect one document to another, activate the first document and choose the Document command from the Format menu. When the Document dialog box appears, click the File Series button to open the File Series dialog box.

Click to choose the document you want to connect to the active document —

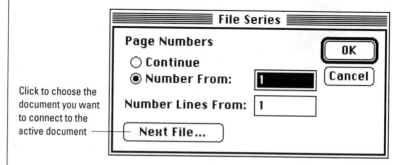

When you click the Next File button, Word displays the Open dialog box (the dialog box that appears when you choose Open from the File menu). Select the document that you want to follow the currently active document, and then click Open or press Return. The File Series dialog box now shows the name of the second document.

Breaks the connection between the active document and the document named at right

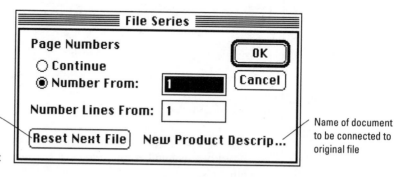

Name of document to be connected to original file

To connect the second document to a third, you open the second document and then repeat the preceding routine. You can continue connecting documents by opening each one in turn and then using the File Series dialog box to specify the next document in the series. You can see how a series of connected documents is like a train: Each document is connected to the next one in the series.

Printing connected documents

When you've connected one document to another and you tell Word to print the first document, Word adds a Print Next File check box to the Print dialog box.

LaserWriter "HP LaserJet IIISi"	7.0	Print

Copies: **1**   Pages: ⊙ All ○ From: [   ] To: [   ]   Cancel

Cover Page: ⊙ No ○ First Page ○ Last Page

Paper Source: ⊙ Paper Cassette ○ Manual Feed

Print: ⊙ Black & White   ○ Color/Grayscale

Destination: ⊙ Printer   ○ PostScript® File

Section Range: From: 1   To: 1   ☐ Print Selection Only

☐ Print Hidden Text   ☒ Print Next File   ☐ Print Back To Front

Uncheck to print only the active document

If you want to print the next document in the chain, check the Print Next File box. If the next document is connected to a third document, Word prints all three. Remember, you can cancel printing by pressing Command-period.

Step-by-Step

This section describes how to connect one document to another, how to break the connection between two documents, and how to accurately number footnotes across connected documents.

To connect documents:

1. Open the first document in the series and be sure its window is active.
You don't have to open the second document.

2. Choose Document from the Format menu.
The Format dialog box appears.

3. Click the File Series button.
The File Series dialog box appears.

4. Click the Next File button.
The Open dialog box appears.

5. Locate the document you want to follow the active document, and then double-click its name or select its name and click Open or press Return.
The File Series dialog box now lists the connected document's name. The Next File button changes to Reset Next File.

6. **If you want to number the pages consecutively across the connected documents, click the Continue button.**

To specify a beginning page number for a document, click the Number From button and then type the desired page number in the Number From box.

7. **Click OK or press Return to close the File Series dialog box.**

8. **Click OK or press Return to close the Document dialog box.**

9. **Save the document and then close it.**

10. **Open the next document in the series and then repeat steps 2–9. Continue connecting documents until you reach the last document in the series.**

To break the connection between two documents:

1. **Open the first document of the connected pair.**

For example, to break the connection between Document 1 and Document 2, open Document 1. Similarly, to break the connection between Document 4 and Document 5, open Document 4.

2. **Choose Document from the Format menu.**

The Format dialog box appears.

3. **Click the File Series button.**

The File Series dialog box appears. The name of the next document in the series appears in the dialog box.

4. **Click the Reset Next File button.**

Word removes the next document's name. The Reset Next File button changes to Next File. If desired, you can now connect the active document to a different document by clicking Next File.

5. **Click OK or press Return to close the File Series dialog box.**

6. **Click OK or press Return to close the Document dialog box.**

7. **Save the document to commit your changes to disk.**

To accurately number footnotes across connected documents:

1. **Open the first document in the connected series.**

2. **Choose Footnotes from the View menu.**

The footnote window opens.

3. **Scroll to the bottom of the footnote window and jot down the number of the last footnote.**

4. **Close the document, saving any changes if desired.**

5. **Open the next document in the series.**

6. **Choose Document from the Format menu.**
   The Document dialog box appears.

7. **In the Footnote area, be sure the Number From button is selected.**

8. **Add 1 to the number you jotted down in Step 3, and type the sum in the Number From box.**
   For example, if the last numbered footnote was 8, type *9*.

9. **Click OK or press Return to close the Document dialog box.**

10. **Save the document.**

11. **Open the next document in the connected series and then repeat steps 2–10.**

Quick Tips

Moving connected documents

When you connect one file to another, Word remembers which disk and which folder contains the second file. If you move the second file to a different folder or disk, Word won't be able to find it. When you tell Word to compile an index or table of contents, or when you try to print the series of connected files, Word displays an Open dialog box that asks you to locate the connected file. When you locate the file and then click Open, Word updates its information to reflect the file's new location.

Memory tips for working with connected documents

Compiling an index or table of contents for a group of connected documents can require a fair amount of memory. To avoid out-of-memory error messages, try any or all of the following:

✦ *Use picture placeholders.* These gray boxes require less memory to display than actual pictures do. Choose Preferences from the Tools menu, click the View option, and check the Picture Placeholders box. You can still see the actual pictures in the Print Preview window.

✦ *Save the first document in the series before compiling the index or table of contents* — a good idea even if you aren't running low on memory.

✦ *Clear the Clipboard.* Select a single character and then choose the Copy command *twice*. This doesn't completely clear the Clipboard — it will still contain the single character you selected — but it's as close as you can get.

Remember, too, that if you're running MultiFinder or System 7, you can use the Finder to increase the amount of memory allocated to Word. See Appendix A for details on allocating memory to Word.

Creating a long document using INCLUDE

By typing a special instruction in a document, you can combine other documents with it, creating a *merge document* that has the contents of each. If a series of connected documents is like a train, a series of *INCLUDE* instructions is like a freeway system, with many roads merging to form the main stream of text. The INCLUDE instruction is one of Word's many document-merging features, which are most often used to create personalized form letters and mailing labels (see Topic 31).

You type an INCLUDE instruction directly into your document, enclosing it within « » symbols, called *print merge* characters.

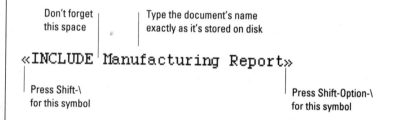

To create the final merge document, choose the Print Merge command from the File menu. Word merges the documents and creates a new document containing the contents of each.

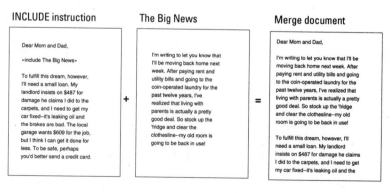

One benefit of using INCLUDE is that you can automatically number footnotes across a series of documents — you don't have to go through the manual routine described in this topic's Step-by-Step section.

The INCLUDE instruction has many applications. You can use it to:

✦ Insert a passage of boilerplate text (standard text that you save and reuse) in a document.

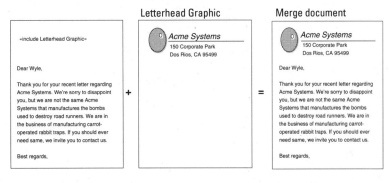

✦ Insert a graphic in a document.

✦ Print a series of documents with just one Print command.

```
«include Mom & Dad»

«include Body Shop Letter»

«include Body Shop Letter»

«include Landlord»
```

Hard page breaks (Shift-Enter) ensure each document will begin on its own page

To create an INCLUDE instruction, type the print merge characters (« »)
and then type *INCLUDE document name*, where *document name* is the
name of the document you want to include. An INCLUDE statement
can summon any Word-supported file format. That means you can
include not just Word documents, but several varieties of graphics
formats, too (see Topic 32).

When you're ready to create the merge document:

1. Choose Print Merge from the File menu.

The Print Merge dialog box appears.

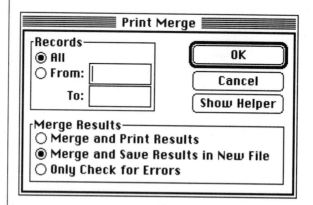

2. Select the desired Merge Results option.

3. Click OK or press Return.

If you clicked the Merge and Print Results button, the Print dialog box
appears. Specify the desired options and then click Print or press
Return. After the merge document is printed, Word discards it.

If you want to save the merge document, use the Merge and Save
Results in the New File option. When you choose this option, the
contents of the merge document appears in a new document window
whose name begins with Merge. You can save this merge document as
you would any Word document — by choosing Save from the File
menu. You might do this prior to compiling a table of contents or index
for the merge document.

If you use INCLUDE instructions often, you might want to add one to
Word's glossary so that you can recall it in a flash and not tangle your
fingers typing the « and » symbols.

Automating document production with INCLUDE

The following illustration shows another use of INCLUDE instructions: to automate the assembly of a report written by many different contributors.

```
«INCLUDE Table of Contents»
«INCLUDE Executive Summary»
«INCLUDE Manufacturing Report»
«INCLUDE Marketing Report»
«INCLUDE R&D Report»
«INCLUDE Human Resources Report»
```

In this scheme, the authors copy their reports to a shared folder, giving them the names required by the INCLUDE instructions. (You could also copy each document to a folder from floppy disks supplied by each contributor.) Assembling the final document is a matter of choosing Print Merge and supplying a few options. The page breaks between each INCLUDE instruction ensure that each document will begin on a new page.

A template for this and other print merge documents is included with Jim Heid's Word Companion disk set (sold separately); see the order page at the end of this book.

You can also automate the production of a document with many contributors by using the Publish and Subscribe features of the Mac's System 7 software. Topic 32 shows how.

Topic 31

Creating Form Letters with Print Merge

Overview

Have you ever wondered how Ed McMahon finds the time to personally address all those publisher's sweepstakes giveaways? Perhaps he uses Word's *print merge* feature, which lets you combine two documents to produce a third document containing the information in each.

Word's print merge feature is most commonly used to create personalized form letters and mailing labels. For each, you can use name-and-address information taken from a database manager such as Claris FileMaker Pro or from a spreadsheet such as Microsoft Excel. Or you can create your list of names and addresses within Word.

Word's print merge feature has some powerful features that go beyond simply inserting a different name and address in each form letter you print. You can create *conditional text* that appears in the merged document only if certain conditions are true. For example, you can tell Word to print a past-due notice if a client's payment is more than 30 days late, or to print a thank-you notice if payment was received.

You can also instruct Word to display dialog boxes that prompt you for information, which Word then inserts into the merged document. A common use of this feature is to fill in a template document for a form letter: When you want to send a copy of the letter, choose Word's Print Merge command, type the recipient's name and address in the dialog boxes Word displays, and Word prints a personalized version of the letter. This topic's Overview section describes other ways you might use this feature.

There's more to Word's print merge features than I have room to describe here. In this topic, I'll outline the basic concepts behind print merge and then examine the most important concepts in detail. A selection of examples that illustrate print merge applications is included with Jim Heid's Word Companion, the disk set (sold separately) that complements this book; see the order page at the back of the book for details.

Print merge basics

Print merging usually involves working with two kinds of documents:

✦ a *main* document. As its name suggests, this is the document containing the main portion of a form letter. The main document contains the text that remains the same in each copy of the letter, as well as *merge instructions* — text codes that tell Word where to insert information that is stored in...

✦ a *data* document. The data document contains the information that changes from one letter to the next. The data document can contain information extracted from a spreadsheet or database program, or information that you enter within Word.

The information in a data document is organized into *fields* and *records*. A field is a single piece of information, such as a person's last name or street address. A record is a collection of related fields — for example, the name-and-address information for one person.

When you use the Print Merge command in the File menu, Word combines the contents of the main document with that of the data document, generating a *merge document*.

Main document

«firstname» «lastname»
«address»
«city», «state» «zip»

Dear «firstname»:

As you know, Acme Systems has been manufacturing the highest-quality gizmos available.

We're pleased to announce the opening of our new branch office in «city». Stop in and browse sometime!

    Best regards,

    Fred Fredericks

+

Data document

firstname	lastname	address	city	state	zip
Joe	Smith	15 5th Ave.	New York	NY	10001
Sue	Buck	325 Sage Dr.	Pittsburgh	PA	15243

=

Merge document

Joe Smith
15 5th Ave.
New York, NY 10001

Dear Joe:

As you know, Acme Systems has been manufacturing the highest-quality gizmos available.

We're pleased to announce the opening of our new branch office in New York. Stop in and browse sometime!

    Best regards,

    Fred Fredericks

Print Merge Helper

First there was Hamburger Helper, then came — gulp — Tuna Helper. Now there's Print Merge Helper, which makes Word's print merge feature palatable. Word has always had a print merge feature, but it has been difficult to use, requiring you to memorize and type arcane instructions and grapple with data records and field delimiters. Print Merge Helper puts a friendlier facade on Word's print merge features by walking you through the process of creating data documents and main documents. Print Merge Helper also eliminates the need to remember and type arcane instructions, and it lets you create data documents using Word's built-in table editor (discussed in Topic 24).

When you choose Print Merge Helper from the View menu, a dialog box appears that enables you to choose an existing data document or create a new one.

Open an existing data document

```
Choose or Create a Data Document:
          ▭ System 7.0 ▼
  ☐ 'Documents                    ⇧        ▭ System 7.0
  ☐ Communications                          378K available
  ☐ Graphics Folder
  ☐ System Folder                          ┌ Open ┐  ┌ Eject ┐
  ☐ Temporary Items
  ☐ Utilities                              ┌Cancel┐ ┌Desktop┐
                                 ⇩          Find File...
List Files of Type: │Readable Files    ▼│  ┌ New ┐  ┌ None ┐
```

Create a new   Don't use a
data document   data document

If you click New, the Data Document Builder dialog box appears.

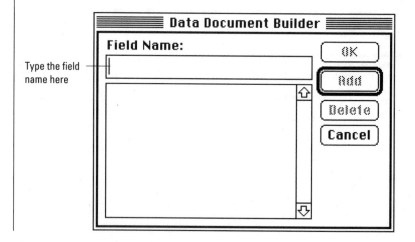

```
              Data Document Builder
  Field Name:                              ┌   OK   ┐
Type the field ── │                    │   ┌  Add   ┐
name here
                  │                    ⇧│  ┌ Delete ┐
                  │                     │  ┌ Cancel ┐
                  │                     │
                  │                    ⇩│
```

You use this dialog box to define each of your data document's fields. You type field names (such as *first name, last name, city, state, zip*), clicking Add or pressing Return after each one.

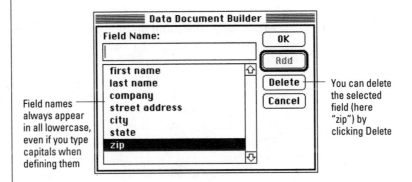

Field names always appear in all lowercase, even if you type capitals when defining them

You can delete the selected field (here "zip") by clicking Delete

When you click OK, Word displays a Save dialog box that you can use to save the fledgling data document on disk. Supply a name for the document and click Save or press Return, and two things happen:

♦ Word creates a table containing columns whose headings correspond to the fields you added in the Data Document Builder dialog box.

This first row is called the *header record*

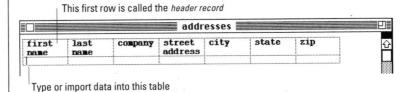

Type or import data into this table

♦ Word creates a new, untitled main document that begins with a DATA instruction. This instruction tells Word which file contains the data that will be used in the merge process.

Print Merge Helper bar

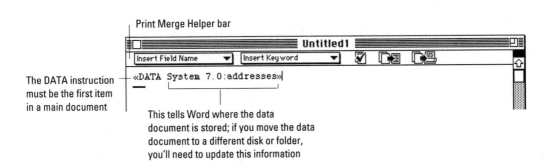

The DATA instruction must be the first item in a main document

This tells Word where the data document is stored; if you move the data document to a different disk or folder, you'll need to update this information

As the preceding illustration shows, print merge instructions are always enclosed in print merge symbols, « and ». The instruction's *keyword*—such as the word DATA—always appears in capital letters. A space always follows the keyword.

Working on the main document

After creating the data and main documents, you can begin working on the rest of the main document, or you can activate the data document window and begin typing the fields and records that will be included in each copy of the letter you print.

Let's assume you want to continue working on the main document. When creating a form letter, your first step might be to type the date at the beginning of the letter, or better still, to insert Word's *date* glossary entry so that Word supplies the accurate date for you each time you print letters.

Business letters then typically contain the recipient's name and address. This is information that will be taken from the data document you'll create. To tell Word to insert information from the data document, use the Insert Field Name pop-up menu in the Print Merge Helper bar.

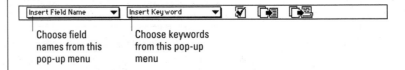

Choose field   Choose keywords
names from this   from this pop-up
pop-up menu   menu

When you choose a field name from this pop-up menu, Word inserts a merge instruction at the location of the blinking insertion point, as shown in following illustration.

Before inserting *first name* field

Insertion point

After inserting *first name* field

«DATA System 7.0:addresses»

«first name»

To complete the addressee information for a form letter, you choose each field name from the Insert Field Name pop-up menu, pressing Return when you want to begin a new line. You can put one field after another on the same line, but you must remember to type a space between them. Similarly, you can include other characters between fields.

This space was typed by hand

«first name» «last name»
«company»
«street address»
«city», «state» «zip»

Comma and spaces added

After completing the address portion of the letter, you can create the salutation.

```
«DATA System 7.0:addresses»


April 21, 1992



«first name» «last name»
«company»
«street address»
«city», «state»  «zip»
```

Salutation —— Dear «first name»: |
—

Then you can begin typing the main portion of the letter, inserting field names where you want Word to insert information from the data document.

IF...ENDIF: Controlling what prints in the main document

As mentioned earlier, conditional text allows Word to tailor a document based on the information in your data document. Let's flesh out the example I presented earlier by adding a conditional instruction that tells Word to print a past-due notice if a payment is late.

The key to conditional text is the IF...ENDIF set of keywords. When you choose IF...ENDIF from the Insert Keyword pop-up menu, a dialog box appears in which you describe the condition that will cause the text to be printed or not printed.

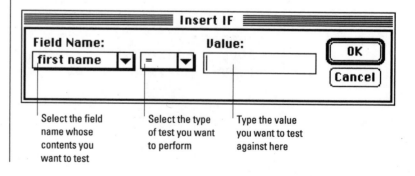

Select the field name whose contents you want to test

Select the type of test you want to perform

Type the value you want to test against here

When you complete the dialog box and click OK or press Return, Word inserts the merge instructions at the insertion point's location.

```
Dear «first name»:

According to our records, you placed an order on «last order
date». «IF «past due»="yes"»«ENDIF»
```
Type the conditional text here

Notice that the blinking insertion point is located between the IF and ENDIF keywords. You type the conditional text here.

```
Dear «first name»:

According to our records, you placed an order on «last order
date». «IF «past due»="yes"»As of today, we haven't received
your payment. Please send it as soon as possible to avoid
late charges.«ENDIF»
```

The Insert IF dialog box's operator pop-up menu also lets you use the greater-than, less-than, and other symbols to tell Word to compare the field and value you specify in other ways. For example, you could test whether customers ordered more than $1,000 worth of merchandise, and then print a "thanks for being one of our best customers" paragraph for those who did. This topic's Step-by-Step section contains more details.

A conditional instruction may also make use of the ELSE keyword. For example, if a client's account *is* paid up, you might want to print the text, "Thank you for your prompt payment — we appreciate your business." To add an ELSE instruction, position the insertion point just before the «ENDIF» instruction's « character and then choose ELSE from the Insert Keyword pop-up menu. Word inserts the ELSE instruction, and positions the insertion point between it and the ENDIF instruction. Type the alternative text here.

```
Dear «first name»:

According to our records, you placed an order on «last order
date». «IF «past due»="yes"»As of today, we haven't received
your payment. Please send it as soon as possible to avoid
late charges.«ELSE»Thank you for your prompt payment--we
appreciate your business.«ENDIF»
```
ELSE instruction

IF...ENDIF operators

The Insert IF dialog box lets you choose from a variety of operators that test the value of a field in certain ways. The following table lists each operator and shows how it works.

Operator	Checks that the field value...	Example
=	Equals the number you specify or exactly matches the text characters you type	«IF amountdue=0»Your account is paid up.«ENDIF»
<	Is less than the number or text you type	«IF amountdue<10»You owe less than $10.«ENDIF»
>	Is greater than the number or text you type	«IF date>"12/25"»Christmas is over.«ENDIF»
<=	Is less than or equal to the number or text you type	«IF amountdue<=10»Your balance is $10 or less.«ENDIF»
>=	Is greater than or equal to the number or text you type	«IF amountdue>=10»Your balance is $10 or more.«ENDIF»
<>	Is not equal to the number or text you type	«IF date<>"12/25"»It isn't Christmas.«ENDIF»
Field not empty	is not blank	«IF company»There is a company name in this record.«ENDIF»

Operators illustrated

When comparing text, Word uses the sorting order to determine whether one piece of text is greater than or less than another. For example, "cat" is less than "dog" because "cat" precedes "dog" alphabetically.

Working with the data document

Filling in the data document is a straightforward process: Simply type each field item, pressing Tab to move from one table cell to the next. Don't bother formatting the data — specifying bold, italics, different fonts and sizes, and so on. Word uses the data document as a source of information only; the formatting of the information is determined by the main document.

Because the information in a data document is stored in a table, you can sort it according to a specific field. You might take advantage of this capability to sort a list of names and addresses according to the State field. For details on sorting, editing, and working with tables, see Topic 24.

Later in this section, I'll describe how to move data from a spreadsheet or database manager into a data document.

Creating the merge document

You've created the data document and entered information into it, and you've created the main document and added merge instructions and field names. Now you're ready to generate the merge document — the document that will contain the personalized form letters.

To create the merge document, you can either choose the File menu's Print Merge command or you can click icons on the Print Merge Helper bar. The icons correspond to options in the Print Merge dialog box.

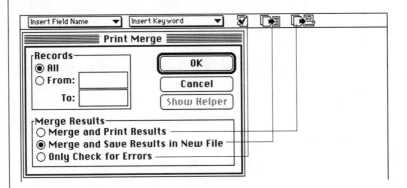

If you choose to merge the documents and save the results in a new file, Word creates a new document whose name begins with *Merge*. If the data document contains more than one record (and chances are it does), Word creates a separate form letter for each record, and separates each letter with a section break, as shown in the following illustration.

```
▤□▤▤▤▤▤▤▤▤▤▤▤ Merge1 ▤▤▤▤▤▤▤▤▤▤▤□▤
```

According to our records, you placed an order on February 12.
As of today, we haven't received your payment. Please send it
as soon as possible to avoid late charges.

We would like to remind you of our new 24-hour hotline
service. If you have any questions regarding our products or
services, call 800/555-1234. As always, you can also call the
Keene office to speak with your local sales representative.

Thanks again for your support.

                                    Best regards,

                                    Trixie Kelly
                                    Manager

Section break —————
separating each
form letter

April 21, 1992

Dave Byrd
Time Management Associates
130 Elm St.

```
P1 S1              Normal
```

Each section break has the New Page section start option. This
enables each form letter to appear on its own page. (See Topic 22 for
details on Word's ability to divide a document into sections.)

ASK and SET: Supplying data at merge time

Two merge instructions, ASK and SET, enable you to supply data to
Word during the print merge process. ASK and SET instructions cause
Word to display a dialog box asking for information during the merge.

This ASK instruction...

«ASK food=?What's your favorite dish?»

...produces this dialog box during the print merge

```
▤▤▤▤▤▤▤▤▤▤ Print Merge ▤▤▤▤▤▤▤▤▤▤

  What's your favorite dish?


  ┌──────────────────────────────────┐
  │                                  │
  └──────────────────────────────────┘


              (     OK     )  ( Stop Merge )
```

The ASK instruction tells Word to get new information from you for each form letter. You might use it to get the name and address information for each letter. The following illustration shows a thoroughly tacky application of ASK instructions: to write personalized form letter thank-you notes.

You can include a field name in an ASK prompt; at merge time, Word substitutes the name with the text you entered previously

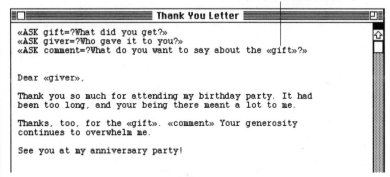

```
▤▱▰▰▰▰▰▰▰▰▰▰▰▰▰▰▰▰▰ Thank You Letter ▰▰▰▰▰▰▰▰▰▰▰▰▰▰▰▰▰▱▤
«ASK gift=?What did you get?»                                    ⇧
«ASK giver=?Who gave it to you?»
«ASK comment=?What do you want to say about the «gift»?»


Dear «giver»,

Thank you so much for attending my birthday party. It had
been too long, and your being there meant a lot to me.

Thanks, too, for the «gift». «comment» Your generosity
continues to overwhelm me.

See you at my anniversary party!
```

The SET instruction tells Word to get information from you only once — at the beginning of the merge operation. The information you supply is used in each form letter you create.

This topic's Step-by-Step section shows how to create ASK and SET instructions.

If you're willing to supply all your data using ASK and/or SET instructions, you don't need a data document at all. When you first choose Print Merge Helper and the Open dialog box appears, click the None button. The main document window will then appear with the Print Merge Helper bar visible.

Using spreadsheet or database data

The data that you want to include in form letters or other merge documents may already be stored in a spreadsheet or database program. You can move this information into Word and use it in a data document in the following ways:

♦ *Text-only files.* Use your spreadsheet or database program to create a text-only file containing the fields and records you want to use. Word's print merge feature can work with tab- or comma-delimited text files. Topic 32 shows how to export data using a variety of popular spreadsheets and data managers.

✦ *The Clipboard.* You can copy a series of spreadsheet cells and then paste them into Word to create a table.

✦ *The Edit menu's Subscribe command* (System 7 only). If you subscribe to a published Microsoft Excel spreadsheet, you can update your data document when the original spreadsheet changes. You might use this technique if you send the same form letter to a client list every month. By updating the data document before you use the Print Merge command, you can be sure that letters will go out to your newest clients.

✦ *The Edit menu's Paste Special and Paste Object commands* (System 7, Microsoft Excel, and the Equation Editor only). With these commands, described in Topic 32, you can create links between a word document and a Microsoft Excel spreadsheet to streamline the process of updating documents when spreadsheet data changes.

Step-by-Step

This section shows how to create main and data documents using Word's Print Merge Helper, how to create IF...ENDIF, ELSE, SET, and ASK statements, and how to merge the main and data documents into a merge document.

To create a new main document using Print Merge Helper:
1. Choose New from the File menu.
A new, untitled window appears. (You can also activate Print Merge Helper for a document that you've already begun working on.)

2. Choose Print Merge Helper from the View menu.
An Open dialog box appears.

3. Locate and open an existing data document, click New to create a new data document, or click None to work with only the main document.
The document window appears with the Print Merge Helper bar visible. If you selected an existing data document, a DATA instruction appears at the top of the window. If you clicked New, the Data Document Builder dialog box appears.

To build a data document using the Data Document Builder:
1. Type the name of the field you want to create.
Field names can be up to 253 characters, including spaces. *Do not use a comma (,) in a field name.*

2. Click the Add button.

Word creates the field and adds it to the list.

3. Repeat steps 1 and 2 until you've created all the fields for the data document.

You can create up to 31 fields. (Note: Be sure to click Add after defining the last field. If you click OK instead, Word won't save the field.

4. When you've defined all the fields, click the OK button.

A Save dialog box appears for the data document. Type a name for the data document and then click Save or press Return. Word saves the data document and then creates a new main document and inserts into it a DATA statement referring to the data document you just created. The Print Merge Helper bar is visible in the new main document.

5. Either activate the data document and enter or import data into it, or continue working with the main document, adding merge instructions, field names, and conventional text.

To enter data into a data document:

1. Type each field item, pressing Tab to move from one field to the next.

When you reach the end of a row (which, in a data document, represents a record) and you press Tab, Word creates a new row (record) for you.

— or —

1. Copy the data from a spreadsheet or database manager and then paste the data into the table in the data document.

See Topic 24 for details on editing tables.

To insert a field name in the main document:

1. Position the insertion point where you want the field's contents to appear.

2. Choose the field's name from the Insert Field Name pop-up menu on the Print Merge Helper bar.

Word inserts the field's name, surrounding it with the merge characters (« and »).

To insert an IF...ENDIF instruction in the main document:

1. **Position the insertion point where you want the instruction's text to be inserted.**

2. **Choose IF...ENDIF from the Insert Keyword pop-up menu on the Print Merge Helper bar.**
   The Insert IF dialog box appears.

3. **In the Insert IF dialog box, choose the name of the field whose value you want to test.**

4. **Choose the desired operator from the Operator pop-up menu.**
   See "IF...ENDIF operators" in this topic's Overview section for a description and example of each operator.

5. **Type the value you want to test the field against in the Value box.**

6. **Click OK or press Return.**
   Word inserts the IF...ENDIF instruction in the main document and positions the insertion point before the «ENDIF» keyword.

7. **Type the text that you want to have printed if the condition you just specified is met.**
   Keep an eye on the word spaces around the text and the IF...ENDIF instructions; it's easy to wind up with an extra space or none at all.

To insert an ELSE instruction in an existing IF...ENDIF instruction:

1. **Position the insertion point just before the «ENDIF» instruction.**

2. **Choose ELSE from the Insert Keyword pop-up menu in the Print Merge Helper bar.**
   The ELSE keyword appears, and the insertion point is positioned between it and the ENDIF keyword.

3. **Type the text that you want to have printed if the condition specified by the IF instruction is not met.**

To insert an ASK instruction:

1. **Position the insertion point where you want the ASK instruction.**
   The ASK instruction can be located anywhere in the main document, provided that it appears after any DATA instruction.

2. **Choose ASK from the Insert Keyword pop-up menu in the Print Merge Helper bar.**

    The Insert ASK dialog box appears.

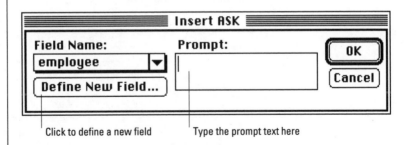

Click to define a new field   Type the prompt text here

3. **Click the Define New Field button.**

    The Insert New Field dialog box appears. As an alternative to performing this and the following step, you can select the name of a new field from the Field Name list.

4. **Type a name for the field and then click OK or press Return.**

    The new field's name appears in the Field Name list.

5. **In the Prompt box, type the text that you want Word to display when asking for information.**

    For example, if you're asking for a client's first name, you might type *Enter the client's first name.*

6. **Click OK or press Return.**

    Word inserts the completed ASK instruction in the document. Don't forget to insert the field name referenced by the ASK instruction where you want its information to appear in the main document.

To insert a SET instruction:

1. **Position the insertion point where you want the SET instruction.**

    The SET instruction can be located anywhere in the main document, provided that it appears after any DATA instruction.

2. **Choose SET from the Insert Keyword pop-up menu in the Print Merge Helper bar.**

    The Insert SET dialog box appears.

3. **Click the Define New Field button.**

    The Insert New Field dialog box appears. As an alternative to performing this and the following step, you can select the name of a field from the Field Name list.

4. Type a name for the field and then click OK or press Return.

The new field's name appears in the Field Name list.

5. Do one of the following:

If you want...	Do this...
Word to prompt you for information at the beginning of the merge	Choose =? from the operator list and then type the prompt in the Prompt box
To specify the field value directly within the instruction	Choose = from the operator list and then type the value in the Value box

6. Click OK or press Return.

Word inserts the completed SET instruction in the document. Don't forget to insert the field name referenced by the SET instruction where you want its information to appear in the main document.

To perform the print merge:

1. Choose Print Merge from the File menu.

The Print Merge dialog box appears. As an alternative to choosing Print Merge, you can click the merge buttons in the Print Merge Helper bar.

2. Choose the desired options from the Print Merge dialog box.

For example, if you want to print form letters for only certain records in the data document, type the record numbers in the From and To boxes.

3. Click OK or press Return.

If you selected the Merge and Print Results option, the Print dialog box appears. Specify the desired options and then click Print or press Return. If you selected the Merge and Save Results in New File option, the contents of the merge document appear in a new document window whose name begins with *Merge*. You can save this merge document as you would any Word document — by choosing Save from the File menu. You might do this prior to compiling a table of contents or an index for the merge document.

Quick Tips

Print merging without a data document

If you're content to supply print merge data during the merge process, you don't actually have to work with a data document in order to use Word's print merge feature. Simply click None when Word asks you to choose a data document and create a new one, and then insert SET and ASK instructions in the main document.

Other print merge features

Here are some advanced print merge features you might want to explore:

✦ *Calculations.* You can calculate values within print merge instructions. For example, say you have an ASK instruction that prompts you for a discount percentage. You can type the percentage, and then have Word calculate the net cost of an item.

✦ *Logical operators.* You can test for more than one condition by using the logical operators AND, OR, and NOT. For example, you might want to test to see whether an account is past due OR dormant.

✦ *The INCLUDE instruction.* This instruction lets you insert the contents of one document into another. It's discussed in detail in Topic 30.

Part III
Advanced Formatting

Part IV
Streamlining Your Work

Topic 32

Exchanging Information with Other Programs

Overview

Why bother exchanging data between Word and other programs? It's often a necessity. You might need to:

+ include an image created with a scanner in a sales brochure or a manual

+ *import* Word documents into a desktop publishing program such as Aldus PageMaker or QuarkXPress

+ include a table of financial information from a worksheet created in Microsoft's Excel or Works, Claris Resolve or ClarisWorks, or other spreadsheet programs

+ use name-and-address information from a database program such as Claris FileMaker Pro to create personalized form letters

Exchanging data means combining the best efforts of all your programs to create documents that you couldn't create with any single program. It's also one of the Mac's less-appreciated strong points.

Data exchange options

Word can exchange text or graphics with other programs by using:

+ *Files*. Many programs — particularly desktop publishing packages — can read Word documents directly, with no special conversion process required. You can also save Word documents in other formats such as that used by WordPerfect Corp.'s WordPerfect word processor. Similarly, Word can directly open documents created with many popular word processors, and it can read popular graphics formats such as TIFF, PICT, and EPS. You can even use the Insert menu's File command to insert files from Word or other programs into an existing document.

+ *The Clipboard.* You can cut and copy information in one program, and then start Word (or switch to Word) and paste the information into a Word document. You can also cut or copy information from a Word document and then paste it into another Word document or into another program.

+ *Publish and subscribe* (System 7 only). If you use Apple's System 7 software, you can make part or all of a Word document available to other Word documents and to other programs by *publishing* it. You or other users can then *subscribe* to the published information, a process that causes the information to be inserted into a document. You can choose to have subscribed information automatically updated when the original document changes.

+ *Linking* (System 7 only). Linking is similar to publishing and subscribing, but has some advantages and disadvantages that I'll discuss in this topic's Overview section.

+ *Embedding* (System 7 only). You can embed information from one document into another document. If you double-click the embedded information, called an *object,* Word opens a window that allows you to modify the object — even if that means starting or switching to a different program. When you close the window, Word updates the document to reflect any modifications you made.

The last three options make use of some of the whiz-bang, Buck Rogers features in Apple's System 7 software. They can be more complex than simply cutting and pasting or opening a disk file, but as we'll see in the next section, they offer power and flexibility that you may find useful for certain data exchange tasks.

Will you need to update the data you exchange?

There are subtle differences among the data exchange options I just presented, but there's also a more basic point of comparison: How easy is it to update transferred information when an original document changes? For example, say your financial report needs to contain a table of financial data from a Microsoft Excel worksheet. If the original worksheet changes while you're working on the report, how many hoops must you jump through to bring the figures in the Word document up to date?

If you won't need to update the data — or if you're simply moving small bits and pieces to cut down on repetitive typing — you'll probably be well served by using disk files or the Clipboard (via the Edit menu's Cut, Copy, and Paste commands, discussed in Topic 3). The Clipboard is simple and straightforward, and it doesn't require you to plumb the nooks and crannies of System 7's data exchange features. But the Clipboard is cumbersome if you frequently need to update information. In that case, consider using publish and subscribe, linking, or embedding instead.

With this in mind, here are a few notes to keep in mind about publish and subscribe, linking, and embedding:

♦ If you want to use subscribe to include information from a different program, that program must support the Apple System 7 Edition Manager. You can tell if a program supports the Edition Manager by looking at its Edit menu: If the Edit menu contains Create Publisher and Subscribe To commands, the program does support the Edition Manager. If a program does not support the Edition Manager, you'll need to use the Clipboard or disk files to transfer the information.

♦ If you want to use linking or embedding to include information created in a different program, that program must support Microsoft's Object Linking and Embedding (OLE) specifications. At this writing, only Word 5.0's Equation Editor and Microsoft Excel 3.0 (and later versions) support OLE.

It's important to remember that publish and subscribe, linking, and embedding can be very useful even if you're working with only Word documents. By applying these features to different Word documents — or even to different parts of the same document — you can save time, simplify document revisions, and help ensure consistency.

Exchanging data with disk files

When you need to move a great deal of information and you probably won't have to update it often in the future, disk files are good vehicles. If you use different word processors — perhaps even ones on IBM PCs — you'll also use disk files to transfer documents themselves.

Word can read documents created by several popular word processors, and it can create documents that these same programs can open:

♦ Claris MacWrite II and MacWrite, versions 4.5 and 5.0

♦ WordPerfect for the Macintosh, version 2.0

+ WordPerfect for DOS, versions 4.1, 4.2, 5.0, and 5.1

+ Microsoft Works for the Macintosh, version 2.0

+ Microsoft Word for DOS (all versions)

+ Microsoft Word for Windows (all versions)

+ and, of course, Microsoft Word for the Macintosh (all versions)

Word can also open the following graphics formats:

+ MacPaint, a monochrome (black-and-white) format supported by all painting programs

+ Encapsulated PostScript (EPS), a format supported by PostScript-based illustration programs, such as Adobe Illustrator and Aldus FreeHand, and also many image scanning and processing programs

+ Tagged-Image File Format (TIFF), a format used to store images created by image scanners and video digitizers

+ PICT, a format supported by many drawing and image processing programs

Word can also open and save several specialized document formats:

+ text only, a format that stores only a document's text and rudimentary formatting such as tab codes and carriage returns. Word can work with several varieties of text-only files.

+ Interchange Format (Rich Text Format, or RTF for short), a variation of text-only format that uses codes to save formatting information and graphics.

+ Stationery, a format that enables you to store common document-formatting settings and boilerplate text in template documents that you can reuse. Stationery is discussed in Topic 33.

In order to read some of the aforementioned formats, Word needs *converters,* files that reside in the Word Commands folder on your hard disk. (See Appendix A for details.)

You use a pop-up menu in Word's Open or Save dialog box to specify the file format you want to access or save as. This topic's Step-by-Step section shows how.

Exchanging data with the Clipboard

Topic 3 shows how to move text within a Word document using the Clipboard. The basic concepts are the same for moving text between different programs: Select the text, and then choose Copy or Cut to place the text on the Clipboard (Cut removes the text from the original document; Copy doesn't). Next, switch to Word and choose Paste from the Edit menu.

If you cut or copy a series of spreadsheet cells from Microsoft Excel, you can paste them into Word and work with them as a table. Similarly, you can cut or copy part or all of a Word table and then paste it into Excel or any other spreadsheet. If you paste into Word part of a spreadsheet created in a program other than Excel, chances are it will appear as a series of items separated by tabs. You can convert the items into a table by selecting them and choosing the Text to Table command from the Insert menu.

You can paste graphics into Word from just about any graphics program. If you want to paste a graphic from a PostScript drawing program such as Aldus FreeHand or Adobe Illustrator, copy the graphic with embedded PostScript for best results. For details, see the tip "Importing EPS graphics via the Clipboard," in Topic 13's Quick Tips section. If you paste a drawing created in a QuickDraw drawing program (such as Claris's MacDraw) into Word, you can modify the drawing using Word's picture window. See Topic 13 for more details about importing and working with graphics.

Exchanging data with System 7's publish and subscribe

Like the Clipboard, System 7's publish and subscribe features enable Word to exchange data with another program. But unlike the Clipboard, the Publish and Subscribe commands enable the exchange to take place automatically, without your having to copy and paste information from one program to another.

Publish and subscribe make possible new ways of working with information and creating documents. Some examples:

♦ A financial report created in Word might include a chart generated by a spreadsheet program such as Microsoft Excel or Claris Resolve. Using publish and subscribe, you can have the chart be automatically updated in the report when its underlying spreadsheet data changes.

♦ A weekly executive status report might include summaries from several different managers. Using publish and subscribe, a secretary could assemble the report automatically by linking the report document to each manager's status report files.

The last example illustrates an important point: Publish and subscribe can work together with System 7's file-sharing features to enable different programs *running on different Macs* to exchange data. Thus, a group of coworkers can collaborate on a document that can be easily updated whenever one of its contributors makes a change in his or her section. Indeed, with publish and subscribe you can create a document in which every single component — text as well as graphics — comes from programs running on other users' computers.

Publishing involves making part or all of a document available to other programs. As a general rule, anything you can select in Word — text, graphics, table cells — you can make available to other programs. You publish something by selecting it and choosing Create Publisher from the Edit menu, and then responding to the Create Publisher dialog box.

A preview of the information you're publishing appears here

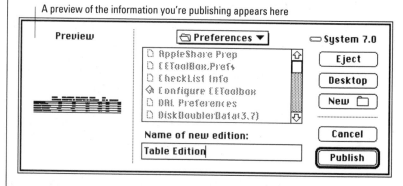

When you publish some information, you create an *edition*, a separate file containing the information itself as well as data that tells the Mac where the information came from. The edition file acts as a conduit between publisher and subscriber: Data always flows from publisher to edition to subscriber. Documents that contain publishers and subscribers don't have to be open at the same time to share data. Whenever you save a document containing a publisher, the edition changes to reflect the current data from the publisher. Any number of subscribers can subscribe to a single edition.

Subscribing involves including in a document information that has been published. To subscribe to an edition that you or others have created, choose Subscribe To from the Edit menu. Locate and choose the desired edition from the dialog box that appears and click OK, and the published information appears in your document; if Show ¶ is active, large gray brackets appear around the information to indicate that it comes from an edition. Information that you've subscribed to is called a *subscriber*.

Using the Edit menu's Subscribe Options and Publisher Options commands, you can specify how the Mac handles the process of updating information that you've published or to which you've subscribed. You might choose to automatically receive new editions as soon as they become available. This update option is useful if you've subscribed to information in a spreadsheet consisting of daily sales figures, for example, where you would want to receive each version of the sales information as soon as it becomes available.

On the other hand, you might choose to receive a new edition only upon request — perhaps if you've subscribed to an edition consisting of an illustration that an artist in your office is working on. You probably don't need to have the illustration updated constantly, so you'd specify manual updating in the Subscriber Options dialog box. With manual updating, the Mac updates the subscriber with a new edition only when you specifically request it.

You can select, cut, and paste a subscriber. You can't edit a subscriber, although you can modify it as a whole. For example, you could underline or italicize subscriber text, but not delete or edit a word. This restriction protects you from losing changes to a subscriber when a new edition arrives.

The concepts behind publishers and subscribers sound complex, and indeed, they are quite a bit more complicated than cutting and pasting. For many tasks, you'll probably continue to rely on the Clipboard to move information between programs. Moving data using the Clipboard requires less memory, disk space, and processing time, and it doesn't require that your software support the Edition Manager. But for those times when you need automatic updating, the Edit menu's Publish and Subscribe commands are the answer.

Exchanging data by linking

Exchanging data through links is similar to using publish and subscribe, in that the data you exchange can be updated when the original information changes. But linking also differs: It doesn't use edition files, and it doesn't work across computers on a network. Also, to establish links between two files created in different programs — such as a Word document and an Excel spreadsheet — you must have enough memory to have both programs open simultaneously. And obviously, you need to have both programs. (This isn't the case with publish and subscribe, where you can use Word to access editions created with any program.) Finally, linking is not supported by very many programs: Among mainstream programs, only Word and Excel support it at this writing. (The Equation Editor that's included with Word 5.0 also supports it.) One additional drawback is that if you rename or move a linked file, Word won't be able to find the linked information; this isn't the case with publish and subscribe.

You establish a link by first cutting or copying some information in a program that supports links, and then using Word's Paste Special command (in the Edit menu). Once you've established a link, you can control how and when the linked information is updated by using the Edit menu's Link Options command. This topic's Step-by-Step section contains more details.

One handy use of linking is to create cross-references to figures within a Word document or across more than one Word document. In the following illustration, the figure title is linked to its title in the text: If the figure number in the text is changed, the number next to the figure changes too.

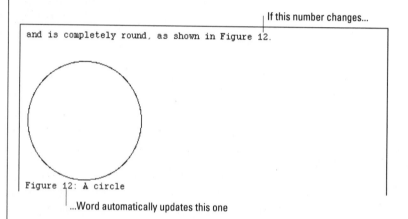

If this number changes...

and is completely round, as shown in Figure 12.

Figure 12: A circle

...Word automatically updates this one

Exchanging data by embedding objects

Embedding is another data exchange option that's currently supported by only Word's Equation Editor and Excel. Embedding is similar to pasting, except that Word keeps track of certain vital details about the information you embed, such as the name of the program that created it and the format of the information. If you need to modify an embedded object, you double-click it and Word opens an *object window* that contains the object. If the object came from Excel, Word starts or switches to Excel, which opens the object window, as shown in the following illustration.

This worksheet was embedded from
Microsoft Excel. If you double-click on it...

The following table compares the performance of these
printers.

	Abaton LaserScript	Apple Personal LaserWriter NT	Apple Personal LaserWriter SC	Fujitsu RX-7100PS
Font document	382	582	191	1003
Courier document	215	308	420	237
MacDrawII document	420	344	212	346
FreeHand document	1293	1274	599	1275
Newsletter document	394	184	167	181

...Word starts Excel and opens the worksheet.

🍎 File Edit Formula Format Data Options Macro Window 10:51

Normal

A1

Personal Printer Performance

	A	B	C	D	E	F	G	H
1		Abaton	Apple Personal	Apple Personal	Fujitsu	GCC		HP LaserJet II
2		LaserScript	LaserWriter NT	LaserWriter SC	RX-7100PS	BLP IIs	GCC PLP II	HP PostScri
3	Font document	382	582	191	1003	345	442	
4	Courier document	215	308	420	237	154	504	
5	MacDrawII document	420	344	212	346	238	101	
6	FreeHand document	1293	1274	599	1275	840	155	1
7	Newsletter document	394	184	167	181	134	264	
8								
9								
10								
11								
12								

After you modify the object and close the object window, Word
updates the object as it appears in the Word document.

If you've embedded an object from Excel and you want to edit the
object, your Mac must have at least 4MB of memory so that both
Word and Excel can be open and running at the same time.

In this topic's Quick Tips section, I'll provide some guidelines that will
help you pick the data exchange technique that is most appropriate to
the task at hand.

Step-by-Step

In this section, you'll find instructions for saving and opening documents in other file formats, and for publishing and subscribing, linking, and embedding.

To save a document in a different format:

1. Choose Save As from the File menu.

The Save As dialog box appears.

2. From the Save File As Type pop-up menu, choose the desired file format.

3. Click OK or press Return.

Word saves the document in the format you specified.

To open a document that's saved in a different format:

1. Choose Open from the File menu.

The Open dialog box appears.

2. Optional: From the List Files of Type pop-up menu, choose the desired format.

This step is optional because Word automatically lists all the files in the formats it supports. Still, you may want to perform this step to narrow down the list.

3. Locate the file you want to open, and then double-click its name (or select its name and then click Open or press Return).

Word opens the file. Depending on the file you're opening, Word may display a conversion dialog box while it's opening the file. If you change your mind and decide not to open the file, you can cancel the operation by clicking the Cancel button.

To publish some information:

1. Select the information you want to publish.

You can publish anything — text, graphics, tables, and any combination thereof.

2. Choose Create Publisher from the Edit menu.

The Create Publisher dialog box appears.

3. Type a name for the edition file; if desired, use the dialog box's buttons and folder icons to switch to a different disk or folder.

4. Click Publish or press Return.

Word creates the publisher. If you activate Show ¶, you'll see gray brackets around the information you published.

To control update options and other publisher settings:

1. **Position the blinking insertion point anywhere within the published information.**

   If you published only a picture, select the picture.

2. **Choose Publisher Options from the Edit menu.**

   The Publisher Options dialog box appears.

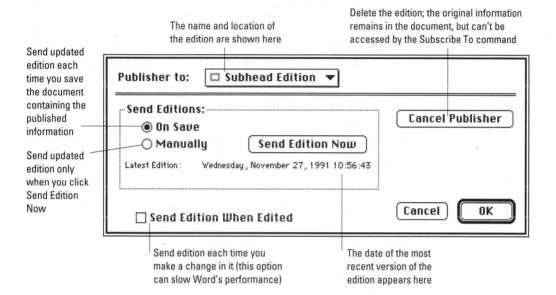

The name and location of the edition are shown here

Delete the edition; the original information remains in the document, but can't be accessed by the Subscribe To command

Send updated edition each time you save the document containing the published information

Send updated edition only when you click Send Edition Now

Send edition each time you make a change in it (this option can slow Word's performance)

The date of the most recent version of the edition appears here

3. **Specify the desired options and then click OK or press Return.**

To subscribe to information:

1. **Position the insertion point where you want the published information to appear.**

2. **Choose Subscribe To from the Edit menu.**

   The Subscribe dialog box appears.

3. **Locate the edition you want to subscribe to, and then double-click its name (or select its name and then click Subscribe or press Return).**

   Word subscribes to the edition, inserting its contents at the location of the insertion point.

To control subscriber options:

1. **Position the blinking insertion point anywhere within the published information.**

   If you published only a picture, select the picture.

2. Choose Subscriber Options from the Edit menu.

The Subscriber Options dialog box appears.

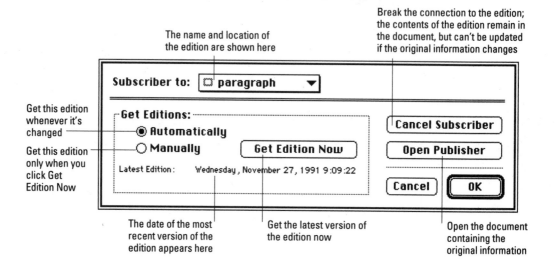

The name and location of the edition are shown here

Break the connection to the edition; the contents of the edition remain in the document, but can't be updated if the original information changes

Get this edition whenever it's changed

Get this edition only when you click Get Edition Now

The date of the most recent version of the edition appears here

Get the latest version of the edition now

Open the document containing the original information

Subscriber to: 🗀 paragraph ▼

Get Editions:
- ◉ **Automatically**
- ○ **Manually**   [**Get Edition Now**]

Latest Edition: Wednesday, November 27, 1991 9:09:22

[**Cancel Subscriber**]
[**Open Publisher**]
[Cancel] [OK]

3. Specify the desired options and then click OK or press Return.

To create a link:

1. In the source program (the program containing the original information), select the information you want to include in your Word document.

Remember that the source program must support Microsoft's OLE specification; see this topic's Overview section for details.

2. Activate the Word document that you want to include the information in.

3. Press Shift and choose Paste Link from the Edit menu.

Word inserts the information into the document. If you activate Show ¶, you'll see gray brackets around the information. If you edit the original information, Word automatically updates the linked version.

To open the original copy of linked information, cancel a link, or change a link's update options:

1. Select the linked information that you pasted using Paste Link.

You'll notice you can't select individual text characters, but only the entire block of information.

2. Choose Link Options from the Edit menu.

The Link Options dialog box appears, as shown in the following illustration.

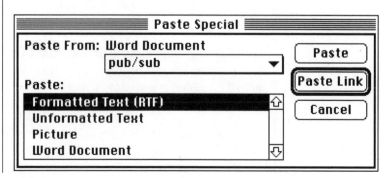

```
═══════════════ Link Options ═══════════════
Link To: LINK3
in:       ┌─────────────────────────┬───┐
          │ pub/sub                 │ ▼ │
          └─────────────────────────┴───┘
Using:    Microsoft Word
┌─Update───────────────────────┐   ┌────────────────┐
│ ⦿ Automatically              │   │  Cancel Link   │
│ ○ Manually    ┌────────────┐ │   ├────────────────┤
│               │ Update Now │ │   │  Open Source   │
│ ○ Never       └────────────┘ │   ├────────────────┤
└───────────────────────────────┘   │   Edit Link... │
                                     └────────────────┘
Format: ┌──────────────┬───┐  ┌──────────┐ ┌──────────┐
        │ Best Format  │ ▼ │  │  Cancel  │ │    OK    │
        └──────────────┴───┘  └──────────┘ └──────────┘
```

3. Specify the desired options and then click OK or press Return.

To embed an object:

1. Select the information you want to embed and then choose Copy from the Edit menu.

2. If necessary, switch to Word.

3. Position the blinking insertion point where you want to embed the information.

4. Choose Paste Special from the Edit menu.

The Paste Special dialog box appears.

```
═══════════════ Paste Special ═══════════════
Paste From: Word Document                   ┌──────────────┐
            ┌─────────────────────┬───┐     │    Paste     │
            │ pub/sub             │ ▼ │     └──────────────┘
            └─────────────────────┴───┘     ┌──────────────┐
Paste:                                      │  Paste Link  │
┌────────────────────────────────┬───┐      └──────────────┘
│ Formatted Text (RTF)           │ ⇧ │      ┌──────────────┐
│ Unformatted Text               │   │      │    Cancel    │
│ Picture                        │   │      └──────────────┘
│ Word Document                  │ ⇩ │
└────────────────────────────────┴───┘
```

5. Select the data type whose name includes the name of the application you used to create the object.

For example, if the data came from Excel, select the data type that contains *Excel* in its name. Similarly, if the data came from a Word document, select the data type containing the word *Word*.

6. Click the Paste button.

The information appears in your document, surrounded by a boundary similar to that used for graphics.

To edit an embedded object:

1. Double-click the object.

Word opens an object window for the object.

2. Edit the object as desired.

3. Click the object window's close box, or choose Close from the File menu.

The object window closes and Word updates the embedded object in the document.

Quick Tips

Publish and subscribe? linking? or embedding?

So you want to take advantage of the hot-link data exchange options Word provides. Which should you use: publish and subscribe, linking, or embedding? That depends. The table on the following page compares the three.

In the end, if you work primarily by yourself and you use Microsoft Excel, you might lean toward linking and embedding. On the other hand, if you work on a network and you use a wide variety of applications, publish and subscribe is probably the better exchange medium.

Transferring documents to or from IBM PCs

If you need to convert word processor documents that are stored on an IBM PC — or if you need to transfer Word documents to PCs — you have a few options.

✦ *Floppy disks.* All Macs made after August 1990 contain Super-Drive floppy disk drives that can work with 3½-inch MS-DOS disks. (One exception is the PowerBook 100 portable, which lacks a built-in floppy drive; an external SuperDrive is available as an option.) In order to work with a DOS disk using the Finder, you need a utility program such as Dayna Communications's DOS Mounter or Insignia Solutions's DOS Access. With such a utility, you can work with MS-DOS disks as though they were Mac disks.

Hot-link techniques compared

	Pros	Cons
Publish and subscribe	✦ Supported by a large number of applications ✦ Doesn't require applications to be open simultaneously ✦ Works across networks; many users can subscribe to a single edition ✦ You can subscribe to an edition created by a different program without having to have that program on your Macintosh	✦ Requires three files; it can be cumbersome to move files to a different machine via floppy disks, since you need to copy and keep track of three files, not one
Linking	✦ Requires a maximum of two files (the source and destination), making transporting linked files more practical ✦ Faster and more convenient than publish/subscribe for linking data within a Word document	✦ Currently supported by Microsoft Excel and Word and Equation Editor only ✦ If you're linking between two programs, you must have the second program and your Mac must have enough memory to open both simultaneously ✦ Other users can't access a linked file simultaneously
Embedding	✦ Requires only one file, making it easy to transport files ✦ Changes in an object are automatically reflected in your document	✦ Currently supported by Microsoft Excel and Word and Equation Editor only ✦ If you're linking between two programs, you must have the second program and your Mac must have enough memory to open both simultaneously ✦ Other users can't access an embedded object

(You can also access DOS disks using the Apple File Exchange utility, included with the Mac. Apple File Exchange doesn't allow you to see the disks on the Finder's desktop, however.) You can add 3½-inch or 5¼-inch disk drives to your Mac such as Dayna Communications's DaynaFile II.

✦ *Cable transfer utilities.* Products such as Dataviz's MacLink Plus/PC and Traveling Software's LapLink/Mac include cables and software that you can use to transfer files between Macs and PCs. Both products also let you transfer files over telephone modems.

✦ *Networks*. Farallon Computing and others offer expansion boards and software that add LocalTalk network compatibility to IBM PCs, PS/2s, and compatibles. With such hardware, you can access Mac folders and disks that have been made available via System 7's Sharing command (in the Finder's File menu).

For more details on Macintosh and IBM PC file-transfer products and techniques, see the *Macworld Complete Mac Handbook* (IDG Books Worldwide, 1991). It's available through the order page at the back of this book.

RTF: For exchanging formatted text

Word supports a special data-exchange format called *Rich-Text Format,* or *RTF*. This format uses text-only codes to represent character and paragraph formatting information. To you and me, an RTF file looks like gibberish, with one arcane code after another. But a program that can interpret RTF data can reconstruct a document's character and paragraph formatting. And because an RTF file contains no special characters, you can transfer it to IBM PCs and other non-Macs.

You can use the Save As dialog box's Save File As Type pop-up menu to save a document in RTF format. Several popular programs can interpret RTF files:

✦ Microsoft Word for Windows and for DOS

✦ Aldus PageMaker for the Macintosh and for Windows

✦ Microsoft Excel for the Macintosh and for Windows

✦ T/Maker's WriteNow for the Macintosh

✦ WordPerfect for the Macintosh and for DOS

Word can also interpret RTF files created by other programs. The Open and Save option of the Preferences dialog box contains a check box called Always Interpret RTF. If this box is checked, Word automatically interprets RTF files when you open them. If the box is unchecked and you open a file containing RTF codes, Word displays a message asking "Interpret RTF text?" If you click No, Word opens the file as a text-only file — you'll see all the cryptic RTF codes that describe the text's formatting. The only reason you might uncheck the Always Interpret RTF option is if you wanted to manually edit an RTF code — or if you're simply curious to see what RTF codes look like.

Saving memory by not copying formatted text to the Clipboard

Word can also copy text to the Clipboard in RTF form. You can then switch to a different program that supports RTF and choose Paste to have the text appear in its fully formatted form. The General option of the Preferences dialog box contains a check box called Include Formatted Text in Clipboard. Normally this box is checked — Word includes RTF data when you copy text to the Clipboard. But this data uses a considerable amount of memory. If you aren't interested in retaining formatting — or, if as is more likely, your other programs can't interpret RTF that you paste — uncheck the Include Formatted Text in Clipboard option.

Incidentally, you can paste formatted text from Microsoft Excel into Word, but you can't paste formatted text from Word into Excel. When you paste from Word to Excel, Excel ignores the formatting information and accepts only the text itself.

Topic 33
Managing Documents

Overview

Keeping track of the thousands of documents a hard disk holds can be, well, hard. Word provides two features that make managing files easier:

✦ *Summary Info dialog box.* By entering descriptive text into this dialog box, you can create an electronic catalog of your documents. You can also use Word's glossary feature to insert the summary information you type directly into a document's text.

✦ *Find File feature.* This lets you search for a document according to a variety of criteria. You can search for a piece of information you entered into the Summary Info dialog box, you can search for text that you know to be in the document itself, and you can search for documents created before or after a certain date or between two dates. (The Find File feature is available only if the Find File plug-in module is located in the Word Commands folder, which is within Word's folder; see Appendix A for details on Word's plug-in modules.)

This topic covers these features and also discusses *stationery* documents — template documents you can use to store often-used margin, page setup, and other formatting settings. If you always create a certain kind of document, you can save time and cut down on repetitive typing and formatting by creating stationery.

Summary Info

When you save a document for the first time, the Summary Info dialog box appears (assuming the Prompt for Summary Info option is checked in the Open and Save portion of the Preferences dialog box). The Summary Info dialog box contains boxes for:

✦ *Title.* The title of your document — for example, *Chapter 2* or *Memo to Fred* or *Trashy Novel Proposal.*

✦ *Subject.* A brief description of your document — for example, *Proposal for expansion of home office.*

+ *Author.* Word automatically supplies this information for you, based on the name you typed when you installed Word. You can change this entry by typing over it. You can also change the author name Word uses for subsequent documents: Choose Preferences from the Tools menu and then type your name in the Your Name box.

+ *Version.* A number or phrase (such as *Draft copy)* that identifies the version of the document.

+ *Keywords.* This box can contain any words that you feel describe the crux of the document — client names, key dates, basic concepts, and so on.

You can change a document's summary information at any time by choosing Summary Info from the File menu and then typing the new information and clicking OK or pressing Return.

You can insert a piece of summary information in a document by using Word's glossary feature. Each item of summary information is stored in its own standard glossary entry. The glossary entries are named *title, subject, author, version,* and *keywords.* See Topic 16 for details on Word's glossary feature.

Locating documents with Find File

You can access the Find File feature in two ways: by choosing Find File from the File menu or by clicking the Find File button that appears in the Open dialog box. Either way, the Search dialog box appears.

You can type up to 255 characters in each text box

Search	
File Name:	**OK**
Title:	**Cancel**
Any Text:	
Subject:	**Drives:**
	System 7.0
Author:	
Version:	**File Types:**
	Readable Files
Keywords:	
Finder Comments:	**Search Options:**
	Create New List

Choose the drive you want to search

Specify the type of file you want to locate

Create a new list of files or narrow down an existing list

┌Created──────────────────────────────
◉ **On Any Day** ○ **From:** 12/ 1/91 **To:** 12/ 1/91 **By:**

┌Last Saved───────────────────────────
◉ **On Any Day** ○ **From:** 12/ 1/91 **To:** 12/ 1/91 **By:**

Specify a date range and, if desired, an author name

Topic 33
Managing Documents

Here are some things to note about the Search dialog box:

✦ You can search for summary information, for any text that occurs within the file itself, and for text entered in the file's Get Info window at the Finder.

✦ You can fill in just one box or you can type something in several boxes. If you type information in more than one box, Word finds only those files that match all the criteria you specify. For example, if you type *Kevin* in the File Name box and *Westport* in the Any Text box, Word will find only those files whose names contain *Kevin* and that contain the word *Westport*.

✦ Word ignores capitalization when searching, so it doesn't matter whether you type capital or lowercase letters in the boxes. If you type *Proposal*, Word finds *proposal, PROPOSAL, Proposal,* and even *PrOpOsAl.*

✦ In the Any Text box, you can type the wildcard character (?) to search for any character. For example, if you type *Sm?th*, Word will find *Smith* and *Smyth*, but not *Smythe* (because *Smythe* contains an extra letter).

After you specify your search criteria, you can conduct the search by clicking OK or pressing Return. The Find File dialog box appears, and the hunt is on. During the search, Word displays a running total of any files that meet your search criteria. You can halt a search in progress by pressing Command-period.

After the search: Find File options

When the search is complete, Word displays the names of any files it finds and selects the first file in the list. The contents of the first file in the list appear on the right side of the dialog box, in the View box. You can select this text and copy it to the Clipboard: Simply drag across the text and then choose Copy from the Edit menu. This can be a handy way to extract some text from a document without having to actually open the document.

You can also use the Find File dialog box's View pop-up menu to get information about the files.

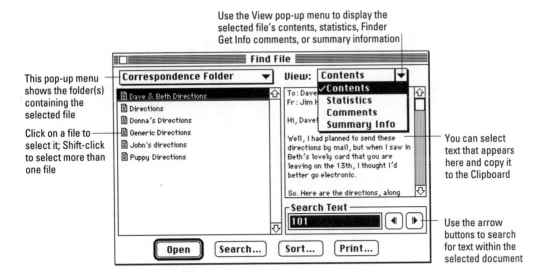

Use the View pop-up menu to display the selected file's contents, statistics, Finder Get Info comments, or summary information

This pop-up menu shows the folder(s) containing the selected file

Click on a file to select it; Shift-click to select more than one file

You can select text that appears here and copy it to the Clipboard

Use the arrow buttons to search for text within the selected document

Then you can click the buttons at the bottom of the Find File dialog box to open or print the selected file, to specify new or additional search criteria, or to sort a list of files according to their name, size, creation and modification dates, and other vital statistics.

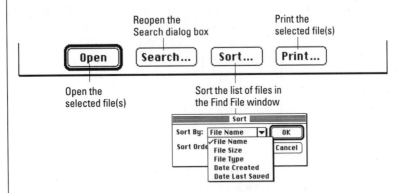

Reopen the Search dialog box

Print the selected file(s)

Open the selected file(s)

Sort the list of files in the Find File window

You can select more than one file in the file list box by clicking the first file you want, and then Shift-clicking each file you want to add to the selection. Use this feature to open or print a group of files in one fell swoop: Select the files and click Open or Print. You can also duplicate one or more files: Select the file or files you want to duplicate, and then choose Save As from the File menu. Word opens each file you selected and then immediately displays the Save As dialog box so that you can give each file a new name.

Stationery documents

You'll save time and cut down on repetitive formatting if you create stationery for the types of documents you create often, whether they're fax cover sheets, memos, business and personal letters, reports, scripts, or book chapters.

You can turn any document into a stationery document: Choose Save As from the File menu and then choose the Stationery option from the Save File as Type pop-up menu. Type a name for the stationery (you might want to include the word *stationery* in the name) and then click Save or press Return.

When you open a stationery document, Word creates a new, untitled document with its settings. You can then begin working on the document without having to slog through your old setup chores. And you don't have to worry about accidentally saving over the original version of the template.

For example, if you create a newsletter once a month, you can set up a stationery document that contains the newsletter's banner, formatting settings, and any boilerplate text that appears in each issue, such as "Table of Contents." When you need to create a new issue, open the stationery document and begin typing the new issue's articles.

Incidentally, many programs allow you to automatically open a certain stationery document whenever you start the program or choose New from the File menu. For example, with Claris's MacWrite II, if you name a stationery document *MacWrite II Options*, it's automatically opened when you start the program or choose New. Word doesn't have a similar feature, but you can accomplish similar results in either of two ways:

◆ Double-click the desired stationery document to open it.

◆ Add often-used stationery documents to Word's Work menu.

A selection of stationery documents for common types of documents is included with Jim Heid's Word Companion, the disk set (sold separately) that complements this book; see the order page at the back of this book for details.

Step-by-Step

This section shows how to search for files using Word's Find File feature and how to save a stationery document.

To search for files:

1. **Choose Find File from the File menu or click the Find File button that appears in Word's Open dialog box.**

   The Search dialog box appears.

2. **To search according to summary information, Finder Get Info comments, or text contents, type search criteria in the appropriate text boxes.**

   You can type up to 255 characters in each box. Each box can display only about 25 characters, but the text will scroll to the left as you type.

3. **To search according to the date the file was created, click the From button in the Created area. Then click the From and To arrows to set the date.**

   You can also specify the name of the person who created the file by typing the name in the By box.

4. **To search according to the date the file was last saved, click the From button in the Last Saved area. Then click the From and To arrows to set the date.**

   You can also specify the name of the person who last saved the file by typing the name in the By box.

5. **Optional: Use the Drives and File Types pop-up menus to specify where you want to search and which types of files Word should look for.**

   If you don't perform this step, Word looks on the hard drive that contains the Word program itself, and looks for all readable files. Topic 32 describes the file formats Word supports.

6. **Click OK or press Return.**

   The Find File dialog box appears and Word begins searching. If files are found that meet your criteria, their names appear. You can use the controls in the Find File window to open and print files, to sort their names, and to view their statistics. For details, see the section "After the search: Find File options" in this topic's Overview section.

To save a document as a stationery document:

1. **Choose Save As from the File menu.**

   The Save As dialog box appears.

2. **Choose the Stationery option from the Save File as Type pop-up menu.**

3. **Type a name for the stationery.**

   You might want to include the word *stationery* in the name — for example, *Memo stationery.*

4. **Click Save or press Return.**

   Word saves the document as a stationery document.

Quick Tips

Searching troubles? Watch for old criteria

If Word's Find File feature doesn't seem to be finding files you *know* are out there, examine the boxes in the Search dialog box. It may be that you didn't clear a box from a previous search. For example, say you searched for a file named *breakfast* this morning, and it's now afternoon and you want to search for a file whose subject is lunch. You choose Find File, but don't notice that the File Name box still contains the word *breakfast*. You type *lunch* in the Subject box (I'm getting hungry), click OK, and frown a moment later as Word reports no files were found. The moral: Be sure to clear old search criteria that you don't want Word to apply to the next search. This applies to the date criteria at the bottom of the search window, too: If you don't need to locate files that were created or modified within a certain date range, be sure the On Any Day buttons are selected.

Be specific: The more criteria, the better

When searching for files, try to be as specific as possible when specifying search criteria. For example, if you write a lot of memos about the XYZ Corporation and you need to locate the memo you wrote last week discussing its takeover bid, don't simply search for files containing the text *XYZ Corporation*. Instead, search for files containing the text *takeover* and use the date options at the bottom of the Search window to narrow the search to files created or modified last week.

How to search more than one drive

You may have noticed that the Search dialog box lets you search for files on only one drive at a time. If you want to search more than one drive, first search for the files on one drive, and then perform the following steps:

1. **In the Find File dialog box, click the Search button.**
   The Search dialog box reappears.

2. **Choose the desired drive's name from the Drives pop-up menu.**

3. **Choose the Add Matches To List option from the Search Options pop-up menu.**
   This tells Word to add any matches on the new drive to the list of matches from the previous search.

4. **Click OK or press Return.**
   Word searches the drive you specified and adds any matches to the list of files it found on the first drive.

I'm just browsing, thanks

Want to browse through the documents on your hard drive without having to open and close each one? Don't specify any search criteria in the Search dialog box: Simply choose Find File and then click OK or press Return when the Search dialog box appears, and Word will "locate" all the files on your hard disk. You can then use the Find File dialog box to examine each file's contents. If you want to narrow the list down a bit — perhaps to only Word documents — choose the appropriate file type from the File Type pop-up menu before you click OK in the Search dialog box.

Topic 34
Customizing Word

Overview

Your wishes are Word's commands. Word is a wonderfully malleable program, offering many options that enable you to customize its operation and its menus to suit your work habits and preferences.

Word's customizing features fall into two categories:

◆ *Preferences settings*. These control basic aspects of Word's operation, such as the default font and type size Word uses in new, untitled documents, and whether or not the ruler and ribbon appear when you open a document. You specify your preferences by using the Tools menu's Preferences command.

◆ *Command settings*. These control which commands appear on Word's menus, as well as the keyboard shortcuts Word responds to. You can remove menu commands you don't use. Better still, you can add menu commands that correspond to options in Word's dialog boxes. Instead of having to choose a command and then thread your way through a dialog box, you can simply choose the desired option directly from a menu — or press a keyboard shortcut. You can also change any or all of Word's keyboard shortcuts, and you can create numerous keyboard shortcuts for a single command. You customize Word's menus and keyboard shortcuts by choosing Commands from the Tools menu or by using shortcut keys when dialog boxes are open. This topic covers both techniques.

The Preferences dialog box

The key to setting preferences is the Preferences dialog box, which appears when you choose Preferences from the Tools menu, as shown in the following illustration.

```
┌────────────────────────────────────────────────────┐
│ ▤▢        ▨▨▨▨▨ Preferences ▨▨▨▨▨                    │
├────────────────────────────────────────────────────┤
│  🔲W  ⇧   Your Name:  │Trixie Norton              │ │
│ General   Your Initials: │tn                     │   │
│                                                      │
│   🔲W     Custom Paper Size   Width: │         │     │
│  View                        Height: │         │     │
│                                                      │
│   🔲W     Measurement Unit: │Inch      ▼│           │
│ Open And Save  ⊠ "Smart" Quotes                      │
│           ⊠ Background Repagination                  │
│    Ef     ⊠ Include Formatted Text in Clipboard      │
│ Default Font  ⊠ Drag-and-Drop Text Editing           │
│                                                      │
│   📚                                                 │
│ Spelling ⬇                                           │
└────────────────────────────────────────────────────┘
  Category panel   Options panel
```

As the preceding illustration shows, the Preferences dialog box contains two *panels:* the *category* panel and the *options* panel. The category panel — the panel on the left — lists preferences categories, each of which pertains to a specific aspect of Word's operation (such as the way it opens and saves documents). When you choose a category, the options panel shows the settings relevant to that category. (This is the way the Mac's Control Panel desk accessory operates in System versions prior to 7.0.)

The following table summarizes the categories and options available in the Preferences dialog box. Many of these options are described in detail elsewhere in this book; consult the index to learn where.

Preferences categories

Category/setting	Description
General	
Your Name	Default name used for summary information
Your Initials	Initials placed next to voice annotations
Custom Paper Size	Dimensions of custom paper size (available for ImageWriter printers only)
Measurement Unit	Preferred unit of measurement (inches, centimeters, points, or picas)
"Smart" Quotes	When checked, Word uses typographically correct quotes

Category/setting	Description
Background Repagination	When checked, Word keeps page breaks accurate during editing
Include Formatted Text in Clipboard	When checked, Word adds RTF codes to cut or copied text
Drag-and-Drop Text Editing	When checked, this text-editing feature is available
View	
Show Hidden Text	When checked, hidden text is visible in the document
Show Table Gridlines	When checked, dotted lines separate table rows and columns; gridlines do not print
Show Text Boundaries in Page Layout View	When checked, dotted borders indicate headers, footers, and framed text areas
Show Picture Placeholders	When checked, Word displays gray boxes instead of pictures for faster performance
Open Documents in Page Layout View	When checked, Word always opens documents in page layout view
Open Documents with Ruler On	When checked, Word always shows the ruler when opening a document
Open Documents with Ribbon On	When checked, Word always shows the ribbon when opening a document
Show Function Keys on Menus	When checked, function key numbers appear in menu keyboard shortcuts
List Recently Opened Documents	When checked, the last four opened or saved documents are listed in the File menu
Use Short Menu Names	Abbreviates certain menu names to shorten the menu bar (useful on small screens)
Open and Save	
Always Interpret RTF	When checked, Word automatically interprets RTF files that you open
Always Make Backup	When checked, Word makes a backup copy when you save a file
Allow Fast Saves	When checked, Word saves documents faster, but documents use more disk space
Prompt for Summary Info	When checked, Word displays Summary Info dialog box when you save for the first time
Save Reminder	When checked, you can specify an interval at which Word reminds you to save
Default Font	
Default Font	Lets you choose the font Word uses in new, untitled documents

Category/setting	Description
Default Size	Lets you choose the font size Word uses in new, untitled documents
Spelling	
Main Dictionary	Lets you choose a language dictionary
Custom Dictionaries	Lets you create, open, and edit custom dictionaries
Always Suggest	When checked, Word always suggests alternatives for words it doesn't recognize
Ignore Words in UPPERCASE	When checked, Word skips over words in all capitals
Ignore Words with Numbers	When checked, Word skips over words containing numbers
Grammar	
Rule Groups	Lets you control which grammatical or style rules Word checks; you can view information about a rule by selecting it and then clicking Explain
Catch	Lets you control how Word examines split infinitives, consecutive nouns, and prepositional phrases
Show Document Statistics	When checked, Word displays information about the document after checking its style and grammar
Thesaurus	
Language	Lets you choose a language for Word's thesaurus
Hyphenation	
Language	Lets you choose a language for Word's hyphenation feature

Customizing menus and keyboard shortcuts

To add commands to or remove them from Word's menus, you can use either of two techniques:

✦ *Shortcut keys provide the fastest way to add or remove commands.* To remove a command, press Command-Option-minus (-) and then choose the doomed command. To add a command, press Command-Option-plus (+) and then click a dialog box option or a button or icon in the ruler or ribbon. Note that you must use the plus and minus keys on the main keyboard, not the ones on the number keypad. (The minus key is also the hyphen key — the key to the right of the zero key.) Also, you don't have to press Shift when using the Command-Option-plus sequence.

♦ *The Commands dialog box, which appears when you choose Commands from the Tools menu, gives you more control over the process of adding and removing commands.* You can, for example, specify where you want a new command to appear. You can also customize keyboard shortcuts using the Commands dialog box.

This topic's Step-by-Step section shows how to use both techniques.

The Commands dialog box

When you choose Commands, the Commands dialog box appears.

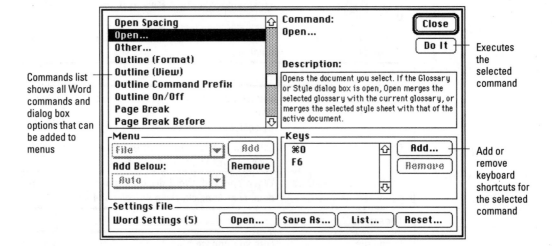

Commands list shows all Word commands and dialog box options that can be added to menus

Executes the selected command

Add or remove keyboard shortcuts for the selected command

The commands list shows all of Word's commands, options, and features. Some of the commands are already present in Word's menus, but most aren't. When you're using the Commands dialog box to add a command to Word's menus, your first step is to locate the command you want to add. You can jump to a particular command by quickly typing the first few characters of its name.

When you select a command, its description appears in the Description box. (This description is the same one that appears if you activate System 7's balloon help feature.) If the command has a corresponding keyboard shortcut, the shortcut appears in the Keys area of the dialog box. Note that a single command can have more than one shortcut assigned to it, as shown in the following illustration.

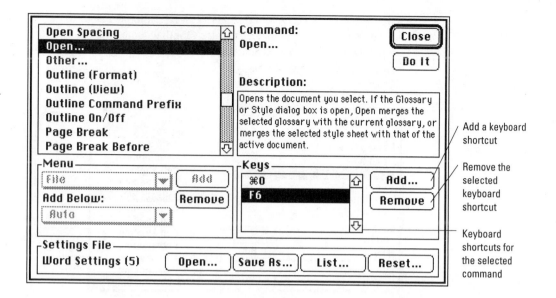

Add a keyboard shortcut

Remove the selected keyboard shortcut

Keyboard shortcuts for the selected command

If the command is already present in one of Word's menus, that menu is listed in the Menu area. You can remove the command from its menu by clicking the Remove button. If the command isn't present in any of Word's menus, the Menu area shows the default menu — the menu where the command will be inserted unless you specify otherwise.

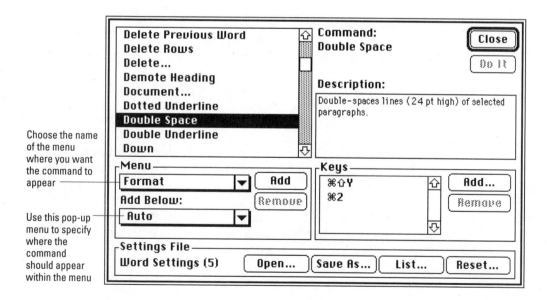

Choose the name of the menu where you want the command to appear

Use this pop-up menu to specify where the command should appear within the menu

When you select a command that has a colon (:) after its name, Word displays a pop-up menu that lists options for that command. For example, if you select the Cell Shading: command, a pop-up menu appears listing various shading options.

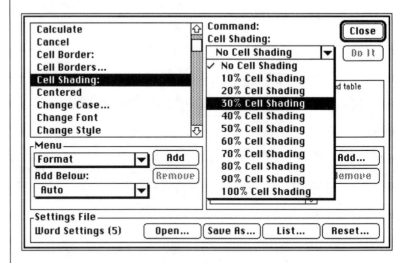

You can add as many options from this pop-up menu as you like; choose an option and click Add, and then repeat the process for each option that you want to have appear in Word's menus.

The Work menu

If you frequently work with particular styles, glossary entries, or documents, you can add their names to Word's Work menu:

✦ To add a style to the Work menu, press Command-Option-plus and then choose the desired style from the ruler's Style pop-up menu or from the list of styles in the Style dialog box.

✦ To add a glossary entry to the Work menu, press Command-Option-plus and then choose the desired entry from the Glossary dialog box.

✦ To add a document's name to the Work menu, press Command-Option-plus when the Open dialog box is open, and then double-click the document's name.

Working with settings files

The preferences and commands settings you specify are stored in a *settings file* named Word Settings (5). The *(5)* is part of the file's name, and indicates that the settings file is for Word version 5. This file is stored in the System Folder. If you're using Apple's System 7 software, the file is stored in the Preferences folder within the System Folder.

When you start up Word, it reads the Word Settings (5) file and adjusts its menus and keyboard shortcuts as needed. When you quit Word, it automatically saves your latest Preferences and Commands settings in the Word Settings (5) file. If you click the Use As Default button present in many of Word's dialog boxes, your choices are also stored in the current settings file.

Having one settings file is powerful enough, but Word doesn't stop there. You can create any number of settings files and switch among them by using buttons at the bottom of the Commands dialog box.

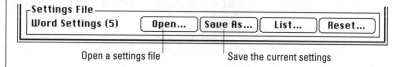

Open a settings file   Save the current settings

Word's ability to switch between settings files enables you to create separate settings files for various tasks. For example, if you frequently create tables using Word's table editor, you might want to customize Word's menus to contain the table-formatting options you use most. You can then save the customized menus in their own settings file — perhaps one called *Table Settings* — and then switch to that settings file when you're working with tables.

A selection of settings files for various tasks is included with Jim Heid's Word Companion, the disk set (sold separately) that complements this book. See the order page at the back of the book for details.

Step-by-Step

This section shows how to set preferences using the Preferences command, how to add and remove menu commands using keyboard shortcuts and using the Commands dialog box, and how to work with settings files.

To set preferences:

1. **Choose Preferences from the Tools menu.**

   The Preferences dialog box appears.

2. **Select the desired preferences category from the category panel.**

   You can select a category using the mouse or using the keyboard's up arrow and down arrow keys.

3. **Specify the desired preference(s) for the current category.**

4. **Repeat steps 2 and 3 until you've specified all the desired preferences.**

5. **Close the Preferences dialog box by clicking its close box.**

To add a command to Word's menus using keyboard shortcuts:

1. **Open the dialog box that contains the option you want to add. If you want to add a command pertaining to the ruler or ribbon, be sure the ruler or ribbon is visible (choose Ruler or Ribbon from the View menu).**

   For example, if you want to add the Keep Lines Together option from the Paragraph dialog box, open the Paragraph dialog box.

2. **Press Command-Option-plus. (You don't have to press Shift.)**

   The mouse pointer turns into a bold plus sign (+). If you decide not to add an option, you can cancel the operation and restore the normal mouse pointer by pressing Command-period or the Esc key.

3. **Click the desired option in the dialog box, or click the desired button or icon in the ruler or ribbon.**

   If the item you clicked has a corresponding command, Word flashes the menu bar and the pointer returns to its normal shape. If the item doesn't have a corresponding command, the pointer remains a bold plus sign.

4. **If you opened a dialog box, close it.**

To remove a command from a menu using shortcut keys:

1. **Press Command-Option-minus.**

   The mouse pointer turns into a bold minus sign (-). If you decide not to remove a command, you can cancel the operation and restore the normal mouse pointer by pressing Command-period or the Esc key.

2. Choose the command you want to remove.

The menu bar flashes and the command is removed.

To add a command using the Commands dialog box:

1. Choose Commands from the Tools menu.

The Commands dialog box appears.

2. In the commands list, select the command you want to add.

When you select the command, a description of it appears in the Description box. If the command has keyboard shortcuts, they appear in the Keys area of the dialog box.

3. Optional: In the Menu area, choose the menu to which you want to add the command.

If you don't perform this step, Word will add the command to the menu that's already listed in the menu area.

4. Optional: In the Menu area, use the Add Below pop-up menu to specify the command's position within the menu.

If you don't perform this step, the command will be positioned at its default location, which is often the bottom of the menu.

5. Click the Add button.

The menu bar flashes and then the menu to which you've added the command flashes.

6. Optional: Specify or change keyboard shortcuts for the command.

If you want to perform this step, see the next set of instructions for details.

7. Click the Close button.

If you click the Do It button, Word executes the command you selected.

To assign or change a keyboard shortcut using the Commands dialog box:

1. Choose Commands from the Tools menu.

The Commands dialog box appears.

2. In the commands list, select the command whose keyboard shortcuts you want to change.

If the command has keyboard shortcuts already, they appear in the Keys area of the dialog box.

3. **To remove a keyboard shortcut, select it and then click the Remove button.**

4. **To add a keyboard shortcut, click the Add button.**

   A dialog box appears telling you to press the key sequence for the selected command.

   Type the keystroke for the "Double Space" command.

   [Cancel]

   If you decide not to add a keyboard shortcut, click the Cancel button.

5. **Type the keystroke sequence that you want to assign to the command.**

   You can use the following key combinations. Note that older Mac keyboards do not contain Control keys. For *character*, substitute any character on the keyboard or number keypad. (Be sure Num Lock is turned off before pressing a keypad key; before choosing Commands, press the Clear key on the number keypad until Num Lock does *not* appear in the lower-left corner of the document window.)

   Command-*character*
   Command-Option-*character*
   Command-Shift-*character*
   Command-Shift-Option-*character*
   Control-*character*
   Control-Shift-*character*
   Control-Shift-Option-*character*
   Command-Control-*character*
   Command-Control-Shift-*character*
   Command-Control-Option-*character*

If the key sequence you type is already assigned to a command, Word asks if it's OK to reassign it.

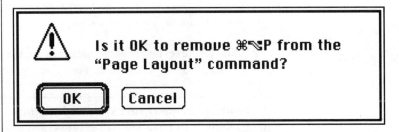

Click OK if you want to reassign it; click Cancel to type a different key sequence.

6. **Optional: To add another key sequence to the same command, repeat steps 5 and 6.**

7. **To modify a different command's keyboard shortcut, repeat steps 2 through 6.**

8. **When you've finished working with the Commands dialog box, click the Close button or press Return.**

To save a settings file:

1. **If you haven't already, choose Commands from the Tools menu.**
   The Commands dialog box appears.

2. **Click the Save As button at the bottom of the dialog box.**
   The Save As dialog box appears.

3. **Type a name for the settings file and then click Save or press Return.**
   Word saves the settings in the new file. The file you just created becomes the current settings file until you quit Word.

To open a settings file:

1. **Choose Commands from the Tools menu.**
   The Commands dialog box appears.

2. **Click the Open button at the bottom of the dialog box.**
   The Open dialog box appears.

3. **Locate the settings file you want to open and double-click its name, or select its name and then click Open or press Return.**
   Word opens the settings file and adjusts its menus to reflect its settings.

To reset the menus and keyboard shortcuts to Microsoft's defaults:

1. Choose Commands from the Tools menu.

The Commands dialog box appears.

2. Click the Reset button at the bottom of the dialog box.

A dialog box appears listing three reset options.

```
⦿ Reset to Microsoft Standard Settings          ⌈  OK  ⌉
○ Revert to Last Saved Settings
○ Add All Commands to Their Default Menus        ⌈ Cancel ⌉
```

3. Select the Reset to Microsoft Standard Settings option and then click OK or press Return.

As a shortcut, you can also simply double-click the option.

To reset the menus and keyboard shortcuts to the last saved settings:

1. Choose Commands from the Tools menu.

The Commands dialog box appears.

2. Click the Reset button at the bottom of the dialog box.

A dialog box appears listing three reset options.

3. Select the Revert to Last Saved Settings option and then click OK or press Return.

To add all commands and options to their default menus:

1. Choose Commands from the Tools menu.

The Commands dialog box appears.

2. Click the Reset button at the bottom of the dialog box.

A dialog box appears listing three reset options.

3. Select the Add All Commands to Their Default Menus option and then click OK or press Return.

It may take Word several seconds to modify its menus — and you'll have some huge menus to wade through once it's finished.

Quick Tips

Think "customize"

As you work in Word, always be thinking about ways to customize the program's preferences settings, menus, and keyboard shortcuts to match the task at hand. If you find yourself traveling to a particular dialog box frequently, chances are you can save time by adding one or more of its options to Word's menus. If Word's keyboard shortcuts tangle your fingers, make up your own. If you always summon a particular style, add it to the Work menu. If you frequently work with a few stationery documents, add their names to the Work menu. Take advantage of Word's customizing features, and you'll streamline your work. Don't agonize — customize!

The Assign to Key command

Word's Assign to Key command lets you quickly create keyboard shortcuts for commands that are already on Word's menus. To issue the Assign to Key command, press Command-Option-plus — but use the plus sign on the number keypad. The mouse pointer turns into a Command symbol (the cloverleaf). Next, choose the command for which you want to add a keyboard shortcut. Word asks you to type the key sequence. If the sequence is already used by a different command, Word asks if it's OK to reassign it to the command you chose. If you can't remember the Command-Option-numeric-plus key sequence, you can use the Commands dialog box to add the Assign to Key command to Word's menus.

Using the Commands dialog box to find a keyboard shortcut

If you'd like to use a particular key sequence for a shortcut but you're not sure if it's already in use, you can use the Commands dialog box to find out. Choose Commands, and then press the key sequence. If the key sequence is in use, Word selects the command that it's assigned to. If the sequence isn't in use, nothing happens.

Creating a table of commands

You can create a list of Word's commands and their keyboard short-cuts by clicking the List button in the Commands dialog box. A dialog box appears that lets you list the current menu and keyboard settings, or all commands and their keyboard shortcuts. You can edit, sort, and print the table using Word's standard table-editing features (discussed in Topic 24).

Opening settings files from the Finder

You can open settings files by double-clicking them at the Finder. If you use MultiFinder or System 7, this technique is faster than choosing the Commands command, clicking the Open button, and then locating and opening the desired file.

A sampler of commands to add

The best way to find out which commands Word can add to its menus is to explore the commands list in the Commands dialog box. The following table lists a small sampling of commands you might find useful on your menus. Not listed here are common formatting commands for editing tables and formatting characters.

Command sampler

Command name	Default menu	Description
Copy As Picture	Edit	Copies selected text to the Clipboard as a picture that you can resize and stretch
Delete	File	Opens a dialog box that lets you delete a file
Save Copy As	File	Lets you save a copy of a document while keeping the editing focus on the original version
1½ Line Spaced	Format	Sets line spacing to 1½ lines
Double Space	Format	Sets line spacing to 2 lines
Fast Save Enabled	Tools	Lets you activate/deactivate Word's fast save feature
Screen Test	Tools	A built-in screen saver that displays geometric patterns on the screen
Sort Descending	Tools	Sorts selection in descending (for example, Z to A) order
Show Table Gridlines	View	Shows/hides table gridlines

Appendix A
Word Installation Tips

Generally, you don't have to worry about how to install Word or where certain files need to be located in order for Word to operate. The Installer program that sets up Word on your hard drive handles these details for you. Still, knowing a bit about how Word is installed can help you fine-tune your Word setup so that the program runs efficiently and doesn't gobble too much memory or hard disk space.

Installing Word

When you run the Installer program, it displays a dialog box that lets you choose between an easy, one-button installation and a custom installation. If you click the Install button, you get a standard Word installation that includes the Word program and all plug-in modules and file converters. Plug-in modules add features to Word, such as its grammar checker; converters enable Word to read and create other file formats. Both are described later in this appendix.

If you click the Customize button, a dialog box appears that lets you select which portions of Word you want. If you're installing Word on a system without a great deal of free hard disk space, you might click Customize and then select those portions of Word you want. If you never exchange files with IBM PCs, for example, don't select the PC converters — you save roughly 800K of disk space. Similarly, if you don't use Word's somewhat gimmicky grammar checker, don't select it. The savings? Again, almost 800K.

If you decide you need a certain converter or plug-in module later, you can run the Installer, click the Customize button, and then install the features or converters you need by selecting each one.

Fine-tuning Word's memory requirements

If you use MultiFinder or System 7, you can use the Finder's Get Info command to specify how much memory Word uses when it runs. By decreasing Word's memory requirements, you may be able to run more programs simultaneously. By increasing Word's memory requirements, you can improve its performance, especially with complex tasks such as compiling a lengthy index or table of contents.

You can decrease Word's memory requirements to as low as 512K. Some of Word's plug-in modules, including the grammar checker and the picture window, won't run well (or at all) in such cramped confines, however. Also, Word may run slower in print preview or page layout modes. Still, these trade-offs may be a small price to pay in order to be able to run more programs simultaneously.

To change Word's memory requirements:

1. Quit Word if it's running.

2. At the Finder, select the Word icon.

3. Choose Get Info from the File menu.

4. Type the desired memory size in the Current Size box.
   In System versions prior to 7.0, this box is labeled Application Memory Size.

5. Close the Get Info window.

Installing Word's files manually

If you have Aladdin Systems's StuffIt Classic or StuffIt Deluxe programs (or UnStuffIt Deluxe, which is free through user's groups and online services), you can install some of Word's files manually. The Word master files whose names are enclosed in [brackets] are actually StuffIt *archives* — special versions of the original files compressed to use less disk space. You might want to install a file using StuffIt if your original Word Install disk has become damaged and is unable to install Word automatically.

Saving disk space by unplugging plug-in modules

Some of Word's features require that separate files be located on your hard disk, within a folder named Word Commands. These files contain software that add features to Word, and are called *plug-in modules*.

You can reduce Word's disk and memory requirements by removing files for commands you don't use. This can be handy if you're using a Macintosh PowerBook or any time you're running low on disk space. The following table lists the names of Word's plug-in modules and their approximate disk space requirements. The disk space figures are based on prerelease copies of Word 5.0, and may differ slightly from the final released product. Entries containing *U.S. English* refer to files that accompany English-language versions of Word sold in the United States; versions sold for other languages or countries will have files whose names reflect that language or country.

Word plug-in modules

File name	Purpose	Disk space used (in K)
Find File	Locates files based on criteria you specify	78K
Mail	Allows exchange of electronic mail via Microsoft Mail (not included)	20K
Picture	Adds Picture window to Word	71K
Spelling	Checks spelling	139K
Symbol	Simplifies accessing accents and special characters	13K
U.S. English Dictionary	Contains spelling checker and dictionary	254K
U.S. English Grammar	Contains grammar and style rules	763K
U.S. English Hyphenation	Contains hyphenation data	25K
Voice Annotation	Lets you attach recorded comments to documents	34K

Saving disk space by removing converters

Word uses files called *converters* to read and create some graphics files as well as files created with other word processors. If you're tight on disk space, feel free to remove converters you don't use. The following table lists the names of Word's converters and their approximate disk space requirements. (The disk space figures are based on prerelease copies of Word 5.0, and may differ slightly from the final released product.)

Word converters

File name	Purpose	Disk space used (in K)
EPS/TIFF/PICT	Enables Word to open EPS, TIFF, and PICT graphics files	25K
MacWrite II Converter	Enables Word to open and create MacWrite II documents	202K
Text with Layout	Enables Word to apply basic formatting to text-only files you open	200K
Windows Metafile Converter	Enables Word to open Windows metafiles, a graphics format used in Microsoft Windows (IBM PC)	81K
Word for DOS 5.x	Enables Word to open and create Microsoft Word for MS-DOS documents (IBM PC)	165K

File name	Purpose	Disk space used (in K)
Word for Windows 1	Enables Word to open and create Word for Windows version 1.x documents (IBM PC)	157K
Word for Windows 2	Enables Word to open and create Word for Windows version 2.x documents (IBM PC)	166K
WordPerfect for DOS 5.x	Enables Word to open and create WordPerfect 5.0 and 5.1 documents (IBM PC)	237K

Saving disk space by removing help files

You can also reduce Word's disk space appetite by removing one or both of its help files:

◆ *Word 5 Command Help* (101K). This file contains the text that appears in System 7 help balloons as well as in the Commands dialog box.

◆ *Word 5 Help* (420K). This file contains Word's detailed on-screen help.

Both files are stored in the Word Commands folder.

Removing Word from your hard disk

Someday you might want to remove the Word program from your hard disk. Perhaps you suspect the program has become corrupted by a virus or a bad spot on your hard disk — or perhaps you've found a word processor you simply like better. Whatever the reason, you can remove Word by dragging its folder to the Trash and then choosing Empty Trash from the Finder's file menu.

But Word also relies on a few files in your System Folder, and if you want to remove all traces of the Word program from your machine, you'll want to remove these files, too. The following table lists the other Word-related files that you'll find on your hard disk.

File name	Where you'll find it
Voice Record	In the System Folder (with System 7, in the Extensions folder, within the System Folder)
Voice Record Help	In the System Folder (with System 7, in the Extensions folder, within the System Folder)
Word Settings (5)	In the System Folder (with System 7, in the Preferences folder, within the System Folder)
Embedding Preferences	In the System Folder (with System 7, in the Preferences folder, within the System Folder)

Appendix B
Keyboard Shortcuts

Command	Key sequence	Menu
Activate Keyboard Menus	Command-Tab	
Activate Keyboard Menus	Keypad-period	
Add to Menu	Command-Option-equals	
Add to Menu	Command-Shift-Option-equals	
All Caps	Command-Shift-K	
All Caps	Shift-F10	
Assign to Key	Command-Option-Keypad-plus	
Assign to Key	Command-Shift-Option-Left arrow	
Backspace	Delete	
Bold	F10	Format
Bold	Command-B	Format
Bold	Command-Shift-B	Format
Calculate	Command-equals	Tools
Cancel	Esc	
Cancel	Command-period	
Centered	Command-Shift-C	
Change Font	Command-Shift-E	
Change Style	Command-Shift-S	
Character...	F14	Format
Character...	Command-D	Format
Close	Command-W	File
Commands...	Command-Shift-Option-C	Tools
Context Sensitive Help	Help	
Context Sensitive Help	Command-/	
Copy	F3	Edit
Copy	Command-C	Edit
Copy as Picture	Command-Option-D	
Copy Formats	Command-Option-V	
Copy Formats	Shift-F4	

Command	Key sequence	Menu
Copy Text	Command-Option-C	
Copy Text	Shift-F3	
Cut	F2	Edit
Cut	Command-X	Edit
Delete Forward	Delete	
Delete Forward	Command-Option-F	
Delete Next Word	Command-Option-G	
Delete Previous Word	Command-Option-Delete	
Delete Rows	Command-Control-X	
Document...	Command-F14	Format
Dotted Underline	Command-Shift-\	
Dotted Underline	Option-F12	
Double Space	Command-Shift-Y	
Double Underline	Command-Shift-[	
Double Underline	Shift-F12	
Down	Command-[	Font
Down	Command-Shift-Option-<	Font
Extend to Character	Command-Option-H	
Extend to Character	Keypad-minus	
Find Again	Command-Option-A	
Find Again	Keypad-equals	
Find...	Command-F	Edit
First Line Indent	Command-Shift-F	
Flush Left	Command-Shift-L	
Flush Right	Command-Shift-R	
Footnotes	Command-Shift-Option-S	View
Footnote...	Command-E	Insert
Glossary...	Command-K	Edit
Go Back	Command-Option-Z	
Go Back	Keypad-0	
Go To...	Command-G	Edit
Grammar...	Command-Shift-G	Tools
Hanging Indent	Command-Shift-T	
Hidden Text	Command-Shift-V	
Hidden Text	Command-Shift-X	

Command	Key sequence	Menu
Hidden Text	Option-F9	
Hyphenation...	Shift-F15	Tools
Insert Formula	Command-Option-\	
Insert Glossary Entry	Command-Delete	
Insert Nonbreaking Hyphen	Command-'	
Insert Nonbreaking Space	Command-spacebar	
Insert Nonbreaking Space	Option-spacebar	
Insert Optional Hyphen	Command-hyphen	
Insert Rows	Command-Control-V	
Insert Tab	Tab	
Insert Tab	Option-Tab	
Insert ¶ Above Row	Command-Option-spacebar	
Italic	F11	Format
Italic	Command-I	Format
Italic	Command-Shift-I	Format
Justified	Command-Shift-J	
Larger Font Size	Command-Shift->	
Larger Font Size	Command-Shift-period	
Line Break	Shift-Return	
Move Down One Text Area	Command-Option-Keypad-2	
Move Left One Text Area	Command-Option-Keypad-4	
Move Right One Text Area	Command-Option-Keypad-6	
Move Text	Command-Option-X	
Move Text	Shift-F2	
Move to Bottom of Window	End	
Move to End of Document	Command-End	
Move to End of Document	Command-Keypad-3	
Move to End of Line	Keypad-1	
Move to First Text Area	Command-Option-Keypad-7	
Move to Last Text Area	Command-Option-Keypad-1	
Move to Next Character	Right arrow	
Move to Next Character	Command-Option-L	
Move to Next Character	Keypad-6	
Move to Next Line	Down arrow	

Command	Key sequence	Menu
Move to Next Line	Command-Option-comma	
Move to Next Line	Keypad-2	
Move to Next Page	Command-Page down	
Move to Next Paragraph	Command-Down arrow	
Move to Next Paragraph	Command-Keypad-2	
Move to Next Paragraph	Command-Option-B	
Move to Next Sentence	Command-Keypad-1	
Move to Next Text Area	Command-Option-Keypad-3	
Move to Next Window	Command-Option-W	
Move to Next Word	Command-Right arrow	
Move to Next Word	Command-Keypad-6	
Move to Next Word	Command-Option-;	
Move to Previous Cell	Shift-Tab	
Move to Previous Character	Left arrow	
Move to Previous Character	Command-Option-K	
Move to Previous Character	Keypad-4	
Move to Previous Line	Up arrow	
Move to Previous Line	Keypad-8	
Move to Previous Page	Command-Page up	
Move to Previous Paragraph	Command-Up arrow	
Move to Previous Paragraph	Command-Keypad-8	
Move to Previous Paragraph	Command-Option-Y	
Move to Previous Sentence	Command-Keypad-7	
Move to Previous Text Area	Command-Option-Keypad-9	
Move to Previous Word	Command-Left arrow	
Move to Previous Word	Command-Keypad-4	
Move to Previous Word	Command-Option-J	
Move to Start of Document	Command-Home	
Move to Start of Document	Command-Keypad-9	
Move to Start of Line	Keypad-7	
Move to Top of Window	Home	
Move to Top of Window	Command-Keypad-5	
Move Up One Text Area	Command-Option-Keypad-8	
Nest Paragraph	Command-Shift-N	

Command	Key sequence	Menu
New	F5	File
New	Command-N	File
New Paragraph	Return	
New Paragraph	Enter	
New Window	Shift-F5	Window
New ¶ After Ins. Point	Command-Option-Return	
New ¶ with Same Style	Command-Return	
No Paragraph Border	Command-Option-1	
Normal	Command-Option-N	View
Normal Paragraph	Command-Shift-P	
Numeric Lock	Keypad-Clear	
Open Any File...	Shift-F6	
Open Spacing	Command-Shift-O	
Open...	F6	File
Open...	Command-O	File
Outline (Format)	Command-Shift-D	
Outline (Format)	Shift-F11	
Outline (View)	Command-Option-O	View
Outline (View)	Shift-F13	View
Outline Command Prefix	Command-Option-T	
Page Break	Shift-Enter	Insert
Page Layout	F13	View
Page Layout	Command-Option-P	View
Page Setup...	Shift-F8	File
Paragraph...	Command-M	Format
Paragraph...	Shift-F14	Format
Paste	F4	Edit
Paste	Command-V	Edit
Paste Link	Option-F4	
Paste Object	Command-F4	
Paste Special Character	Command-Option-Q	
Plain Text	Command-Shift-Z	Format
Plain Text	Shift-F9	Format
Print Preview...	Command-Option-I	File

Command	Key sequence	Menu
Print Preview...	Option-F13	File
Print...	F8	File
Print...	Command-P	File
Quit	Command-Q	File
Remove From Menu	Command-Option-minus	
Renumber...	Command-F15	Tools
Repeat	Command-Y	Edit
Replace...	Command-H	Edit
Revert To Style	F9	Format
Revert To Style	Command-Shift-spacebar	Format
Ribbon	Command-Option-R	View
Ruler	Command-R	View
Save	F7	File
Save	Command-S	File
Save As...	Shift-F7	File
Scroll Line Down	Command-Option-/	
Scroll Line Down	Keypad-plus	
Scroll Line Up	Command-Option-[	
Scroll Line Up	Keypad-multiply (*)	
Scroll Screen Down	Page down	
Scroll Screen Down	Command-Option-period	
Scroll Screen Down	Keypad-3	
Scroll Screen Up	Page up	
Scroll Screen Up	Keypad-9	
Section Break	Command-Enter	Insert
Section...	Option-F14	Format
Select All	Command-A	Edit
Select All	Command-Option-M	Edit
Shadow	Command-Shift-W	
Shadow	Option-F11	
Show/Hide ¶	Command-J	View
Small Caps	Command-Shift-H	
Small Caps	Option-F10	
Smaller Font Size	Command-Shift-<	

Command	Key sequence	Menu
Smaller Font Size	Command-Shift-comma	
Spelling...	F15	Tools
Spelling...	Command-L	Tools
Split Window	Command-Option-S	
Strikethru	Command-Shift-/	
Style...	Command-T	Format
Subscript 2 pt	Command-Shift-hyphen	
Superscript 3 pt	Command-Shift-equals	
Symbol Font	Command-Shift-Q	
Thick Paragraph Border	Command-Option-2	
Unassign Keystroke	Command-Option-Keypad-minus	
Underline	F12	Format
Underline	Command-U	Format
Underline	Command-Shift-U	Format
Undo	F1	Edit
Undo	Command-Z	Edit
Unnest Paragraph	Command-Shift-M	
Up	Command-]	Font
Up	Command-Shift-Option-<	Font
Update Link	Option-F3	
Word Count...	Option-F15	Tools
Word Underline	Command-F12	
Word Underline	Command-Shift-]	
Zoom Window	Command-Option-]	

Appendix C
Glossary

This glossary contains definitions of common word processing terms as well as Word-related terminology. More specifically, it contains definitions of the appropriate italicized terms in this book. (And that shows how useful Word's ability to search for formatting attributes is: To create the list of terms for the glossary, I searched through each topic looking for italic text.)

For details on where the following terms are covered in this book, see the index.

antonym A word with the opposite meaning: *Bad* is an antonym for *good*.

ascending sort A sort in smallest-to-largest order; for example, A to Z or 0 to 9.

background pagination The process of keeping page breaks and page numbers accurate as you edit a document.

background printing Printing with a spooler active. See *spooler*.

bitmapped graphic A graphic created with a paint-type program such as Claris's MacPaint, Aldus's SuperPaint, SuperMac's PixelPaint Professional, or Deneba's UltraPaint, or with an image scanner or video-frame grabber. Contrast with *object-oriented* graphic.

border A horizontal or vertical line positioned adjacent to the left, right, top, or bottom edge of a table cell, paragraph, or graphic.

border sample The small preview page in the Border dialog box, used to create borders.

cell In a table created with Word's table editor, a single storage area located at the intersection of a row and column.

cell selection bar An invisible area to the left of a cell's contents, used for selecting lines and paragraphs within a cell.

Clipboard A temporary storage area in the Mac's memory that holds information you cut or copy.

close To put away a document window or dialog box by clicking the close box in its upper-left corner.

collapse In outline view, to cause a heading's subheadings to be hidden.

column In a table created with Word's table editor, a vertical series of cells.

column selection bar An invisible area at the top of a table column, used for selecting entire columns.

contents code A code that denotes a table of contents entry.

continuation notice A notice for footnotes that span more than one page.

continuation separator A horizontal line that separates footnote text from a continuation notice.

converter A file, located in the Word Commands folder, that enables Word to read and create files in formats other than Word's.

crop To adjust the frame that surrounds a graphic to remove white space or unwanted portions of the graphic.

custom dictionary A spelling checker dictionary to which you can add technical terms, names of companies and people, acronyms, and other words not present in Word's dictionary.

data document A document that contains information (such as a list of names and addresses) that is inserted into a merge document using Word's print merge feature. See *print merge*.

decimal tab A tab stop that aligns the decimal points in columns of numbers.

delimiter A code (such as a tab) or character (such as a comma) that separates one piece of information from the next.

demote In outline view, to make a heading or paragraph subordinate to the heading above it. Demoting a heading or paragraph indents it to the right.

descending sort   A sort in largest-to-smallest order; for example, Z to A or 9 to 0.

diacritics   Accent characters such as the tilde (as in *Piñata*) and the umlaut (as in *üblichen*).

document   The information that you enter, modify, look at, save on disk, and print. A document that you save on disk is also often called a *file*.

drop cap   A large capital letter that begins a paragraph and whose baseline is below that of the rest of the first line.

edition   A file containing published information. An edition file acts as a conduit between the publisher and subscriber: Data always flows from publisher to edition to subscriber. See *publish* and *subscribe*.

expand   In outline view, to cause a heading's subheadings to be visible.

export   The process of moving information from Word to another program.

field   A single piece of information, such as a person's last name or street address.

first-line indent   A paragraph format in which the paragraph's first line is indented from the left margin.

first-line indent marker   The upper triangle that appears at the ruler's left edge, used to change the indent of a paragraph's first line.

font   A collection of characters in a given design.

footer   The portion of a document that appears at the bottom of every page.

footnote reference   The number or character that appears in the main body of text and refers to a footnote or endnote.

footnote separator   A horizontal line that separates the footnote from the body text on the printed page.

frame   An invisible box that holds text or graphics; in the Print Preview window, you can drag a frame around on the page until it's positioned where you want it.

glossary   A set of often-used text or graphics that you've saved for fast recall.

glossary file   A disk file that contains glossary entries.

gutter margin   The extra space added to the inside margin to compensate for binding. Also, the space between columns on multicolumn pages.

hanging indent   A paragraph format in which all of a paragraph's lines except the first are indented from the left margin. Often used to align runover lines in bulleted or numbered lists.

hard page break   A formatting code that overrides Word's automatic pagination, used to force a page to end where you want it to. You can create a hard page break by choosing Page Break from the Insert menu or by pressing Shift-Enter.

header   The portion of a document that appears at the top of every page.

hidden text   A character format used to indicate glossary and index entries.

import   The process of reading information created by another program and converting it to the format used by Word, allowing you to further edit and modify it.

indent scale   A ruler scale that lets you adjust paragraph indents by clicking and dragging.

index code   A code that denotes an index entry.

inside margin   The margin adjacent to the binding in a bound document.

justification   Aligning text against the left and right margins.

Keep paragraph options   Paragraph-formatting options, accessed through the Paragraph command in the Format menu, that enable you to specify that Word keep certain lines of a paragraph together, or to keep a given paragraph on the same page as the one that follows it.

leader characters   A series of characters, usually a row of periods, that guides the eye across a line of text. Leader characters are often used in tables.

left indent marker   The lower triangle that appears on the ruler's left edge, used to change a paragraph's left indent.

margin scale   A ruler scale that lets you adjust document margins by clicking and dragging.

merge document   A document that contains information from a data document and from a main document.

negative indent   A paragraph format in which a paragraph extends into the left or right margin of the page.

nonbreaking hyphen   A hyphen, inserted when you press Command-tilde (~), that Word will not use to end a line. When Word encounters a nonbreaking hyphen in a word, it moves the entire word down to the next line instead of breaking the line after the hyphen.

nonbreaking space   A space that won't be used to end a line. You might want to use a nonbreaking space between a person's initials and his or her name—for example, E. B. White. To type a nonbreaking space, press Command-spacebar or Option-spacebar.

normal view   The most commonly used of Word's three viewing modes. In normal view, Word makes a few display compromises that allow you to scroll and manipulate text more quickly; for example, Word indicates the breaks between pages with a dotted line and displays text in one continuous column.

object-oriented graphic   A graphic created with a draw-type program such as Claris's MacDraw series, Aldus FreeHand, or Adobe Illustrator.

open   To retrieve a saved document from disk and display it on the screen.

optional hyphen   Also called *a soft* hyphen, a hyphen that appears only when Word breaks a line where the optional hyphen is inserted.

outline bar   The bar that appears at the top of the screen when you're working in outline view. You use the outline bar to arrange an outline's components and control how they're displayed.

pagination   The process of dividing a document into pages based on the margin, line spacing, page setup, and other formatting options you choose.

paragraph mark   A code that Word inserts when you press Return or Enter. A paragraph's formatting is stored in its paragraph mark.

paragraph properties mark   When Show ¶ is active, a symbol Word displays to indicate that a paragraph has special formatting attributes that may not show up unless you print the document or view it in the Print Preview window.

point   A unit of measurement equal to $\frac{1}{72}$ inch.

print merge helper bar   An icon bar, visible when the Print Merge Helper feature is active, that lets you insert print merge instructions and field names.

print merge instruction   An instruction in a main document that tells Word to insert information from a data document or to display a dialog box asking for information.

print merge   To combine two documents, a data document and a main document, to print or produce a third document (a merge document) containing the information in each. See *data document, merge document, print merge instruction.*

printable area   The area of a sheet of paper within which a printer can apply an image.

printer driver   A program, selected through the Chooser desk accessory, that acts as an intermediary between the Mac and the printer. A printer driver teaches the Mac how to communicate with a specific type of printer, and it enables the Mac to display the appropriate Page Setup and Print dialog box options for that printer.

promote   In outline view, to move a heading or paragraph to the left.

publish   To make part or all of a document available to other programs using the Edition Manager in Apple's System 7 software.

pull quotes   Excerpts of a document's body text set off in a larger type size to attract a reader's attention.

ribbon   The set of icons and controls you use to choose fonts, type styles, and sizes, and to open the picture window and specify multicolumn formats.

record   A collection of related fields — for example, the name-and-address information for one person.

reverse type   White or light-color text on a black or dark-color background.

row   In a table created with Word's table editor, a horizontal series of cells.

row selection bar   An invisible area to the left of a table row, used for selecting entire rows.

rule   A horizontal line or border.

ruler   The on-screen ruler you use to select styles, set margins, paragraph spacing, and tabs, and specify paragraph alignment.

runaround   A layout effect in which text margins flow around the contours of a nearby graphic.

save   To store a document on disk for future recall.

scale   To adjust the size of a graphic.

scrolling   Accessing portions of the document that aren't currently visible within the document window's boundaries by clicking the scroll bars or using the keyboard's scrolling keys.

section   A portion of a document that can have its own page-numbering arrangements, headers and footers, and column arrangements.

section break   A formatting code that divides one section from another.

section mark   The double-dotted line that denotes a section break. The section mark stores all the section-formatting information for the text that precedes it.

select   To mark text or graphics for a subsequent action, such as reformatting, resizing, cutting, or copying.

selection bar   The invisible area along the left edge of the document window, used to quickly select lines, paragraphs, and an entire document.

separator characters   In a series of numbered paragraphs, characters such as a period or parenthesis that surround or follow each number and separate it from the text.

settings file   A file that holds your preferences and commands settings.

snaking columns   Newspaper-style columns in which text "snakes" from the bottom of one column to the top of the next.

soft page break   The page break that Word inserts automatically as you work on a document. Soft page breaks appear as dotted horizontal lines when you're in the normal document view. Contrast with *hard page break*.

soft return   A paragraph formatting code Word inserts when you press Shift-Return.

split bar   The black rectangle at the top of the document window's vertical scroll bar. You can split a document window into two *panes* by dragging or double-clicking the split bar.

spooler   A program that intercepts and stores on disk the data the Mac transmits to a printer, and then works behind the scenes to send the data to the printer in bursts while you continue to work.

stationery   A template document that stores often-used margin, page setup, and other formatting settings. If you always create a certain kind of document, you can save time and cut down on repetitive typing and formatting by creating a stationery document.

style   Variations within a font such as *italic* or underline. Also a named set of character and paragraph formats that you can apply throughout a document; see *style sheet*.

style sheet   A set of styles stored within a document.

subscribe   To include in a Word document an edition file created with System 7. See *edition* and *publish*.

summary information   Descriptive information about a document: its author, title, version, comments, subject, and keywords. You can enter summary information when you save a document or by choosing Summary Information from the File menu. You can use Word's Find File option to locate documents based on their summary information.

synonym   A word with the same or similar meaning: *Upright* is a synonym for *good*.

tab stops   Formatting codes that enable you to indent text or graphics and align columns of numbers in tables.

table scale   A ruler scale that lets you adjust table cells or column widths by clicking and dragging.

text-only file   A document that contains only text characters and rudimentary formatting information such as tab codes and carriage returns.

true color images   Graphics that can contain millions of colors and provide photo-realistic detail.

watermark   Text or graphics that appear superimposed over a document's main text, such as the word *CONFIDENTIAL* appearing superimposed over the text on each page.

wildcard character   In the Find and Change dialog boxes, a question mark (?) character that means "any character."

word wrap   A word processing feature that brings a word that doesn't fit at the end of a line down to the beginning of the next line, eliminating the need to press Return at the end of each line as you would with a typewriter.

Appendix D
Task Index

Appendix E
Word 5.1 Update

Overview

In October 1992, Microsoft released Word 5.1, a minor upgrade to Word 5 that provides some new capabilities. There are no earth-shattering new features in the new version, but there are several noteworthy enhancements, which are described in this section.

Word 5.1's improvements include:

✦ A new toolbar that provides buttons for many of Word's commands:

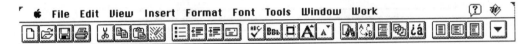

With the toolbar, you can open, save, and print documents, format bulleted lists, create envelopes, and much more. As this topic's Step-by-Step section shows, you can use the Preferences command to customize the toolbar, adding buttons for the commands you use the most and removing buttons for commands you don't use.

✦ Easier table creation. The Insert menu's Table command is still available, but the ribbon now provides a table button that enables you to specify the number of rows and columns in a table by simply dragging:

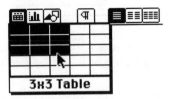

When the insertion point is within an existing table and you click the table button, the Table Layout dialog box appears. (And speaking of tables, Word 5.1's toolbar provides buttons that let you easily add borders to tables.

✦ Easier envelope printing. You can use the Toolbar option in the Preferences dialog box to create any number of addresses that Word automatically uses as the return address:

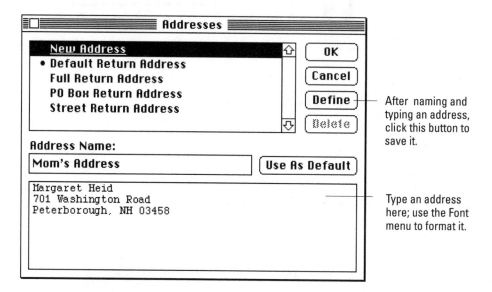

After naming and typing an address, click this button to save it.

Type an address here; use the Font menu to format it.

You can then use the toolbar's envelope button to create the envelope:

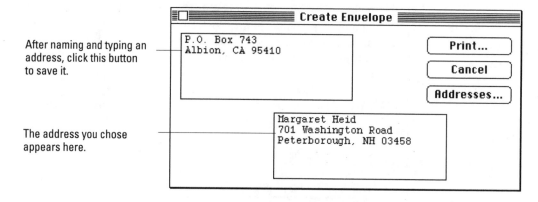

After naming and typing an address, click this button to save it.

The address you chose appears here.

✦ Text annotations. A new plug-in module enables you to attach the electronic equivalent of PostIt notes to your documents.

✦ An improved Find File command. Find File now lets you restrict a search to a particular folder. Simply choose the folder you want to search for from the Location pop-up menu.

✦ A Drop Caps plug-in module that streamlines the process of creating drop-capital letters (described in Topic 23).

✦ An odd/even printing option in the Print dialog box that lets you print only odd- or even-numbered pages of a document. This makes it easier to print double-sided documents.

✦ An improved picture window that provides a Group command, which enables you to group multiple objects together so they can be moved or resized as a unit.

✦ Improved spelling and grammar checking features. Word 5.1 includes the revised Spelling and Grammar plug-in modules described later in this section.

✦ QuickTime support. Word 5.1 includes a QuickTime plug-in module that lets you insert and play QuickTime movies in Word documents.

✦ A three-dimensional ribbon and ruler. If you have a color or grayscale Mac, you can tell Word to display a 3-D version of its ruler and ribbon. Choose Preferences, select the View option, and check the Show 3-D Ribbon and Ruler box.

✦ More installation options, including a PowerBook installation option that minimizes disk space and power requirements. (Another plus: The ribbon now provides a battery-life indicator that lets you keep tabs on your PowerBook's battery charge.)

Word 5.1 also includes a simple graph-generating program, Microsoft Graph, that lets you add charts and graphs to documents. Microsoft Graph supports the Object Linking and Embedding specification, so you can easily link graphs to Word documents (OLE is described in Topic 32). If you use Microsoft Excel, chances are Word's graphing program won't be of much use to you, since Excel also supports OLE and has better graphing features. However, if you don't have Excel — or if your Mac doesn't have enough memory to run Word and Excel simultaneously — Graph could be useful.

The Word 5.1 upgrade is available to registered Word users for $14.95. For details, contact Microsoft product support.

Unless otherwise noted in this update, the instructions and information in Macworld Guide To Word 5 (as well as in Jim Heid's Word Companion disk set, sold separately) still apply to Word 5.1.

The toolbar

If you prefer issuing commands using the mouse instead of the keyboard, you'll love the toolbar. Its buttons provide one-click access to commonly used Word commands (see the quick reference card at the front of this book for a list of the toolbar's standard buttons).

The toolbar menu — the down-pointing triangle at the end of the toolbar — lets you specify the toolbar's location: at the top of the screen (the default location), at the left edge, or at the right edge:

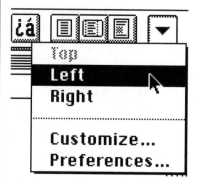

Note that on most monitors, more toolbar buttons appear when the toolbar is positioned at the top of the screen.

You can also use the toolbar menu to open the Preferences dialog box and to customize the toolbar. The Toolbar option in the Preferences dialog box lets you create your own toolbar, with buttons that correspond to the commands you use the most:

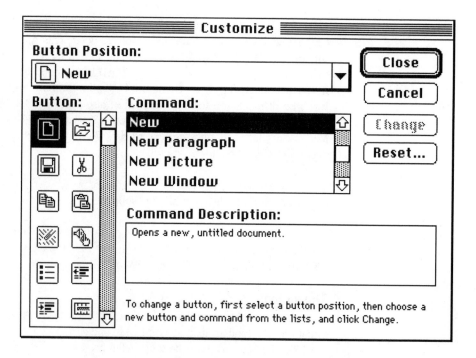

Improved spelling and grammar checkers

The version of the Grammar plug-in module that accompanied Word 5.0 had bugs that could cause Word to crash when run on a Mac Plus, SE, Classic, Portable, and PowerBook 100. In June 1992, Microsoft released an updated version of the Grammar plug-in module, version 5.0.1, and made it available free through on-line services and user groups. The updated module is included with Word 5.1; if you're still using Word 5.0, you can also obtain the new Grammar module free of charge by contacting Microsoft product support at 206-635-7200.

While it was fixing the grammar checker, Microsoft also fine-tuned the spelling checker plug-in module. The revised spelling checker offers numerous improvements, including:

✦ Better feedback. When you choose the Spelling command, the message *Loading Spelling Dictionaries* appears on the screen to let you know that Word has started the checking process.

✦ The ability to cancel a spelling check. You can cancel a spelling check by pressing Command-period or the Esc key.

✦ Page number feedback. When the spelling checker highlights a suspect word, the page number where the word is located appears in the lower-left corner of the document window.

✦ Percentage-complete feedback. When Word is searching for the next suspect word, the percentage of the spelling check that has been completed appears in the lower-left corner of the document window.

✦ Improved performance when editing large custom dictionaries. The new Spelling module deletes words from custom dictionaries more quickly, and in general, handles custom dictionaries better than its predecessor.

✦ Improved handling of ignored words. With the new Spelling module, clicking the Ignore All button tells Word to ignore that word for the balance of your Word session — that is, until you quit Word. A new option in the Preferences dialog box lets you clear the list of ignored words: choose Preferences and select the Spelling option, and then click the Reset "Ignore All" List button. When Word asks you to confirm the operation, click OK or press Return. (You can also access the Spelling Preferences dialog box by clicking the Options button in the Spelling window.)

QuickTime support

You've probably heard of *QuickTime*— it's the new extension for the Mac's system software that enables Macintosh programs to work with dynamic data such as digitized video clips and sound. You can create *QuickTime movies,* as they're called, using video digitizing hardware such as SuperMac's VideoSpigot.

Word 5.1 includes a plug-in module that enables you to include QuickTime movies in documents. The QuickTime plug-in module adds a Movie command to Word's Insert menu. Imported movies can be played using the standard QuickTime movie controller buttons:

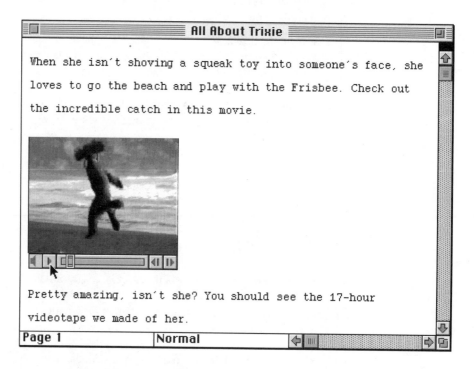

Text annotations

Do you know anyone who used Word 5's voice annotation feature? I don't either. Voice annotations take up too much disk space and memory to be practical — and who wants to whine into a microphone?

Voice annotations are still available in Word 5.1, but the program also provides a more useful text annotation feature that lets you attach typed comments to documents. When you choose Annotation from the Insert menu, a small window appears into which you can type a comment:

At the annual shareholder's meeting, the Board of Directors presented the corporation's goals for the coming year.

✪ Increase Sales by 20% — Double-click to read the annotation
    ✪ New Promotional Techniques
        ▫ Direct mail
        ▫ Radio advertising

The annotation is inserted at the location of the blinking insertion point, and is indicated by a small icon:

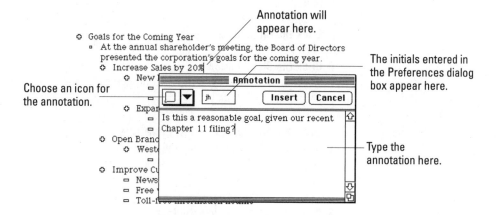

Annotation will appear here.

Choose an icon for the annotation.

The initials entered in the Preferences dialog box appear here.

Type the annotation here.

The annotation icon is formatted as hidden text (notice the gray dotted line beneath it). This means you can hide annotation icons if you don't want to see them: choose Preferences, select the View option, and then uncheck the Hidden Text option.

You can cut or copy an annotation by selecting it and then choosing Cut or Copy from the Edit menu. (When an annotation is selected, a box border appears around its icon.) You can also move a selected annotation by using Word's drag-and-drop editing feature (described in Topic 3).

You can copy all of a document's annotations to a new, untitled document by clicking the Copy To Document button. Clicking this button displays a dialog box that lets you choose to copy only the annotations (which appear with page number references) or the entire document.

Step-by-Step

This section describes how to customize the Word 5.1 toolbar, how to use Word 5.1's envelope-printing features, and how to format a drop capital using the new Drop Cap plug-in module.

To customize the toolbar:

1. Choose Customize from the toolbar menu.

You can also choose Preferences from the Tools menu, scroll to the Toolbar entry, and then click the Customize button.

2. Open the Button Position pop-up menu and then select the location where you want the new button to appear.

3. In the Command box, select the command you want for the new button.

4. In the Button box, select a button for the command.

Unfortunately, Word doesn't automatically select the button that corresponds to the command you chose — you have to locate the button yourself.

5 Click the Change button.

6. Click the Close button.

Word saves the changed toolbar automatically when you quit the program.

To store an address for use in envelopes:

1. In a document window, type the address as you want it to appear.

2. Select the entire address.

3. Choose Addresses from the Insert menu.

The Addresses dialog box appears:

The address you selected appears automatically in the Addresses dialog box.

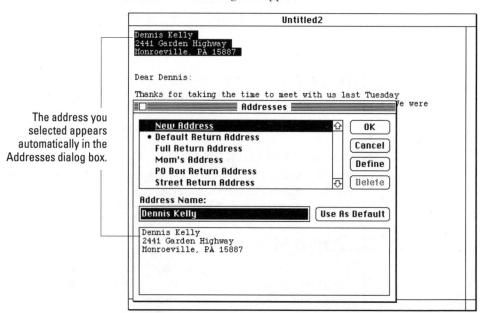

4. Click the Define button.

Word saves the address for future use.

5. Click OK.

To insert an address in a document:

1. Choose Addresses from the Insert menu.

2. Select the name of the address you want to insert.

3. Click OK.

As an alternative to selecting the address and then clicking OK, you can simply double-click the name of the address you want to insert.

To create an envelope for a letter:

1. Select the address as it appears in the letter.

2. Click the toolbar's Envelope button.

The Create Envelope dialog box appears:

If you specify a default return address, it appears here automatically.

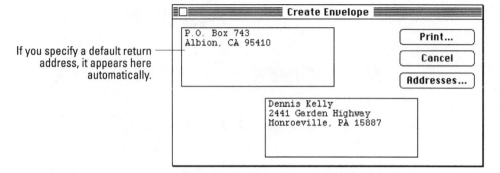

3. Optional: Insert or type a return address.

If you specified a default return address, it appears automatically.

4. Click the Print button.

The Print dialog box appears, with special options for envelopes:

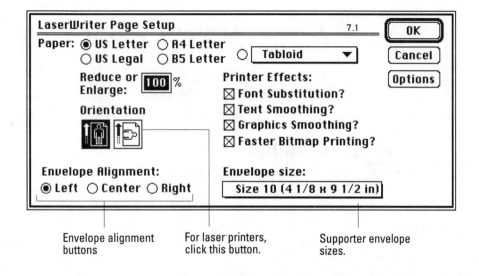

Envelope alignment buttons

For laser printers, click this button.

Supporter envelope sizes.

5. **Specify the desired print options and then click Print or press Return.**

To create a drop capital for a paragraph:

1. **Be sure the paragraph in which you want to place the drop capital is single-spaced.**
   The Drop Cap command works only with single-spaced text.

2. **Select the first character of the paragraph.**
   Don't worry about changing the character's formatting — you'll get a chance to do so in the next step.

3. **Choose Drop Cap from the Insert menu.**
   The Drop Cap dialog box appears:

Specify the drop
cap's height.

```
═══════════════ Drop Cap ═══════════════

Font:                    Height:        ┌──────────┐
┌─────────────────┬───┐  ┌──────┬───┐   │    OK    │
│ Futura          │ ▼ │  │ 3 li │ ▼ │   └──────────┘
└─────────────────┴───┘  └──────┴───┘   ┌──────────┐
☐ Small Caps                            │  Cancel  │
                                        └──────────┘
┌─Position──────────────┐  ┌─Apply To──────────────┐
│ ◉ Dropped      ⊞════   │  │ ◉ First Character     │
│ ○ In Margin    ⊞════   │  │ ○ First Word          │
│                        │  │ ○ Whole Selection     │
└───────────────────────┘  └───────────────────────┘
```

4. **Specify the height of the drop cap and, if desired, the font in which it should appear.**

5. **Click OK or press Return.**
   Word frames the character, changes its size, and switches to page layout view so that you can see the drop capital in position.

Quick Tips

Accommodating the toolbar

When the toolbar is at the top of the screen, the document window is shorter, meaning that fewer lines of text can appear within it. For this reason, you may prefer to position the toolbar on the left or right edge of the screen — even though fewer buttons will probably be available as a result.

Disabling the toolbar

If you prefer using the keyboard — or you just don't want to clutter your screen with all the buttons — you can turn off the toolbar by using the Preferences command. After choosing Preferences, scroll to the Toolbar option and then uncheck the View Toolbar box.

You can also disable the toolbar permanently by removing the Toolbar plug-in module from the Word Commands folder.

What does that toolbar button do?

Have you forgotten what a particular toolbar button does? Jogging your memory is easy — just turn on balloon help and then point to the button. As an alternative, display the toolbar's Customize dialog box and open the Button Position pop-up menu. Next to each button appears the name of the command assigned to that button.

Bulleted lists made easy

Topic 5 describes how to create a hanging indent so that runover lines in a bulleted list align properly. Word 5.1's toolbar provides a bullet list button that makes all those gyrations unnecessary. Simply type the items that you want to appear in bullet list form, and then select them and click the bullet list button:

Word automatically inserts the bullet and formats the hanging indent so that runover lines align correctly.

Fine-tuning disk requirements

Many of Word 5.1's new features — the toolbar, text annotation, QuickTime, drop cap, and envelope generator — operate as plug-in modules. If you don't need a particular feature, you can reclaim some disk space by deleting its plug-in module from the Word Commands folder, located within the Word folder. The Microsoft Graph program is also located within the Word Commands folder; if you don't use it, you can reclaim 622K of disk space by deleting the Microsoft Graph folder.

Searching for annotations

You can scan a document for annotations by using the next and previous annotation buttons that appear in the annotation window. The Word 5.1 manual doesn't mention it, but you can also use the Find or Replace command to search for annotations by performing the following steps:

1. Select the icon for an existing annotation and then choose Copy from the Edit menu.
   This puts the annotation icon on the Clipboard.

2. Choose Find or Replace.

Use Replace if you want to delete the annotations or replace them with something else.

3. With the insertion point in the Find What text box, choose Paste.

A square box appears in the Find What text box. If you're using the Replace window and you want to delete all annotations, leave the Replace With box empty.

4. Click Find (or Replace or Replace All).

Index

Notes

Notes

Notes

Notes

Notes

Notes

Get the most out of Word 5 with Jim Heid's Word Companion disks.

This two-disk set includes an on-line guide to Word and a library of stationery documents, glossary and settings files, style sheets, and more.

Jim Heid's Word Companion puts Jim Heid's Word expertise on your Mac with:

+ *Word Guide Online,* an electronic guide to Word containing selected Overview and Step-by-Step sections of this book — organized for fast electronic retrieval. On-screen navigation buttons let you browse topics and steps, or use the Find command to locate a specific section by typing keywords. Page numbers refer you to relevant sections in *Macworld Guide to Microsoft Word 5.* It's perfect for PowerBooks. Whether you're at your desk or cruising at 35,000 feet, you can master Word without leaving your Mac.

+ *Word Toolkit,* a library of files that will help you put Word to work. Stationery and print merge documents for fax cover sheets, business and personal correspondence, envelopes, labels, and other common documents. Settings files let you customize Word's menus to simplify creating and editing tables, add borders and shading, and exchange files with other programs. Style sheet documents automate complex formatting. Glossary files for creating forms, letters, memos, and more. Graphics files give the special effects you crave.

+ *Word Guide Plus,* a printed supplement to this book that spotlights late-breaking Word developments and includes news and tips on using and customizing Word, exchanging files, and available plug-in modules.

An on-line guide and a library of hard-working Word files — for just $17.95.
Jim Heid's Word Companion is available to *Macworld Guide to Microsoft Word 5* readers for just $17.95, including postage in the United States and Canada.* Use the coupon below to order — and make Word work for you!

System Requirements

+ Macintosh Plus, Classic, or above with a hard disk and 1MB of memory (2MB recommended) running System 6.0.5 or a later version

+ Microsoft Word isn't required, but you'll probably want a copy.

Please allow 4–6 weeks for delivery. (Please print or type.)

*Foreign orders add $5. No CODs or credit card orders.

Yes! Send me Jim Heid's Word Companion!
Send your check or money order for $17.95 (drawn on a US bank in US funds*) along with this coupon or a photocopy to Navarro Software, P.O. Box 743, Albion, CA 95410. California residents add sales tax (total $19.25).

Name _____

Address _____

_____

City, State, ZIP _____

Macworld Authorized Editions

Designed specifically for the Macintosh user, Macworld Books are written by leading *Macworld* magazine columnists, technology champions, and Mac gurus who provide expert advice and insightful tips and techniques not found anywhere else. Macworld Books are the only Macintosh books authorized by *Macworld*, the world's leading Macintosh magazine.

Macworld Guide To Microsoft System 7.1, 2nd Edition
by Lon Poole, Macworld magazine's "Quick Tips" columnist

The most recommended guide to System 7, updated and expanded!

$24.95 USA/$33.95 Canada/£22.92 UK & EIRE, ISBN: 1-878058-65-7

Macworld Guide To Microsoft Word 5
by Jim Heid, Macworld magazine's "Getting Started" columnist

Learn Word the easy way with this *Macworld* Authorized Edition. Now updated for Word 5.1.

$22.95 USA/$29.95 Canada/£20.95 UK & EIRE, ISBN: 1-878058-39-8

Macworld Guide To Microsoft Works 3
by Barrie A. Sosinsky

Get inside the new Works so you can work more productively—the perfect blend of reference and tutorial.

$22.95 USA/$29.95 Canada/£20.95 UK & EIRE, ISBN: 1-878058-42-8

Macworld Complete Mac Handbook
by Jim Heid

The most complete guide to getting started, mastering, and expanding your Mac.

$26.95 USA/$35.95 Canada/£24.95 UK & EIRE, ISBN: 1-878058-17-7

Macworld PageMaker Bible
by Jo Ann Villalobos

The ultimate insiders' guide to PageMaker 5, combining an authoritative and easy-to-use reference with tips and techniques. Includes 3 1/2" disk of templates.

$39.95 USA/$52.95 Canada/£37.60 UK & EIRE, ISBN: 1-878058-84-3 — Available July 1993

Macworld Networking Handbook
by David Kosiur, Ph.D.

The ultimate insider's guide to Mac network management.

$29.95 USA/$39.95 Canada/£27.45 UK & EIRE, ISBN: 1-878058-31-2

Macworld Guide To Microsoft Excel 4
by David Maguiness

Build powerful spreadsheets quickly with this *Macworld* Authorized Edition to Excel 4.

$22.95 USA/$29.95 Canada/£20.95 UK & EIRE, ISBN: 1-878058-40-1

Macworld Music & Sound Bible
by Christopher Yavelow

Finally, the definitive guide to music, sound, and multimedia on the Mac.

$37.95 USA/$47.95 Canada/£34.95 UK & EIRE, ISBN: 1-878058-18-5

Macworld QuarkXPress Designer Handbook
by Barbara Assadi and Galen Gruman

Macworld magazine's DTP experts help you master advanced features fast with this definitive tutorial, reference and designer tips resource on QuarkXPress.

$29.95 USA/$39.95 Canada/£27.45 UK & EIRE, ISBN: 1-878058-85-1 — Available July 1993

For More Information Call 1-800-762-2974

PC World Handbook

Expert information at your fingertips. Perfect for readers who need a complete tutorial of features as well as a reference to software applications and operating systems. All PC World Handbooks include bonus disks with software featuring useful templates, examples, and utilities that provide real value to the reader.

PC World DOS 6 Handbook, 2nd Edition
by John Socha, Clint Hicks, and Devra Hall

Completely revised and updated! Includes extended features of DOS and the 250 page command reference that Microsoft excludes. A complete tutorial and reference PLUS Special Edition of Norton Commander software.

$34.95 USA/$44.95 Canada/£32.95 UK & EIRE, ISBN: 1-878058-79-7

PC World Microsoft Access Bible
by Cary Prague and Michael Irwin

This authoritative tutorial and reference on Microsoft's new Windows database is the perfect companion for every Microsoft Access user.

$39.95 USA/$52.95 Canada/£37.60 UK & EIRE, ISBN: 1-878058-81-9

Official XTree MS-DOS, Windows, and Hard Disk Management Companion, 3rd Edition
by Beth Slick

The only authorized guide to all versions of XTree, the most popular PC hard disk utility.

$19.95 USA/$26.95 Canada/£18.45 UK & EIRE, ISBN: 1-878058-57-6

QuarkXPress for Windows Designer Handbook
by Barbara Assadi and Galen Gruman

Make the move to QuarkXPress for Windows, the new professional desktop publishing powerhouse, with this expert reference and tutorial.

$29.95 USA/$39.95 Canada/£27.45 UK & EIRE, ISBN: 1-878058-45-2

PC World You Can Do It With Windows
by Christopher Van Buren

The best way to learn Window 3.1!

$19.95 USA/$26.95 Canada/£18.45 VAT UK EIRE, ISBN: 1-878058-37-1

PC World Excel 4 for Windows Handbook
by John Walkenbach and David Maguiness

Complete tutorial and reference by PC World's spreadsheet experts, with a FREE 32-page Function Reference booklet.

$29.95 USA/$39.95 Canada/£27.45 UK & EIRE, ISBN: 1-878058-46-0

PC World WordPerfect 6 Handbook
by Greg Harvey

Bestselling author and WordPerfect guru Greg Harvey brings you the ultimate tutorial and reference – complete with valuable software containing document templates, macros, and other handy WordPerfect tools.

$34.95 USA/$44.95 Canada/£32.95 UK & EIRE, ISBN: 1-878058-80-0 — Available July 1993

PC World Q&A Bible, Version 4
by Thomas J. Marcellus, Technical Editor of The Quick Answer

The only thorough guide with a disk of databases for mastering Q&A Version 4.

$39.95 USA/$52.95 Canada/£37.60 UK & EIRE, ISBN: 1-878058-03-7

PC World You Can Do It With DOS
by Christopher Van Buren

The best way to learn DOS quickly and easily.

$19.95 USA/$26.95 Canada/£18.45 VAT UK EIRE, ISBN: 1-878058-38-X

For More Information Call 1-800-762-2974

Order Form

Order Center: (800) 762-2974 (8 a.m.-5 p.m., PST, weekdays) or (415) 312-0600

For Fastest Service: Photocopy This Order Form and FAX it to : (415) 358-1260

Quantity	ISBN	Title	Price	Total

Shipping & Handling Charges

Subtotal	U.S.	Canada & International	International Air Mail
Up to $20.00	Add $3.00	Add $4.00	Add $10.00
$20.01-40.00	$4.00	$5.00	$20.00
$40.01-60.00	$5.00	$6.00	$25.00
$60.01-80.00	$6.00	$8.00	$35.00
Over $80.00	$7.00	$10.00	$50.00

In U.S. and Canada, shipping is UPS ground or equivalent.
For Rush shipping call (800) 762-2974.

Subtotal _____

CA residents add applicable sales tax _____

IN residents add 5% sales tax _____

Canadian residents add 7% GST tax _____

Shipping _____

TOTAL _____

Ship to:

Name _____

Company _____

Address _____

City/State/Zip _____

Daytime Phone _____

Payment: ❏ Check to IDG Books (US Funds Only)   ❏ Visa   ❏ MasterCard   ❏ American Express

Card # _____   Exp._____   Signature _____

Please send this order form to: IDG Books, 155 Bovet Road, San Mateo, CA 94402.
Allow up to 3 weeks for delivery. Thank you!

BOBMW93

IDG BOOKS WORLDWIDE REGISTRATION CARD

IDG
BOOKS
THE WORLD OF
COMPUTER
KNOWLEDGE

Title of this book: _____

My overall rating of this book: ❑ Very good [1] ❑ Good [2] ❑ Satisfactory [3] ❑ Fair [4] ❑ Poor [5]

How I first heard about this book:

❑ Found in bookstore; name: [6]

❑ Advertisement: [8]

❑ Word of mouth; heard about book from friend, co-worker, etc.: [10]

❑ Book review: [7]

❑ Catalog: [9]

❑ Other: [11]

What I liked most about this book:

_____

_____

What I would change, add, delete, etc., in future editions of this book:

_____

_____

Other comments:

_____

Number of computer books I purchase in a year: ❑ 1 [12] ❑ 2-5 [13] ❑ 6-10 [14] ❑ More than 10 [15]

I would characterize my computer skills as: ❑ Beginner [16] ❑ Intermediate [17] ❑ Advanced [18] ❑ Professional [19]

I use ❑ DOS [20] ❑ Windows [21] ❑ OS/2 [22] ❑ Unix [23] ❑ Macintosh [24] ❑ Other: [25]_____
(please specify)

I would be interested in new books on the following subjects:
(please check all that apply, and use the spaces provided to identify specific software)

❑ Word processing: [26]

❑ Data bases: [28]

❑ File Utilities: [30]

❑ Networking: [32]

❑ Other: [34]

❑ Spreadsheets: [27]

❑ Desktop publishing: [29]

❑ Money management: [31]

❑ Programming languages: [33]

I use a PC at (please check all that apply): ❑ home [35] ❑ work [36] ❑ school [37] ❑ other: [38] _____

The disks I prefer to use are ❑ 5.25 [39] ❑ 3.5 [40] ❑ other: [41]_____

I have a CD ROM: ❑ yes [42] ❑ no [43]

I plan to buy or upgrade computer hardware this year: ❑ yes [44] ❑ no [45]

I plan to buy or upgrade computer software this year: ❑ yes [46] ❑ no [47]

Name: _____ Business title: [48] _____ Type of Business: [49] _____

Address (❑ home [50] ❑ work [51]/Company name: _____)

Street/Suite# _____

City [52]/State [53]/Zipcode [54]: _____ Country [55] _____

❑ **I liked this book!** You may quote me by name in future
IDG Books Worldwide promotional materials.

My daytime phone number is _____

RETURN THIS
REGISTRATION CARD
FOR FREE CATALOG